Anthony Colombo was born and raised in Brooklyn, NY. He worked along side his father with the Italian American Civil Rights League and was featured on CBS, NBC, FOX, and ABC and numerous other TV and radio stations. After over 40 years of remaining silent, Anthony Colombo decided to speak about his life beside his father.

Don Capria was born in Westchester County, New York. After high school he began working as a writer, and music video director. He has written, produced, and directed content in both scripted and non-scripted film & TV. In 2013 Capria made his directorial debut with his short film, *Eulogy*.

To My Wife and Kids,
You Mean The World To Me.

Dedicated in loving memory of my brother,
Joseph Colombo Jr.

Colombo
The Unsolved Murder

Written by

Don Capria
&
Anthony Colombo

UNITY PRESS

Don Capria & Anthony Colombo

Copyright © [2013] by [Carol Colombo]

Unity Press Copies may be purchased in bulk at a discounted rate for special promotion, corporate gifting, and educational purposes. For more information contact Unity Press at: colombobook@gmail.com

www.colombobook.com

All rights reserved. No part of this book may be reproduced, scanned, or distributed in any printed or electronic form without permission of

Unity Press
The Senator Building,
105 West F Street 3rd Floor, San Diego, CA 92101.
First Edition: [2015]

ISBN -13: 978-0692583241
ISBN – 10: 0692583246

Printed in the United States of America

Contents

Preface ix

Author's Note xiii

Prologue xvii

Chapter 1 (1928-1945) 1

Chapter 2 (1945-1959) 28

Chapter 3 (1959-1963) 54

Chapter 4 (1963-1966) 80

Chapter 5 (1966-1969) 110

Chapter 6 (1969-1970) 141

Chapter 7 (Summer 1970) 175

Chapter 8 (Fall 1970) 217

Chapter 9 (Winter 1971) 238

Chapter 10 (The Godfather) 251

Chapter 11 (March & April 1971) 269

Chapter 12 (May & June 1971) 289

Chapter 13 (Unity Day 1971) 315

Chapter 14 (Post-shooting) 335
    The Lone Gunman Theory 338
    The B.R.A.T. Theory 341
    The Gallo Theory 343
    The Gambino Theory 347
    The FBI-CIA Theory 354

Epilogue 366

Appendix 369

Bibliography 371

Selected Articles 375

Selected Government Articles 375

Index 376

Notes 386

Photo Credits 401

Preface

By

Anthony Colombo

It has been over forty years since my father Joe Colombo was murdered. On June 28, 1971, he was shot three times in the head at a peaceful rally in New York City. I still haven't recovered. In this book I will tell you the story about my father's life, from his father's murder in 1938 to his own assassination in 1971. As a reader, I know you may have encountered a number of books and articles about my father. In every story, Joe Colombo is characterized as a Mob boss who fell out of favor with other members of organized crime, specifically Carl Gambino and Joey Gallo. Gambino and Gallo purportedly hired a black man, Jerome Johnson, to carry out his assassination. This account of his death is a myth perpetuated by the FBI and the media. Over the years, my father's assassination attempt brokered plenty of generous offers for a book or movie. The problem was they all wanted a "shoot 'em up" gangster story. My answer was always the same; I don't have that story. Since his murder, I have tried instead, to tell the true story of my father's life and how he came to found the Italian-American Civil Rights League. This is the only story I have; the one you are about to read.

For years, I was motivated by profound pain and a desire for some sort of vindication for my father. I now realize that vindication lies in simply telling the truth about his life. In this book you will read about the complex life of Joe Colombo Sr., from his tumultuous childhood experiences in Brooklyn to his rise as a pioneering and passionate civil rights leader. This book contains stories you have never heard and presents extensive research never before revealed. I will share with you my life experiences with my father, a man who assembled 200,000 supporters in Columbus Circle in 1970, and was named the "most powerful man in New York City" alongside Mayor Lindsay and Nelson Rockefeller. It is my hope that after reading this book, you will have some sense of the true Joe Colombo Sr.; an extraordinary and profoundly misunderstood man.

ANTHONY E. COLOMBO
BLOOMING GROOVE, NY
JUNE 2012

Don Capria & Anthony Colombo

Author's Note
By
Don Capria

When Joe Colombo's oldest son Anthony began discussing his vision for the book with me, he offered no stories about his father's criminal lifestyle. While he did not deny they existed, he was insistent that he could offer me no support in researching or referencing them. He wanted to depict the father he'd known; charismatic, intensely devoted to his family, fiercely principled, ferociously hard working. Nonetheless, he gave me permission to examine his father's criminal past and allowed me to introduce anything I found, as long as I had supporting evidence. Along with Anthony's first person stories of life with his father, I included many italicized portions in this book. I reconstructed these stories from factual events that were gathered during the many personal interviews I conducted, and documents I secured from law enforcement and press.

In addition to FBI and press reports about Colombo, much of the material in this book came from my own resources in Brooklyn. One man, an "old timer" who wished to remain anonymous, regaled me with stories from the era of Prohibition, when he and Joe were youngsters in south Brooklyn. He vividly described the neighborhood during this time and explained how the young men living there both created, and were shaped by the subculture. At one point, I remarked that it sounded like a world one might recognize in any number of gangster movies. He snapped back irritably, "These men were gangsters, not Hollywood caricatures. They were not colorful clowns that strolled around the streets with Tommy guns and cigars. These men were sharp, refined, businessmen that obeyed a code and respected their own laws." He continued, "That's where we grew up, and those were the men Joe grew up watching. Brooklyn changed hands many times before Joe Colombo became a leader there. And after he was shot, it was never the same again."

DON CAPRIA
ASTORIA, NY
APRIL 2012

Don Capria & Anthony Colombo

Prologue

By

Don Capria

The Colombo crime organization is believed by the FBI to be Brooklyn's largest criminal assembly in both members and territory. Its predecessor, the Profaci Gang was "the oldest and most established crime organization in the genealogy of Brooklyn crime."[i] This organization took root at the close of the bloody Prohibition Era, after the three-year "Castellamarese War." After the war ended, Charlie "Lucky" Luciano and Meyer Lansky established what was known as the Commission, a council intended to keep peace among criminals through negotiation. The council was comprised of bosses from various organizations who would meet to settle territorial and financial disputes, thereby eliminating the need for violent displays and reprisals. Luciano and Lansky wanted the Commission to encourage the evolution of a more restrained, business-oriented gangster. Representatives of the first five organized gangs in New York were: Charlie "Lucky" Luciano, Vincent Mangano, Joseph Bonanno, Gaetano "Tommy" Gagliano, and Giuseppe Profaci.

The Profaci lineage was established after the demise of Brooklyn crime boss Frankie Uale. Though he did not achieve the notoriety of his former apprentice and ally Alphonse "Al" Capone, Frankie Uale was indisputably the largest and most feared racketeer in New York during the Roaring Twenties. Francesco Ioele (which he later changed to Uale, and pronounced "Yale") was born in Longobucco, Calabria, and immigrated to the United States just after the turn of the 19th century. As a teenager, he joined the infamous "Five Points" Gang, to which he contributed his fighting skills and his criminal perspicacity. Uale bore a number of characteristics in common with Joe Colombo. Colombo's family roots were also in Calabria, a region that many men in organized crime disdained. Uale, like Colombo, was a short man with a strong build who was always seen in public dressed to the nines. Their shoes were always shined, hands manicured, gold and gemstones twinkled from their jewelry. Both men were gracious and personable, with inviting faces and dark eyes that betokened some danger. These contradictory qualities were reflected in their reputations. Uale was not only known for his accomplishments as a killer of killers; he was also given the handle "Prince of Pals" for his extraordinary personality and relationships with the many Brooklyn residents he helped.

As a gang leader and a public figure, Uale was feared by men, not only for his willingness to issue a death sentence, but because he frequently completed the job himself. He is believed to have committed some of the most pivotal murders in Mob history, including those of "Big" Jim Collosimo, and Richard "Peg Leg" Lonergan of the White Hand Gang, and most notably, the Irish-American North Side Gang leader, Charles Dean O'Banion. Uale is most famous however, not as a killer, but as the mentor of

Al Capone, whom he took off the streets and employed as an enforcer at the infamous Harvard Inn. Uale moved Capone up through the ranks during his teenage years, and later sent him to work for Johnny Torrio in Chicago to help him avoid a murder rap in Brooklyn. But years later, when Capone had become the biggest gangster in the nation, he and Uale disagreed bitterly over the selection of leadership for the very powerful political group, Unione Siciliana. And so it is believed that Capone ordered the death of his old tutor.

Frankie Uale's final day was July 1, 1928. He was sitting in one of his speakeasies in Brooklyn, the Sunrise Club, next to one of his most trusted men, a vicious killer and feared lieutenant[ii], Giuseppe Piraino. Uale received a phone call of curious urgency and grabbed his keys to rush out the door. Piraino offered to drive him, but Uale refused and left in his new Lincoln armed with only a small revolver. Uale may have felt confident, he had eluded death many times before; once just four months prior, when he was chased in his vehicle by assassins armed with machine guns, but emerged unscathed. Uale's car was equipped with a bulletproof chassis, this precaution Capone made famous, but likely he learned it from Uale. This time, as Uale drove, he was tailed by a black Buick, inside of which were Capone's elite; Fred "Killer" Burke, "Machine Gun" Jack McGurn, John Scalise and Albert Anselmi.

By the time Uale finally made the men behind him, it was too late; he floored the pedal, speeding down New Utrecht Avenue and made a turn down 44th Street with hopes of a getaway, but the steel-loaded Lincoln couldn't outrun the stock Buick. As his killers rolled up alongside him, the hit men sprayed Uale's car with shotgun fire and machine gun bullets. Uale, unable to drive and defend, caught a bullet in the head, and as he lay slumped over the wheel, his vehicle went fumbling down the road. The hunters would not take a chance at being duped by a man who was known to cheat death. They continued to ride alongside the Lincoln and from a few feet away, riddled the interior of the car and Uale's body with more bullets. Finally, satisfied with their work, the killers sped off, never to be apprehended. The Lincoln continued to roll unsteadily until it finally, and dramatically crashed into the front porch of 923 44th Street, whereupon the car door swung open to give bystanders a full view of the dead gangster as he slipped out of his seat, falling lifeless to the ground.

Throughout the Prohibition Era, Uale had absolutely dominated the racketeering business, so disputes arose immediately over who would inherit Uale's territory and financial holdings. Salvatore "Toto" D'Aquila, a gangster who was poised to take over Uale's territory, was murdered. The death rate surged in Brooklyn as various factions grappled for control. The crime wave caused a great public stir, and soon district attorneys issued pleas for police intervention: "Every day three or four men are flung from flying automobiles, shot through their backs. Everyday some new chieftain is caught before the muzzle of a machine gun."[iii]

On December 5, 1928, in an effort to reach some sort of armistice, a small group of men organized a secret meeting at the Slater Hotel in Cleveland to devise a plan for greater stability. At the meeting, it was decided that Uale's territories were to be apportioned among a number of leaders, with Giuseppe Profaci receiving the largest stake. Only one gangster back in Brooklyn rejected this arrangement and refused to relinquish control of Uale's old rackets. He had been one of Uale's most loyal and most vicious associates; an old school Sicilian with an insatiable appetite for murder and power, Giuseppe Piraino.

This oversized killer was convicted of murder in Palermo in 1911, but he'd managed to escape from prison and flee to the United States. Piraino had beaten cases and avoided prosecution for dozens of murders since his arrival in the United States. In one such instance, the body of a Coney Island man, who was last seen with Piraino, was found butchered, lying supine in a creek, faceless, with his body slashed and mutilated. He was also suspected to have committed the 1918 Barrel Murder of Gaspare Candello. The victim's body was found lacerated by close to forty knife wounds in the face, neck and chest[iv]. The killer had folded the body in half and stuffed it into a barrel in a vacant South Brooklyn lot. It was one of the city's most gruesome murders.

Piraino did serve time in Sing Sing for shooting a detective during a bootlegging raid on the Brooklyn waterfront. He was nicknamed "the Clutching Hand" not only for his greed for money and power, but also for his deformed right hand with its three knotted fingers. Piraino had sustained the injury in prison, when another inmate attacked and attempted to stab him. He defended himself by grabbing hold of the shank and locking his grip on the blade. His hand was paralyzed, but he'd managed to save his own life in the process. His attacker was not as lucky.

In 1930, right around the time young Joe Colombo was learning to swing a three wood, two assassins were summoned to a Sackett Street building to kill the Clutching Hand. Once Piraino was murdered and Uale's territory uncontested, Giuseppe Profaci assumed control of Brooklyn's underworld; a position he maintained for the next thirty years. Gangsters from the Profaci organization, of which Colombo's father, Anthony, was a member, greatly influenced Joe Colombo as a child and young adult. These were the most feared and respected men in Brooklyn.

Chapter 1.

"Young at Heart"

(1928-1945)

"Hey, Joe, what's wrong with you?" The question issued from a lanky teenager who was standing on a stoop with some of his chums. Joe paused for a moment, thinking about his response. He knew this kid and his friends; they had been teasing him since he'd transferred to their high school a few weeks prior. "Come here, I wanna ask you a question." Joe stared at the teen with a combination of fear and anger. "Loosen up, Joe. I just wanna ask you something." The boy's tone was cloying; obviously disingenuous, but Joe Colombo would not turn away from the group. As Joe approached, he noticed that one of the boys on the stoop was holding a newspaper. The teens chuckled in unison as they anticipated Joe's reaction. The lanky boy pointed to the photos under the bold headline and asked innocently, "Hey Joe, you bastard, isn't that your father's hand sticking out right there?" It was his father's hand, hanging out of a car door. Other photos showed the rest of his corpse stuffed in the backseat. Joe was trembling.

As the boys cackled, delighted with the success of their mockery, Joe slipped half a broom stick out from his back pocket, and without hesitation he stepped forward and whacked the lanky

1

kid in the legs. Joe continued swatting him with the stick until he fell to the ground. While the boy writhed around, Joe turned to the chubby kid who was holding the newspaper, and belted the backside of his hand with the stick. The boy screeched in pain. Joe then smashed his other wrist and whacked the loose fingers as he yelped. Then Joe stood back from the stoop to square off with the other two teens. They backed away fearfully as Joe barked at them, "I dare you, now, say something! One word, I dare yous'!" An old woman screamed something about the police from an open window above. Joe ignored her and continued; "Say something about my father again. Call me a bastard one more time and I'll whack yous' till you bleed." They were silent. Joe gave them one last look; a menacing stare he had seen his father cast at many men. No further words were needed. The lesson was over.

Joe sprinted up 16th Avenue before the cops got wind of the fight. But the cops never bothered Joe, and those kids never even dared look at him again. The word got around quick about Joe Colombo: he wasn't anyone's prey. In time he would become known around Brooklyn as a defender of kids who got bullied, especially those who weren't strong or brave enough to defend themselves.

✷✷✷

Joe Colombo was born on June 16, 1923 in Brooklyn, New York. Anthony Colombo, Joe's father was a well-known racketeer in South Brooklyn, who found work in the crime organization run by Brooklyn gangster Giuseppe Profaci. Forty years later, Joe himself would be identified by the FBI as the leader of this same association.

Joe's mother Catherine was born and raised in the Dyker Heights section of Brooklyn, where she met Anthony, an Italian man born in Brazil whose family originated from the Calabria region of Italy. Anthony and Catherine were married in the summer of 1922. They lived in a small apartment on 86th Street in Gravesend, Brooklyn. When Joe was old enough to attend school he would walk to PS 216 on Avenue X, just around the corner from his home.

On March 7, 1928, Lawrence Colombo, Joe's only brother was born. The family moved a few blocks away to a larger apartment. While home life was flourishing for the Colombos, the nation was on the brink of economic disaster. In October 1929, the Black Friday and Black Tuesday market crashes plunged the United States into the Great Depression, an economic and social calamity that would persist for the next twelve years.

Joe's father, however, was in a line of work that was not as affected by the stock market crash. In fact, during the era of Prohibition, men who made their livings through money lending and the sale of illegal liquor prospered. The bootlegger was often a very well-respected individual in his community. When liquor sales became illegal in 1920, it enabled many enterprising young men in the U.S. to build elaborate empires. Anthony Colombo, like many of his contemporaries, profited from the new laws, which allowed him to earn steady money without having to resort to more malignant crimes like stick-ups and burglaries.

As a young kid, Joe Colombo would faithfully follow his father around the streets of Brooklyn. Joe observed that his father was a man to whom people gave their fullest and most reverent attention. Joe, too, worshipped the man, particularly when it came to his legendary golf game. Young Joe caddied for his father at the Dyker Beach Park public golf course; he began playing alongside him at the age of six. According to both Joe and numerous hapless opponents, Anthony never once lost a game.

Joe's father taught him everything about golf, from the clubs to the etiquette. He was a very strict man, so when his father spoke, Joe listened attentively. Anthony explained to his son the importance of being on time for a match. Showing up early to tee time was critical; this way you never kept any of the players behind you waiting. His father told Joe this should apply to all of his engagements. He didn't want him to build a reputation for being late. The dress code was also an essential aspect of the game. Anthony taught Joe that people would judge him by his appearance. On the course and in life, one needed to look the part. In fact, he advised Joe that a man should always wear a suit when out on the town; the only place appropriate for leisure attire was one's own home.

Honor and respect for protocol were the guiding principles of both Anthony's golf game and his life. He taught Joe that even though he might be anxious to move ahead, if it wasn't his turn, he must always patiently wait for those in front of him. Everyone's time will come sooner or later. Perhaps the most important lesson Joe learned from golf was, "play it as it lies." This meant wherever the ball lands, it couldn't be adjusted; it has to be played from the exact location and condition into which it fell. Joe's father impressed upon him the importance of accepting things in life as they are. He should expect to be dealt some bad hands and must learn to manage them; some things he would not be able to change, regardless of the intensity of his efforts. This was one of the hardest lessons for Joe to learn.

Joe wondered where his father would go during his frequent trips away from their home. Although Anthony claimed to be golfing upstate, he wouldn't allow young Joe, his faithful caddy, to accompany him. At the age of seven, Joe felt he could be a great asset to his father during those three-and four-day trips to the Catskills. Although he didn't understand exactly what his father was doing, he suspected that these weren't merely golf trips. He couldn't imagine, of course, that during the late 1920's his father was embroiled in one of the biggest gang wars in the nation's history.

***

In the winter of 1932, Joe's brother Lawrence contracted influenza. After New Year's Day he was admitted to the hospital. His condition only worsened and his doctor feared the illness was fatal. Joe would cut school to help his mother around the house and, when permitted, he would visit his brother at the hospital. On January 17, 1933, at the age of five, Lawrence died of pneumonia. He was buried a few days later at St. John's Cemetery in Queens.

Lawrence's death introduced both grief and disruption into Joe's life. His mother and father needed some time as a couple to mourn the loss of their son, so Joe was sent to live with his mother's sister, Anna, in Bensonhurst, Brooklyn. He was transferred to PS 201 and spent the remainder of January at his aunt's home. Joe found it difficult to adjust, and had frequent run-ins with school officials. He spent more and more time away from school and preferred activities such as handball and golf. He purchased a set of dice and would run small games with other kids in building basements or alleyways. He also began to work odd jobs, running errands for his father's friends who congregated at their social club in Bensonhurst. On 13th Avenue, he earned some quick change working at a shoe shine spot. Joe observed that earning money brought immediate rewards, as opposed to the monotonous hours spent cooped up in the classroom. A few months after Lawrence's death, Catherine became pregnant with another child.

On March 21, 1934, Loretta Colombo was born in Brooklyn Hospital. The arrival of a new baby helped to console the grieving family. The previous summer, when Joe wasn't staying with his Aunt Anna in Bensonhurst, he had been stuck at home, witnessing the turmoil between his parents, who were struggling with their son's death. The Colombos skipped the family vacation to upstate New York that had been a tradition since Joe's earliest years. After his sister's birth, Joe began to feel the bonds of his family strengthen. The following summer, he was back in Orange County and the fairgrounds with his father watching races, attending to the farm animals, playing carnival games and enjoying the shows.

That fall, with his father's permission, Joe began skipping school more and spending more time with him riding around the Brooklyn streets. His aversion to school only intensified as he spent more time with his father. The world that his father inhabited was enchanting for Joe and he wanted nothing more than to accompany him on his mysterious excursions. Joe repeatedly noticed the effect it had on strangers when he would tell them that Anthony was his father. He discovered that being the son of Anthony Colombo, or Tony Durante, as he was known, immediately elevated him in the esteem of not only local citizens and shop owners, but also of the men who ran Brooklyn; the "criminal" elite.

***

One cold morning in February 1938, two late-model cars, the first a Pontiac, rounded the corner of 3rd Avenue, and gently coasted north on Shore Road in the Bay Ridge section of Brooklyn. The front car's headlights revealed only a fraction of the road, as the thick fog rose from the bay and hovered over the streets. As the Pontiac slowed to a crawl, the driver peered down the misty blocks to his right. He braked after 93rd Street, and turned down Oliver Street with the second car still close behind. In a secluded spot behind a large apartment building, the lead car pulled over to the right side of the street, and carefully backed into an empty parking space. The driver stepped out, and slid into the passenger seat of the idling getaway car. The car pulled off unrushed and quietly disappeared into the mist.

Joe would wake that morning and help his mother around the house. He was not looking forward to the long, cold walk down Ocean Parkway to Abraham Lincoln High that day. If his father were home, he knew he could persuade him to drive him to school, but it had been over a week since his father walked out the door to meet some of his friends for a drink. The car was gone and his mother's mood was less than friendly. He couldn't wait until springtime when he could skip school and caddy at the park for his father. Joe glanced at the front door every few minutes, hoping his father would be back in time for Sunday dinner.

While Joe waited anxiously for his father's return, a fifteen-year-old boy was taking his terrier out for a stroll in Bay Ridge. As the boy turned up Oliver Street, he noticed two men peering into a parked car. It was the same late-model Pontiac that had parked there hours before in the thick of the morning fog. When they saw the boy looking at them, they hurried off down the street. The boy slowed his pace as he approached the car. He inched up, and through the back window he saw dead bodies. As fast as he could, he ran into the entrance of a nearby apartment building and found the janitor.

"Strangulation by rope" was the official statement the coroner printed on their death certificates. The two bodies stuffed in the backseat of the Pontiac were identified as Anthony Colombo and Christine Oliveri. A detective recognized Colombo: he was known as a racketeer in South Brooklyn. The woman, Christine Oliveri, was a mother of two who lived a few doors down from a tavern in Bensonhurst Anthony would frequent. This was the last place he was seen in public alive. The police assumed the woman was

Colombo's girlfriend, who was simply unfortunate enough to be with Colombo at the wrong moment and killed to be kept silent.

Anthony's wife Catherine was driven to the police station for an interview. Their grandfather brought Joseph and his sister Loretta there later. After answering some questions about her husband's recent activities and business dealings, about which she knew very little, Mrs. Colombo was taken into a garage to identify the body. When they pulled back the cover, Anthony still had dried blood crusting his face. Catherine looked at his body and sobbed: "That's him! That's him!" Blood flushed her face and she fainted.

***

At his father's funeral, although Joe was consumed by anger and grief, he was momentarily distracted by a man who pulled him aside. Joe knew this man to be a close friend of his father's. He lived right around the corner from their home in Gravesend. He was someone Joe had met and often seen his father visiting. This man had promised Anthony that he would look out for his son if anything ever happened to him. Joe almost immediately trusted him: his decorum and candor reminded Joe of his father. After their encounter, however, Joe was once again overwhelmed by his loss. Now, his father would expect him to become the man of the house.

Immediately after Anthony's murder, Catherine sent Joe and his sister to live with her mother in Bensonhurst. Although it was against the gangster's "code", she was fearful that more violence might be directed towards her family. Joe was transferred from Abraham Lincoln to New Utrecht High School. While still mourning the loss of his father, he was immediately subjected to the torment of kids in the new neighborhood. Photos of his dead father clipped from newspapers were passed around in classrooms, and bullies teased Joe mercilessly. Joe's mother continued to be fearful after her husband's murder. Finally she concluded that it would be safer to move the family to California, closer to her three brothers and sister. Angered by his mother's plans to leave Brooklyn, Joe told her she would have to leave without him. He argued with her for weeks until she relented; she would take Loretta and leave him again with her sister Anna. Joe felt deserted, but he could not imagine leaving Brooklyn. After a few more miserable months of school, Joe decided to drop out and look for full-time work. At fifteen this wouldn't be easy, so Joe sought guidance from the man he'd spoken to at his father's funeral.

Anthony's friend welcomed Joe with open arms and kept good on his promise to help him. Joe was given a job as delivery boy with a butcher named "Gino", who owned and operated a shop on 13th Avenue, not far from where Joe was staying. Joe was eager to work and made fast deliveries, always rushing back to the shop to help Gino with other duties. Joe was a quick learner and worked as an apprentice or "half-butcher," de-boning and chopping meat. He earned fifteen dollars a week. Gino treated him well and often sent Joe home with cuts for his family, knowing the man who'd brought Joe to him was a powerful figure in the underworld of South Brooklyn.

Joe began to supplement his income by hustling. Along with a few friends from his neighborhood, he started boosting meat deliveries. Their rackets were juvenile in nature, but turned a quick profit. They would follow the meat delivery truck, make a steal off the back, and then sell the meat to people close to home, keeping a full profit. In the same fashion, he and his friends began working other meat and merchandise trucks in South Brooklyn. They would call in for a delivery to a building in the neighborhood and make it for an apartment on the fourth or fifth floor. When the driver would enter the building they would raid the back of the unmanned truck and dash off with the goods.

Joe also spent time running crap games around his neighborhood. He loved everything about crap games: organizing them, playing in them, and talking about them after they were done. If he had an addiction, it was to the dice. The joy he derived from gambling was not only from the game itself, but also from the connection he felt with his father whenever he played.

During his teenage years, Joe began to assemble his coterie of lifelong friends. Among these was a towering tough kid from South Brooklyn, Joseph "Joe Notch" Iannaccia, a good-looking Italian kid with a mean heart, Dominic "Mimi" Scialo, and a dedicated pal for years, short and stocky Joseph "Joe Smash" Gambale. Joe and his young friends were not organized criminals, but rather a part of the counterculture in Brooklyn that survived on petty rackets of deception and services that catered to others' vices. The more friends Joe made, and the more men he introduced himself to, the more he expanded his hustle and territory throughout South Brooklyn.

The young crew drove around Brooklyn, running dice games and taking trips to Coney Island to hang out on the boardwalk. They would play handball at Raven Hall, and, in making new friends, Joe would also find new players for his crap games. His love for the dice and his affable personality made him a great salesman. What extra cash Joe earned for himself wasn't spent on anything frivolous, he invested it back into his trade. These games were played mostly in apartment building basements and alleyways. They were always run professionally, a lookout would check for adults or police. As soon as someone came, the kids didn't panic and run away, they buried the dice and instantly started a handball game or innocently flipped baseball cards. Other times there was a chase. Joe and his friends would be spotted, and patrolmen would pursue them through the alleyways and in and out of the apartment corridors and basements. The boys were good at escaping, and so they loved the chase. The police, too, liked to make a sport of disrupting dice games; cruising past the boys, they would use their vehicle's loudspeaker and yell, "Run!" The kids of course were scared of the bust and scattered, dropping change on the ground as they went. The cops would then swipe up the abandoned coins. Joe encountered corruption at an early age.

***

In 1941 Joe was living in Dyker Heights on 86th Street with his maternal grandmother. Her home was directly across from the golf course where he'd spent summers caddying for his father. His mother and sister had returned from California, and Joe was now working both a full-time job and a side job in order to earn enough money to support his family. His mother had come back penniless and needed help taking care of Loretta. Joe would do whatever he could to make sure they had everything they needed.

In New York City at this time, the unions were always looking for young, strong men to help run the work crews. Joe's reputation for being a disciplined and effective employee earned him a job as a steward at A.W. Franklyn on 175 Varick Street in Manhattan. By the age of 18, the young, handsome and resourceful Colombo was the youngest person of authority in the factory. Joe was adored and respected by his boss, Mr. Vanauzi. Vanauzi paid him thirty dollars a week and even gave him the power to hire some of his own men, so Joe hired his friend Joe "Smash" Gambale and a few others to work in the power press plant. It was not uncommon for union stewards and foremen to have violent exchanges on the job. Indeed, union workers were often hired based on their experience as fighters and their ability to intimidate management. Joe, in contrast, often settled confrontations and kept peace in the workplace. He was young, but exceptionally diplomatic and skillful in resolving conflicts. Those who worked under his supervision seemed relatively happy, and were productive. One evening after work, he was invited to a meeting by a group of people who sought to recruit him for something more politically radical than the union.

***

In early 1941 Joe was invited to a dinner with some of his co-workers. They wanted to talk about politics and community, topics in which Joe was very interested. The organizer of the evening, Mary Gottlieb, appeared to be a communist who hoped to recruit Joe into the group as an organizer and speaker. She and some of her associates had recognized Joe's ability to lead others and resolve problems in the workplace. She wooed Joe, telling him that his voice and character destined him for something much greater than a union steward at a local factory.

Joe listened attentively to their discussion about the Party. While communism was a scary word for many immigrants after the Red Scare of 1919, Joe did not approach anything with fear, but rather with objectivity. This new political trend could potentially offer empowerment for the subjugated workingman. Joe and Mary continued to discuss politics at the factory, and then in the summer of 1941 she invited him to a camp in upstate New York. Joe was told to pack nothing but some clothing and a toothbrush for the two-week stay. He was given leave by his bosses at the factory, and took the ride upstate with his trusted friend, Joe Smash.

When they arrived at the campgrounds after the long ride from Bensonhurst to Pawling, both Colombo and Joe Smash felt anxious. Two men stood by the camp gates with assault rifles and asked for their names and identification before radioing in and allowing them to enter. Given the presence of weapons and the desolate location, Joe immediately feared what could happen to them if something were to go wrong. He had other reasons to be nervous: the place they'd arrived at was called Camp Webatuck, and was known by the government as a Communist indoctrination facility.

The two Joes met Mary at the main building and after they settled in to their quarters; she took them for a walk around the camp with some of her associates. She introduced Joe Colombo with great pride to her friends, and they met him with equal enthusiasm. They walked and Joe listened as they spoke about the current state of affairs in New York and the nation, from political corruption to community activism. As they made their rounds through the property, Joe Smash walked alert and mindful as he saw more and more armed men, most of whom were staring at them with intensity.

After attending some classes and listening to speeches, Joe decided they should enjoy some of their time away from the city and make use of the leisure activities the camp had to offer. They rode boats on the big lake, shot rifles at the range, and feasted on the fresh foods driven up daily from the city.

Joe Smash was uneasy and expressed his concerns to Colombo; "Joe, these people could kill us and leave us in the woods up here and no one would ever know about it." Joe replied, "They're not going to do anything to us, they're looking to recruit us." "Well what about the classes, don't you think they're going to get mad that we aren't showing up? We're eating the food, and doing all the other stuff. You don't think Mary notices we aren't there?" "I told her I would come up here and listen to her people and check the place out, and that's exactly what I'm doing."

Without finishing the two-week indoctrination, Joe told Mary he had to head back to the city for personal reasons. Even knowing he missed much of the education being offered, Mary and her colleagues still wanted Joe involved. They asked him to sign a logbook and make a commitment to the Party, and they hoped he would continue to meet with them back in Brooklyn. Joe did not sign anything and politely told Mary: "I am sorry, but I love my country and cannot make an alliance with this movement."

***

Back at the pocketbook factory in Brooklyn, while getting acquainted with some of the new workers, Joe was introduced to a beautiful young Italian girl with fair skin, sparkling green eyes, and long blonde hair. Her name was Lucille Faiello and she was one of the many Faiello girls employed by the factory at that time. Joe first gained Lucille's attention through his reputation as a figure of authority in the factory, but it was his charm that won him his first date with her. Lucille was striking from a distance and captivating up close. But what struck Joe more profoundly was her strength and composure. Lucille didn't fawn over Joe, nor did she seem intimidated by his superior status; she challenged him in a way that no other woman had before. This remarkable blend of beauty and self-assurance had Joe completely enamored.

After a few dates on the weekends and dinners together after work, Joe and Lucille, or "Jo-Jo", as she was called, became virtually inseparable. He began driving her to and from work every day, and spent almost every weekend with her family, enjoying Sunday dinners while getting acquainted with her eight sisters and one brother. She lived in downtown Brooklyn with her mother and a few of her sisters, on the corner of 4th Avenue and Sackett Street, not far from the factory where they both worked. Joe befriended some of her sisters' husbands, and then the couples began double-dating and taking trips together around the city.

During the summer of 1941, the couples would take trips to a somewhat secluded beach just east of Coney Island. It was a small peninsula and park called Plum Beach, where young couples and families would go to picnic and tan. The area was dubbed Plum Beach for the many plum bushes that adorned the landscape, and for many years was known as a "lovers' lane" in South Brooklyn. The women would set up blankets and food and the men would barbeque steaks and sausages on one of the grills. They played cards and took dips into the water. Joe would rent horses for him and Jo-Jo so they could ride up and down the beach together. In the evenings if they weren't at the beach, they stayed in downtown Brooklyn at one of Jo-Jo's sisters' homes playing cards and listening to the radio. On special nights, they would ride into Manhattan to watch shows at the Copacabana. Joe and Jo-Jo loved to dance, both in the clubs and at social events in local churches. A few blocks away from Jo-Jo's home the couple would watch films at the Garfield Theater. Life with Jo-Jo was filled with leisure activities and love, and her family became a part of his life that Joe had been missing.

On December 7, 1941, Japanese missiles, machine gun fire, and suicide airplanes besieged the United States Naval base at Pearl Harbor. After the attack that killed close to 2,500 Americans, President Roosevelt declared war on Japan. That same day, Germany and Italy would declare war on the U.S. in response. The U.S. was now entirely committed to fighting the Axis powers in the Second World War.

For many patriotic U.S. citizens this time of conflict would prove terribly confusing. Not only were 110,000 citizens of Japanese descent confined to internment camps following the Pearl Harbor attacks, but injustices to Italian and German Americans surged as well. Herds of these same young men were enlisting and being shipped off to war while simultaneously suffering from prejudice and alienation at home. The government began imposing a curfew on Italian-Americans in the state of California. Italian-American members of the longshoreman's unions in New York, New Orleans, and California were isolated into working gangs so a special watch could be maintained. Across the United States, but principally in New York, the FBI forcibly entered the homes of ordinary Italian American citizens, in a purported search for contraband. Excuses were made to justify the discrimination against Italians, but with no real representation, it was up to State led committees to defend the workers. It was understood that in order to protect the United States from espionage and spying, special steps within the military needed to be taken, but to turn away Italian-American garment workers from a plant that manufactured army uniforms in the name of national security was ludicrous.

Joe felt himself pulled in opposite directions. He felt loyalty towards the U.S. and its efforts in the war overseas, but was deeply distressed by his country's treatment of its own citizens. At eighteen years old Joe Colombo was ineligible for the draft, since he was the sole provider for his mother, grandmother and sister. He did not wish to escape the draft, however; he was adamant about fighting for a just cause, and Pearl Harbor had stirred up so much anger he was determined to get into the fight. On February 28, 1942 Executive Order number 9082 was passed and the Services of Supply (S.O.S.) was created as a branch of forces in the U.S. Army. Joe tried ignoring the draft rules and joining the forces on March 31st, but he was never called for active duty.

Following the one-year anniversary and vigil for Pearl Harbor, Joe realized he could not remain on the sidelines of the war. On December 14th, he walked down to the Coast Guard offices and tried to enlist. Since he was the sole provider at home after his father's death, Joe needed consent from a parent or guardian to become an apprentice seaman. Joe convinced his mother against her wishes to sign an agreement, which allowed him to enter the Coast Guard. Additionally, he promised to pay his entire 22 dollar a month sailor's salary towards her 38 dollar a month rent. During the next three months while they were apart, Joe and Jo-Jo's bond grew stronger. The thought of losing her boyfriend in battle made Jo-Jo terribly anxious, and Joe, too, began to understand how profoundly attached he was to her. The Faiellos were his family now and Jo-Jo was his true love. He was committed to the fight but his heart belonged in Brooklyn.

Before leaving to fight in the war, there was one last thing Joe wanted to do. He wanted to ask Jo-Jo for her hand in marriage. Insistent on gallantry and honor, Joe asked to meet with her father first. Dinner was arranged at the Faiello home one Sunday, and Jo-Jo's father, Sabatino, came over to meet the young Italian man who was courting his daughter.

When Joe arrived at the house he greeted Mr. Faiello with a warm show of respect and was met by a cold coarse man who did not return any politeness. They sat down at the table to a large meal with pasta and meats with gravy. The girls had cooked; Jo-Jo made Joe his favorite meatballs with raisins and pignoli in them. The family knew Joe was leaving for the war soon and flooded him with questions. Joe avoided the subject of war and focused on the girls and their personal lives, always interested in hearing how they were getting along in everyday life in Brooklyn. Joe watched as Sabatino sipped his wine, making occasional disdainful comments, and barely showing any interest in the girls' dialogue. He could only think of his own father and the decorum he'd always demonstrated as the head of the household. When dinner was through Joe shook hands and left for home, disappointed by the man he'd just met, wondering how he could have such little interest in such a warm and loving family.

That following day when Joe picked Jo-Jo up for work she spoke about her father and his impressions of Joe. Joe asked, "What did he say about me?" She answered, "Well, he said he asked you if you wanted a glass of wine and you told him you didn't drink, then he asked you if you wanted a cigarette and you told him you didn't smoke, so he says to me, 'What kind of man did you bring home? This guy doesn't drink or smoke?'" Joe listened and paused and told Jo-Jo, "Make sure you tell your father the next time you see him, I'm a better man than he'll ever be." Joe said it with passion and anger. He did not respect Jo-Jo's father. At a young age he learned in order to earn respect you had to show it first. How Sabatino treated his family and the history explained to him by Jo-Jo was enough to make Joe mad. He loved Jo-Jo and in time he would show her how much. She knew this in her heart, and when Joe proposed that following weekend, she accepted immediately.

***

On March 10, 1943 at the age of nineteen, Joe began Coast Guard training at Manhattan Beach, directly across from Plum Beach, his former lovers' hangout. By the fall, after training for three months at Holgate Station, Joe achieved the rank of Seaman 1st Class. His first assignment was working aboard the *USS Norfolk*, a new ship stationed in Philadelphia. After two months on the *Norfolk,* he was reassigned to the *Falgout*, a destroyer escort destined for a convoy mission off the coast of Africa. On December 4, 1943, the *Falgout* was sent to the aid of the *Tochet*, a steam tanker sunk near Bermuda by a German torpedo. The escort then began missions from Virginia to Africa. When the *Falgout* docked in New York, although allotted a three-day furlough, Joe extended his leave to seven days in order to see Jo-Jo. For the infraction, he received twenty days confinement and lost his twenty-two dollar a month salary for two months.

In the early morning of April 20, 1944 while the *Falgout* was escorting a convoy from Hampton Roads to Bizerte, the crew intercepted a transmission that revealed an enemy submarine was tailing them from 30 miles away. The convoy continued on its course but throughout the day Joe and his shipmates were anticipating battle. At 9:00 p.m. that evening Joe manned his battle station as close to thirty German airplanes launched a torpedo attack on the convoy. Within minutes the Germans had sunk the *USS Lansdale* (DD-426). The Germans also destroyed the *SS Paul Hamilton*, an ammunition freighter on its way to Operation Shingle in Italy. All six hundred of its crewmen were lost. The *SS Samite*, the *SS Stephen F. Austin* and the *SS Royal Star* were also torpedoed. After the battle subsided, while other ships searched for survivors and escorted damaged boats to Algiers, the *Falgout* continued to successfully escort the convoy to Bizerte. On its return trip to the US, the crew of the *Falgout* survived yet another German assault. Other vessels in its convoy were hit and close to fifty crewmen were killed before the attacking German sub was finally sunk.

On their return to America, the *Falgout* and its convoy were engaged in battle again. On May 3rd, while sailing just North of Africa, a German bomber flew over the USS *Menges* (DE-320) a destroyer escort on the opposing wing of the *Falgout*. The bomber did not engage with the ship, but after witnessing the low pass, the convoy manned their battle stations anticipating the bomber's return, knowing it wouldn't be alone. At 1:18 a.m. the *USS Menges* was hit in the stern by a torpedo from a German submarine. After two minutes of chaos aboard the ship, as the torpedo lay wedged in the ship's steel, depth charges began to explode. The torpedo killed 31 crewmembers and demolished a huge portion of the *Menges*. After a 26-hour attack the German Sub was abandoned and sunk by its crew. The *Falgout* captured many of the Germans sailors, and took the POWs to North Africa.

Once the escort passed the Alboran Sea, it docked in Casablanca. After the prisoners were released, Joe and his crewmates decided to take a leave before the *Falgout* made its voyage home. This excursion meant that they would not be permitted to go ashore when their ship returned to New York. Joe and many of his fellow seamen planned to leave the ship anyway when they returned to port, and concocted plans to cover for each other to avoid getting caught.

When Joe returned to New York he escaped from the docks to meet Lucille, insisting they be married before he headed back out to sea. Jo-Jo agreed. On May 28, 1944, before Reverend Alfonso Parziale, and both their families, Joe Colombo and Lucille Faiello joined hands at Our Lady of Peace Church on Carroll Street. While the marriage would last Joe's entire life, the immediate joy was short-lived. In fear of being court-martialed, and still needing to cover for some of his shipmates, Joe had to leave Jo-Jo with her sisters and return to the ship, and the war.

Upon returning to the ship, Joe and many of his crewmates received disciplinary action, but were not court-martialed. Joe pled his case, showing off his wedding photo and taking responsibility for the other men who'd left with him. He thanked the commanding officer for his leniency and they celebrated Joe's marriage on the boat with some of the other crewmen. When Joe finally left Brooklyn on his cutter, he was very torn. He had just made vows to love and protect Jo-Jo for the rest of his life, and he had every intention of doing so. But on the other hand, he had made vows to serve his country. One week after Joe's marriage, Operation Neptune began and 160,000 Allied troops landed along the German-controlled coastline of France. Before the day was through, there would be an estimated 20,000 casualties on both sides. A victory would be declared for the Allies but the loss was devastating.

After hearing about the carnage of D-Day and having seen conflict at sea, Joe was quickly realizing the precarious nature of a soldier's life. On board the ship he began to have nightmares, which he hadn't suffered since his father died. His fellow seamen would discover him in the middle of the night, apparently engaged in some chore, but actually fast asleep. His sleepwalking disorder was something Joe neglected to tell the officers during the application process for the Coast Guard.

To complicate matters further, a letter from back home reported disastrous news in Brooklyn: A fire had burned the Faiello's Sackett Street building to the ground. Jo-Jo, her mother and six of her sisters were without a home and had lost everything. Jo-Jo found shelter with her older sister Emily, but insisted that he come to see her as soon as he returned to Brooklyn. She told him she had some very important news for him, but that she needed to disclose it to him in private. Joe became distressed; he knew that he was still on confinement and ineligible for another furlough. Desperate to see his wife, again he arranged for some friends to cover for him as he snuck off the island to see her. Joe knew his next vessel would be dry-docked for the month and this time he planned to spend the entire time with Jo-Jo. After a few days of being off the ship, word was sent to Joe that he was to be court-martialed.

In fear of having the police show up at the Faiello home, Joe took Jo-Jo, loaded up the car and they drove upstate to her uncle's farm in the Catskills. It was there Jo-Jo told Joe that she was pregnant with their first child. They spent the rest of their time together discussing their plans for the future. Joe let Jo-Jo know he would have to leave her again, but left her with his promise, "No matter what might happen to me when I go back to that ship, I will be back to take care of you. It might not be right away, but when I do come back, it'll be for good."

Joe returned to his cutter on August 30th and was immediately brought into custody. After a few days in the brig, he was brought before a court martial and found guilty for being absent without leave. His record stated he had two other disciplinary actions for prior AWOLs, as well as warnings for gambling activities on the ship. Joe avoided the most severe consequences, since he had returned to the ship before it left port. This spared him from the much more serious charge of desertion. For being AWOL, Joe was sentenced to twelve months on Hart's Island, and would be given a dishonorable discharge after he completed the term. After his superior officers spoke on his behalf they agreed that if Joe could complete six months of satisfactory confinement, the dishonorable conduct discharge would be lifted.

After a week on Hart's Island, Joe began sleepwalking again. Out of his element and battling with multiple stresses, he was hospitalized for psychoneurosis. He spent almost three weeks in the hospital as doctors ran tests on him, trying to find a cure for his condition. Joe refused medications or any type of psychotherapy and insisted it would be better to just let the illness run its course as it had many times before. Soon, his condition did improve. For a number of months, he didn't suffer any episodes.

He spent Thanksgiving and Christmas with the rest of the prison population, and wrote letters to Jo-Jo about his anticipation of their first child in February. However, just before Jo-Jo gave birth, Joe found himself back in the hospital, and spent almost a full week under supervision. Three days after his release back into population, on February 25, 1945, their first child, Anthony Edward Colombo was born.

Anthony recalls, "When I was born, my father was still locked up on Hart's Island. I knew he had spent time in the psychiatric unit, but I never questioned him about any of that. I never really got to question him about his time spent in the Coast Guard, but I know he loved his country very much. It was the reason his insisted I go to military school when I finished high school, and the reason he was so fervent about politics and government. He shared a few stories with me, and told me he saw action during the war. He lost friends; some from the neighborhood, some with whom he had served in the Guard. Years later, as a result of these experiences, my father vehemently opposed my decision to join the war effort in Vietnam."

***

About one month later on March 24th, after two years with the Guard and after completing seven months of his sentence, Joe Colombo received an honorable discharge from the Coast Guard. He had full privileges to wear his American, European, Middle Eastern and African campaign ribbons for his service in the war.

The Coast Guard offered him disability checks for his condition but Joe refused, knowing that once he was back in Brooklyn he could earn his own money. He would join his wife and one-month old boy at their home on President Street, and he would start a new life with his new family.

Chapter 2.

"The Good Life"

(1945-1959)

Joe Colombo strode slowly across a lot in the Brooklyn docks towards one of the warehouses near the train tracks. He had been called to meet his supervisor, but the message was cryptic. He knew the building he was about to enter was hardly used for legitimate purposes. It had a few back offices that housed some almost invisible personnel. He had seen men escorted here and emerge with limbs out of place and colorful faces. Joe did not expect the same for himself. He had no debt; he never used drugs or drank, he did not repeat rumors, and he was well respected by the men who ran these docks.

The long wooden planking of a narrow passageway leads him into a large office in the back of the machine shop. The man he saw standing there needed no introduction. Umberto Anastasia was his name; Albert to his paesanos. Anastasia's roots were in Calabria, a heritage of which he was fiercely proud, and which he shared with other gangsters like Frank Costello, Frankie Uale, Big Jim Colosimo, and Joe's own father. He was a union leader whose infamy as a hit man earned him the handle "The Mad Hatter." He must have come in through a back entrance so the rest of the dockworkers wouldn't discover his arrival. Although he was *known everywhere in New York as the leader of the longshoreman, he liked to move in silence, especially when out of his territory. Anastasia leaned on a desktop; his heavy frame sagging slightly as he examined the young Colombo. His face was clean-shaven and his eyes beamed straight ahead in an odd fashion that made men uncomfortable. Joe had been forewarned that Anastasia would ask for him. Now he stood only a few feet away from the man the entire city spoke about in hushed and nervous tones.*

Anastasia began to speak in a gravelly voice laden with an almost impossibly thick accent. "You're Tony Durante's boy?" Colombo answered with respectful pride, "Yes, I am." "What is your name?" "Joseph Colombo." Anastasia nodded and glanced meaningfully at his cohorts who stood quietly around him. They envied the way his mere presence invoked fear in every man that faced him. "Your father, he was a real testa duro. A very tough man." Joe smiled. "They call him Tony 'Two Guns.' You know that?" Although reluctant to give the wrong answer, Joe did not know. "No," he replied. Anastasia stood in order to elaborate. "He always wear' a vest with he suit. In these two pockets he keeps his pistols." Anastasia made two finger pistols on both sides of his belly where the rib pockets would be. He stopped and looked at Joe. "Always!" Anastasia paused and looked out the windows, as a ship passed by in the upper bay. Colombo did not know then that Anastasia had met his father while they were doing hard time together in Sing Sing in the early 1920's. "He was a man's man, your father. A good man."

***

It would only take Joe Colombo a few months to get his business in order after leaving the Coast Guard. The solid reputation he'd earned as a young steward in the union enabled him to find work easily. He began working as a stevedore on the waterfront at the Fort Hamilton Army Base in Bay Ridge, and soon became a member of the Local 1814 International Longshoreman's Association. But Joe already had enough experience with strikebreaking and running work cadres, and was ready for more challenging endeavors. He added to his pay by moonlighting for a bakery in Brooklyn earning a few extra dollars for deliveries and even began making sales for the company.

By the spring of 1946, Jo-Jo was pregnant with their second child. On Christmas Eve that year at Methodist Hospital in Brooklyn, they welcomed Joseph Junior into the Colombo family. While expanding his immediate family, Joe was also still taking care of his mother and twelve-year-old sister. To supplement his income, he had to revive some of his old hustles around Brooklyn, taking down delivery trucks and running crap games. It would also be the first time he had a run-in with law enforcement. During that summer Joe was arrested with a few of his pals by Brooklyn cops for shooting dice in the street. For the offense he received a ticket and had to appear before a judge with his co-defendants. They were all called at the same time and each of them pleaded guilty and were fined four dollars for the offense—never knowing it was a stigma that would harm him decades later.

On the waterfront it was common knowledge that a certain few men within the ranks of organized crime wielded control over the unions. The docks in Brooklyn were firmly in the grip of one of the most feared men in New York City, Albert Anastasia. Law enforcement connected Anastasia with over sixty murders, thirty of them by his own hand. Albert Anastasia was known as the architect of the infamous Murder Inc. organization. For years, he'd wriggled out of indictments, arrests, and even convictions. Anastasia shared a number of attributes with Joe's father. They were both Prohibition-era gangsters with family lineage in the southern region of Calabria. And both husky men had frequented the City Democratic Club in South Brooklyn, a haunt young Joe had visited with his father. With men like Anastasia running the action and controlling the unions, Joe would be furnished with new opportunities to make money.

Where the NYPD was concerned, the docks of Brooklyn weren't an easy place to infiltrate. Irrespective of what went on inside the gates or the warehouses, the police were required to announce themselves whenever they showed up. No business owner wanted cops hanging around the workplace; it drew unwanted attention and slowed the workflow. The cops could only obtain information about the docks and the rackets inside from very low-level informants, and most of it was second and third hand. Still, Colombo's name began popping up in various Brooklyn police stations for suspected involvement in the policy racket and as an organizer of floating crap games. Police saw Colombo with other union bosses at Andy's Bar and Grill during work breaks, speaking with or leaving with assumed "wise guys", increasing their suspicions.

Police believed Colombo was handpicked by Mob bosses to strong-arm union workers on the docks. Men like Joe were also typically involved in undertakings such as loan sharking, bookmaking, crap games, cargo theft, extortion, and assorted shakedowns. The only difficulty for law enforcement was proving it. Finding a victim brave enough to testify in an open court against a man like Joe Colombo was virtually impossible.

The shakedown racket on the waterfronts was designed to keep "kick backs" of cash flowing into the pockets of gangsters. The avocation of men like Joe was to keep tabs on the most productive dockworkers, and to inform the boss who should be chosen each morning for the "shape up." In a "shape up" workers with debts to a loan shark, or who liked to gamble were likely to be selected. They were expected to cough up a percentage of their pay to their bosses as a "contribution," and tabs were kept on simple things such as which local shops the men had spent their money. Tracking expenditures in this manner enabled the bosses to control which businesses would make money on popular products such as olive oil, cheese, and cigarettes.

With the war behind him and financial prospects favorable, Joe began to share with his family the many traditions his father had shared with him. Colombo began taking summer vacations in upstate New York. During these trips, Joe would periodically leave his wife and children to travel back to Brooklyn for several days to handle business.

***

"Some of my earliest memories with my family were when my father would take us upstate for the summers. It was a tradition that my father was introduced to when he was a young kid and that persisted until we all eventually moved up there. My grandfather used to take my father upstate to Orange County every summer to vacation in the woods and visit the fairgrounds. I remember driving around the fairgrounds in our car, and my father would point out all of the different houses he used to stay in as a kid. He would tell us the name of the grocer they bought provisions from and he would point out places where they used to eat. We would stop by an old farmhouse and he would tell us, 'They used to rent horses here, this is where my father first taught me how to ride a horse when I was a kid.' Every year the story was exactly the same. It was almost like he forgot he'd told them to us the year before."

"Years before he purchased the summer home in Blooming Grove, we would stay at a bungalow colony with my aunt and uncles up by Kingston, New York. The place was called Martella's; a quiet family-owned getaway nestled in the top of a mountainside along the edge of the Hudson River. When we first rolled down the long dirt road, there was a big house with a nice wooden porch with lots of country decorations dangling from a shed roof. The family who operated the place lived inside this building, and we would stay in little bungalows further down the dirt road. My father had been taking us there since I was a baby, and would bring other family members up to stay with us to keep my mom company when he went back to work in the city during the week. There I started spending lots of time with my Aunt 'Sugar' and her husband Banjo, my Aunt 'Ray Ray,' and her husband, Uncle 'Do-Do,' and another aunt and uncle who weren't blood relatives, but who were as close to us as family; they were my Aunt Nelly and Uncle Dick.

My mother and her sisters would do most of the cooking while we were away. Our bungalows had small kitchens and there were grills outside where we could fix burgers, hot dogs, steaks, and chicken. Occasionally we would go up to the main house, which had a kitchen and dining area, and for about fifty cents the owners would make us pizza pie. After we had a dinner, the whole family would sit by the radio and listen to the shows. I remember listening to Amos and Andy and comedians like Red Foley. We built campfires and the adults would just sit and talk for hours. I can remember watching my mother and father playing gin against each other. All of the adults were constantly playing card games up there; as a little boy I learned how to play games like casino and canasta with them.

Life upstate was very relaxing for my father; looking back now I see how it must have been therapeutic. I remember he would get up early in the morning and go off hiking or jogging into the woods. Then when he was through, he would go down to the pool to swim laps. He was a very athletic person and Brooklyn must have been very restrictive for him. He was limited to playing golf and handball; he wasn't the type to put on jogging clothes and run on a track or along the sidewalks. He was a different man altogether when we were upstate, something I'm sure my mother noticed too. I don't think it was her desire to move out of Brooklyn when we did, but she knew for my father, it was something he needed to do.

Every morning I would wake up and run out of the bungalow to go find my father and my uncles and see what they were doing. I remember down by the pool area on the side of the cabana hung a heavy bag they would punch, and since they were doing it, I wanted to also. It was too high for me to reach so my father would hold me up to it so I could take swings. He made sure he taught me the right way to make a fist and how to use my body when I swung. Even when I was too young to fight, he wanted to make sure I was doing things the right way. He didn't waste time with us growing up, and he didn't treat us like babies; he always treated us like young men. Some lessons were easy to learn, others took lots of practice, but he never gave up on us.

When my father taught us how to swim, he would take us over to the edge of the pool and just throw us in, and yell, 'Now swim!' That was it, sink or swim. No showing us a stroke as he held us in the water, he just stood on the edge and watched us while we figured it out. This was how he was taught when he was a kid, and this was how we would learn too. I think it made my mother nervous, but she never stepped in to undermine him. When he would go jogging in the woods I would try to trail him. I remember trying to keep up with him a few times but I figured out at a very young age that long distance running just wasn't my thing. I did follow him during his long walks down to the river. There was a Coast Guard station at the bottom of the mountain and we sometimes went fishing there. The station was rarely active, but a few times while we were there a cutter would pull up and drop off supplies. Sometimes we would go down there with golf clubs and hit balls off the pier into the Hudson. I wasn't a big fan of golf but I did like whacking long shots. I preferred the shooting ranges.

The woods were very thick so we would walk down the mountain on the dirt road. I remember once I was walking with my Uncle Banjo over the mountain to go fishing and when we turned a corner, lying right in the middle of the road, bathing in the sun, was a four-foot-long Copperhead snake. I had never seen a snake that size in my life, and to this day I've never seen one that big outside of captivity. I was absolutely frozen. I asked my uncle what we should do. My uncle wasn't a big outdoorsman like my father. He leaned down and said, 'You know what, Anthony, Let's leave that snake alone.' And that was the end of our fishing trip down at the pier.

When we packed up to head back to Brooklyn my father was very nervous about the brakes on our car. They had been giving out the whole ride up from the city, and had gotten really bad the few times he took the car into town. Once we got the luggage strapped to the roof and we climbed in, my dad knew there was no way we could make it back safely. The whole ride out of Martella's, we were on the brink of crashing and he was constantly pumping the brakes just to get it to slow down a little. All the way down at the bottom of the mountain on the main road was a service station. He decided he was going to let the women and children out of the car and drive alone to the station. My Aunt Nelly and Uncle Dick were riding in the backseat of our car, and Dick was a pretty heavy drinker. The afternoon we left he hadn't wanted to let any of his cold beers go to waste so he finished them all. Once everyone got out of the car my father looked at Dick and said, 'Come on Dick, hop in. We'll ride down together.' Dick said, 'I'm not getting in that thing.' 'What are you worried about? We'll be fine.' Dick and my father got into the car and went down the hill, no brakes. This was no little hill; it wound down and around a mountain and then dumped out on to a major road. I didn't get the pleasure of seeing what happened exactly on their way down to the bottom, but I know one thing for sure, by the time They'd made it down to the service station, my uncle Dick was sitting white-faced on a bench next to the Coke Machine. The ride had made him stone cold sober"

***

Vincent Michael Colombo was born on October 16, 1950. The two-bedroom apartment in Jo-Jo's sisters' home on President's Street couldn't accommodate the three young boys, so Joe bought a three-story home on 77th Street in the Bensonhurst section of Brooklyn. Joe rented the second floor to Jo-Jo's youngest sister, Malayla "Sugar" Faiello and her husband, "Banjo". On the top floor in a large space that could have served as an attic, Joe set up a dream train set for his sons. The boys would escape up there for full days, running the electronic toys around their private utopia. Joe's family occupied the first floor and the basement, which contained a small kitchen and dining area. It was here that Anthony would witness his father's first confrontation with a man outside the family. This was Anthony's introduction to the unyielding ferocity that his father could display when provoked.

***

"My father was a very strict disciplinarian. He could just give you a look with his eyes." Anthony vividly recalls the first time he witnessed his father's anger. "I used to walk down 15th Avenue to get to P.S. 204, which is now called Vince Lombardi Grammar

School. I was new in the neighborhood and back then whenever you were a new kid and no one knew you, you were likely to have a run-in of some sort with the neighborhood bully. A few older kids would tease me on my way to school in the mornings. They started with little things like name calling and some minor pushing and shoving, loud threats about kicking my ass. Then one morning in the spring two bullies decided to take things a little further. They were taunting me and I snapped back with some remark and they both grabbed me and we wrestled around until they had my arms pinned behind my back. While one kid held my arms, the other punched me in the stomach. One of the kids I remember was named Ralphie; he used to tower over me. After the beating was through, the bullies ran off to school, but I was hurt so I turned around and went home crying. I showed up at the house and my father was there. He asked me what happened. When I told him the story, he said, 'So, what are you crying about?' I said, 'Dad, two kids just beat me up!' He said, 'Ok, so two guys beat you up. I'll tell you what to do. First of all, don't ever come into this house crying again! If you do, I'm going to give you the rest of the beating they didn't give you. What you do is, you get a bat, and you hit them back. You don't let them walk away. You get back at them, and you go fight them but you don't ever come home crying. You defend yourself!'

So back on 15th Avenue there was a house there that had tall hedges in front of it. I got myself a little stickball bat and I went over there and hid in the hedges. I knew Ralphie and his friends would pass me on the way to school. I sat nervously as I heard them approaching and right when they came to me I jumped out from the bushes. They got startled and before they had time to see what was going on I whacked Ralphie a couple of times with the stick. I was whacking him all over his body. Not that I didn't want to hit him in the head, but I knew this was going to be enough. Ralphie's friends didn't stick around to see if I was going to work them over too, so I stayed on Ralphie real good. Soon, he started to cry and scream. I pounded away until he finally broke free and ran. I was done; I'd made my point and didn't need to chase him. I never said anything to my father about it afterwards, and he never asked.

That night, around six o'clock we were eating dinner in our kitchen. The kitchen in our apartment was in our basement, a few feet below the ground, with those small Jalousie crank out windows facing the driveway. There was a little step down from the driveway and if you opened the door you would be right in the middle of our kitchen. My father would always sit facing those windows and the door. He was the first to see a large man walking into the driveway and up to our screen door. He opened it and came right into the house.

The man stood in the doorway and he looked at my father and said, 'I want to see you.' My father looked at him and said, 'Excuse me, I am eating dinner here with my family. What are you doing walking into my house? I didn't invite you here.' The man started raising his voice to my father, saying,' I got to talk to you about your son.' I knew at that moment that this was Ralphie's dad. He looked down at my father and saw a small Italian man and someone he was sure he could handle; he acted very gruff and tough when he spoke. My father was only about 5 foot 6 inches, 165 pounds, an easy man to size up, but not so easy to fight. Ralphie's dad was belligerent and my father was civil. He said quietly, 'We shouldn't have any discussion as men in front of my wife and my children. Let's walk outside of the house and talk like

39

grown men.' Ralphie's dad took a deep breath and decided to follow my dad's lead.

As soon as they got outside, my father shut the door, and with a speed I couldn't believe, he had this man by the throat and brought him down to his eyelevel. He had a tight lock on his throat and choked him as he yelled at him. For the first time in my life I saw the animal come out of my father. He spat, 'Don't you ever dare come walking into my house. Who the fuck do you think you are?' The man completely lost his composure. He was frightened, and wore a face of a thousand apologies now. As he tried to speak, my father loosened his grip to let him get a few words out. He cried for mercy and said, 'Your son hit my son with a bat, and my son came home crying.' My father snapped back, 'Your son and his friend beat my son up yesterday, punched him in the stomach until he almost threw up, and when he came home crying did I come and tell you anything?' The guy whimpered back, 'No!' 'So what are you doing here? Tell your son that if he's going to do those kinds of things, he's going to get paid back. And I'll tell you another thing, if your son and his friend ever go near my son again; he is going to open them up with that bat. The man whimpered and tried to look away from my father during his rage. 'Look in my eyes!' The man shook and looked eye to eye with my dad. 'You hear me good. The next time you walk in my house without my permission I'm going to open your head up with a bat.' He screamed, 'You hear me? You understand what I'm telling you?' My father was boiling. Ralphie's dad just helplessly repeated, 'I'm sorry. I'm sorry. I'll never bother you again. It's all over, my son will never bother your son again.'

Once my father sent the message to this guy, he let off the chokehold and let the guy breathe in the driveway for a few seconds. He looked at the man and said 'It's over then.' My father fixed the sleeves on his shirt and looked down at Ralphie's Dad knowing he still feared my father might hurt him. So my father asked him in a friendlier tone, 'What's your name?' The guy gave him his name and my dad said 'This is all to be forgotten now, right?' Ralphie's dad agreed and my Dad helped him up and they shook hands and the man left and that was that. That was the first time I saw how he interacted with another man during a feud. I had seen him get angry in the house and I knew what a strict man he was but I had never seen his behavior towards people outside of our home life until that day. When my father came back inside the house, no one at the table said a word. Then after a minute of awkward silence he said to me, 'If that kid ever comes at you again you better put him in a hospital.' I answered, 'Okay dad.' But Ralphie never bothered me after that, and I never came home crying again."

***

Anthony tails his father closely. Wisps of white smoke issue from every exhale into the February air. It is always a few degrees colder in the graveyard. Anthony takes judicious steps on the grass so as not to dirty his dress shoes. The frost on the grass blades crunch beneath him.

They stop at a headstone and Joe bends forward and places a flower in front of it. Joe turns to Anthony with darkened eyes, "This is your Grandfather's grave." Anthony looks at it. He tries to understand its meaning. He sees his name engraved in the stone, a bit obscured by age and grit. He does not know how this makes him feel and decides to stay quiet. Joe bows his head in silent memoriam. Anthony mimics his father, carefully peeking every few seconds, hoping to finish his prayer simultaneously.

When his father finally lifts his head, he wears an expression that Anthony has never seen before. Had it lingered a few moments more, it might have appeared almost soft; sentimental. Instead, the familiar austere gaze returns. "Now, Anthony," he begins with a small breath of cold air. "You're my oldest son. That means God forbid anything ever happens to me you will become the man of the house. You will have to go out and find a job and take care of your mother and brothers." Joe looks intently at his son for confirmation, "Do you understand me?" Trying valiantly to conceal the fact that he is freezing, the nine-year-old boy replies, "Yes, Dad." "If something bad in life falls on you, you just accept it. You take care of your family, no matter what you gotta' do!" Anthony nods dutifully. He senses there is much more than a father buried beneath the cold earth at their feet. A few decades later he would realize this wasn't simply a father's advice to a son. Joe is preparing Anthony for the shadowy legacy that he must inherit, despite terrible reluctance.

✳✳✳

Joe sought to create a childhood for his sons that embodied the many experiences he'd shared with his father. Saturday evenings they would pile into the car and drive into Manhattan for a night of entertainment. Dinners were enjoyed at Lindy's Steakhouse or sometimes Ratskeller's Chinese restaurant. The boys would joyfully examine the giant lobster tank in front of Lindy's before sitting down at the table. The boys were sometimes taken to see movies at the Rio Paramount Theater. Like their father, the boys donned their best sport jackets and ties, along with shiny new shoes. Going to see a film was always an occasion. The theaters were magnificent displays of interior design, surrounded by towering columns, illuminated by thousands of lights, and ornamented with lavish murals and opulent decor. Joe would also purchase tickets every year to the circus and sideshows that visited the city. One of the family's absolute favorite spectacles was the rodeo. The boys and their father shared a love for cowboys and horses, and never missed a chance to attend when Roy Rogers and Dale Evans put on a show.

After church every Sunday, the Colombos would take a ride into downtown Brooklyn to visit Jo-Jo's mother and sisters. Joe's mother-in-law, Maria was the portrait of an Italian grandmother raised in the Depression era. Mariucci, as she was called, was short and stout. She wore her grey hair knotted tightly in a bun and when she smiled she showed gums where her teeth used to sit. She never felt burdened having all ten of her children and their children over to the house for family dinner. She would cook every meal from scratch. If Joe brought over some nice steaks for the grill, she would prepare a fresh salad and serve the meat with fresh cut potato fries. Pasta and pizza dough were always made from scratch, and pies and cakes made with fresh fruits and creams. Joe had a sweet tooth. He would always ask Jo-Jo to get him something sweet after every meal at home, sometimes just a candy from a stash she kept hidden from him. For most Sunday dinners he would pick up pies and cakes from his favorite bakery just off the Bay Ridge Parkway on Third Avenue. He would select the favorite desserts of Jo-Jo's mother and two uncles, Sal, and Tony. After dinner the men would retire in the living room with their black coffees and cakes to discuss social and political affairs. Joe would do anything for his older-generation compatriots. He was an attentive listener and would spend hours discussing the injustices that afflicted the Italian-American immigrant. He was a proud union man, firmly believing that the courage of a few men could prevent the suffering of thousands.

In the summers, Joe continued to enjoy the tranquility of upstate New York with his family. After a few years at Martella's, they began staying at the Warwick Pines, a more upscale establishment with a larger swimming pool and grand dining hall. This new rental had more amenities, including Joe's most loved avocation, horseback riding. Along with his immediate family, Joe would always invite Jo-Jo's sisters upstate to keep her company. He would lure Ray Ray, Sugar, or Fanny there for a weekend, and then, with his charm and good salesmanship, coax them into staying for weeks at a time. In the summer of 1955, Joe found himself the perfect piece of property in a nothing of a town called Blooming Grove, about sixty miles from New York City. The land was about three acres and on it sat a small knotty pine house. The property and house were in need of lots of work but its great potential and reasonable price were too much for Joe to resist. For $8,500, Joe acquired a modest summer home with land that held a small pond, a stream and plenty of fields to build stables and ride horses.

Already an excellent rider, Joe shared his passion for horses with his sons. Just like Joe, Anthony and Joe Junior fell in love with horses and were natural riders. The older boys would ride every day at the summer ranch. Joe taught them how to ride with the same precision that was inculcated in him by own his father in this same place about two decades prior. His passion for horses was reflected in the care he took with every detail. He showed his sons how to properly mount and dismount a horse. He showed them the correct placement of the bridle, the need for a blanket, and the securing of the saddle. He taught them how to handle a horse if it attempted to rear up on them. The first horse he bought was for Anthony when he was eight years old; a pony named Prince. A few years later he purchased two Western-Broke Quarter horses. Anthony's second horse was a reddish bay, named Major. Joe Junior's was a whitish grey colored horse that he called Champ. Joe also purchased an English-Broke thoroughbred mare for himself and named her Joey's Girl. Jo-Jo and Joe would ride with their two sons every chance they got.

For Joe, there was a specific and correct approach to everything. He fastidiously maintained his appearance, and not just in public; it was an obsession and had to be attended to constantly. Every morning, Joe followed the same routine. He would sit down in the kitchen to read his daily newspapers and sip coffee in silk pajamas with matching slippers. His undershirt was neatly pressed and his hair was combed back the same as it would be at dinner. He would snack on a piece of Melba toast with light butter or biscotti, but he rarely had a full breakfast. He ate small meals throughout the day in order to stay trim and healthy. He took walks as often as possible and played regular games of handball with his longtime friends. Joe was a very competitive opponent and had great skill with his hands. The game was played with a smaller, heavier ball in those days, so Joe would wear a black glove to protect his palm. Even leisure for Joe was like work, it must be engaged in with great discipline and purpose.

By the mid 1950's the waterfront was beginning to heat up with investigations. Before the police spotlight could be shone on Joe, his mentor, the man he'd first met at his father's funeral, advised him to switch his line of work. Joe was set up with a job across town on Atlantic Avenue as a salesman for the Pride Meat Company. He would work fewer hours than he did on the docks, and with the more than decent pay rate from his boss Peter Castellano, he was able to quit moonlighting altogether. Joe was earning money faster now. He traded in his two-year-old Cadillac for a brand new 1955 powder blue model. He opened the Café Royal, a social club on New Utrecht Avenue and 80th Street. The club was frequented by a group of Bensonhurst regulars, including Joe "Smash" Gambale, Rocky Maraglia, Joey "Notch" Iannaci, Dominic "Mimi" Scialo, Johnny "Bath Beach" Oddo, Frank "Pee Wee" Campagna, and John "Sonny" Franzese. A veteran friend of Joe's managed the club full-time; he was a tall, limping man called "Brother," There was a small kitchen in the back where a close friend of Joe's, nicknamed, "Fat Steve" made pasta and sauce for the members while they played cards. Joe tried to obtain a beer and wine license in 1955 but was promptly denied. The activities and members of the Café Royal were being closely monitored by the NYPD, who believed the establishment was a numbers racket headquarters. In the summer of that year, Joe and Jo-Jo attended the wedding of Carmella Profaci and Anthony Tocco, at the Commodore Hotel in Manhattan. Carmella was the daughter of Mob boss Joe Profaci; the ruthless, despotic leader of the biggest crime organization in Brooklyn. Colombo's attendance was viewed by law enforcement as an indisputable sign of rank. Joe's sense of persecution and alienation grew as he increasingly encountered police shakedowns and raids.

***

"While we were living on 77th Street my father would give us an allowance of one dollar a week. I would usually spend it at the movies with my brother Joey. We would go with a few of our friends from school to the Lowes Oriental Cinemas on 86th Street. If nothing we liked was playing there, we would check out something at the Deluxe on Cropsy Avenue. For about fifteen cents we could see like thirty or forty different cartoons. There was a story written not too long ago about this time in my life, when Sammy the Bull boasted about how he beat me and Joey up.

I want to set the record straight about what actually happened. I was at the Lowes Oriental with my brother, flirting with the girls and trying to get a kiss or some other kind of little thrill. Joey would wander off sometimes, and there were a few occasions when he got into it with other kids. This one day he came running up to me all upset saying, 'Anthony, this kid just smacked me in the face!' It didn't take much for me to fight back then, especially for my brother. I said, 'Who? Show me.' He walked me down the aisle and points out this kid. He was in the middle of the row talking with some girls, not paying any attention. So, normally when you step into a row to get into your seat you are facing the big screen with your back to the row directly behind you. I walked down this row facing everyone behind me, so they could get a good look at my eyes. When I got to Sammy he had a tough expression on his face. But he didn't recognize me, and he definitely didn't expect what was coming next. I let loose on him. I opened up on his face until my arms got tired. You could say I 'Jap' attacked him, fine, but don't say anything else.

I remember bumping into Sammy years later in Brooklyn. By then we were both young adults. I joined a street gang called the Ramparts that he was also in. We all used to hang out in front of a candy shop across from New Utrecht High School. There was never any mention of that fight we had. And I know he knew it was me in the theater that day. One time we were hanging out and someone said to him right in front of me. 'Hey Sammy, there's Anthony Why don't you give him that beating now?' He didn't say anything. Not a word. He didn't want any part of me. He was definitely a good brawler, there's no doubt about that, but I took the starch out of him that day in the movie theater and he didn't want that to happen again, especially not in front of all our crew."

✳✳✳

By the age of twelve, Joe's son Anthony was already well aware of the underworld of New York City. He got his first glimpses of its brutality and infamous figures from reading the newspapers. In May 1957, the shooting of Frank Costello in Manhattan made headlines, and forecasts of a Mob war appeared in the city ledgers. Almost all of America saw the bloody photos printed in the newspaper on October 26, 1957, when the "Lord High Executioner" Albert Anastasia was killed in the barbershop of the Park Sheraton Hotel. At the time Anastasia was in the newspapers daily, and his death would go down in history as one of the most publicized Mob hits in America.

For years, the police and newspapers speculated about who was behind the brutal killing. While Santo Trafficante could not be questioned after his abrupt departure from New York City the day Anastasia was killed, rumors began to fly about a Gambino, Lucchese, and Genovese coup. Joey Gallo alluded many times to people that it was his gang behind the slaying, Carmine "Junior" Persico stated, "The FBI knew who really hit Anastasia... but that fag Crazy Joe Gallo took the credit"[v]. At that time Gallo was a suspected soldier in the Profaci crime organization of Brooklyn.

About three weeks after Anastasia's death, at the estate of Joe "The Barber" Barbara in Appalachian, New York, close to one hundred men gathered to discuss a number of undisclosed subjects. Potential topics ranged from casino investments in Havana, to narcotics trade, to the possible breaking down of properties in unions and garment industries. But many theorists agree there must have been discussions regarding the Anastasia gang and the possible war brewing with the Genovese crew. The state police, after receiving tips, rallied their troopers and raided Barbara's house, sending men scattering through the woods. Many of these men were suspected members of organized crime's secret board of directors, commonly known as "the Commission." The Appalachian raid was a turning point for J. Edgar Hoover and the FBI in their mounting pursuit of organized crime.

In the spring of 1958 the FBI paid its first visit to Joe to question him about the deaths of two young Brooklyn thugs. They wanted to know about Joe's relationship with "Mimi" Scialo. They told Joe about two young men in East Brooklyn, both beaten with chains and then finished off with bullets. Miraculously, with five bullets in his head, chest, and stomach, one of the youths managed to cling to life long enough to mention the names "Mimi" and "Shelly" on his deathbed at Coney Island Hospital. NYPD issued warrants for Dominick "Mimi" Scialo and Angelo "Shelly" Pero. Joe Colombo's name also surfaced early in the investigation. If Mimi were behind the brutal double murder, Colombo would have to know. Street informants and scared locals gave up what they thought was harmless information about Mimi and Joe. Colombo was best man at Mimi's wedding, and a few years later became the godfather of his son. While Mimi and Pero had both disappeared, the FBI began making visits to Joe at the Café Royal, pressing him to disclose Mimi's whereabouts. Joe told them he didn't know. At that time, the FBI's Organized Crime Task Force (OCTF) was so unacquainted with the underworld layout that they did not know which informants they could trust, but they tended to believe any man who wasn't willing to talk was probably guilty. Joe answered only the questions he could; he told them where he went to work and that he was a friend of Mimi's. Beyond this, he knew nothing about the murders or where Mimi might be. Police pressure intensified. Joe was busted twice for vagrancy within two weeks. His second arrest was at the grand opening of Club 13 on

East 13th Street and Avenue U. While the charges against Joe were eventually dismissed, he and thirteen others were held at the station for their failure to reveal information.

The FBI file on Joe continued to expand. Agents tracked all of his potential business interests, popular haunts and associates. They learned Joe was a silent partner in the Como Lounge on 86th Street and 15th Avenue. When the FBI questioned the manager, a tall, well-built Italian man by the name of Joe LaRosa, they failed to obtain any pertinent information. LaRosa was not only the operator of the restaurant lounge; he was also married to Joe's younger sister Loretta. Loyalty was the guiding and inviolable principle in Joe's family and personal life.

That winter, Joe received a distressing call from Louie Gazolla. Louie had been watching over Joe's summer home in Blooming Grove while they were in Brooklyn during the winter months. The knotty pine house Joe had just finished renovating had completely burned down. He lost a lot of personal belongings in the fire and was visibly distraught when he visited the ruins. The bright side came in the form of an insurance policy Joe had on the home. Since 1955 when he made the purchase, the value of the property had appreciated considerably. After investigations by the fire department revealed no signs of arson, Colombo was able to collect a $23,000.00 check from his broker. He was also paid an additional $14,000.00 for his furniture, clothing, and possessions.

That spring, as a consequence of incessant police harassment, Joe was forced to shut down the Café Royal for good. Within a week he opened a new spot on 13th Avenue and 78th

Street, only a few doors down from his aunt's home where he'd lived as a child. This began a sort of cat and mouse game between Colombo and the NYPD that would persist for the next few years. When police presence became a problem, Joe would close one establishment and open another. While patrolmen were indifferent to neighborhood clubs that housed gambling and numbers running, higher officers were increasingly criticized by politicians and the FBI for their failure to control the multi-million dollar gambling industry in New York. Law enforcement would soon adopt more aggressive tactics.

***

The new house Joe built was complete by August of 1959. It was much larger than the small, cottage-style summer home. It was a four-bedroom white brick ranch, which boasted a large living room with fireplace and finished basement with an entertainment center. Joe bought more land around the property. This last purchase would extend the Blooming Grove estate across a total of forty-seven acres. He would use some of the extra insurance money to build fully equipped horse stables with six individual stalls and a professional tack room for the saddles and equipment. He bought a big wagon for his hefty new pony, and in addition, he was given two Sicilian donkeys from his dear friend, Carmine Persico.

The family would spend the last few weeks of that summer together in their new home. The boys caught up on horseback riding and helped Jo-Jo organize all of the new furnishings and decorations. Joe was living the good life; as far as he was concerned, everything was going according to plan. That fall in downtown Brooklyn, however, a single murder became the virus that would infect all of his illegal activities.

Chapter 3.

"My Blue Heaven"

(1959-1963)

The faint sound of footsteps echoes in the darkness of Carroll Street in Red Hook, Brooklyn. A beam of lamplight illuminates the ghostly forms of two men; one of them immense, hulking. Their fedoras are pulled down tightly to their heads, and their red bandanas are fastened just beneath their eyes. These modern-day grim reaper uniforms foment more terror than the weapons the men carry. Their mark exits a small red tavern door and immediately the executioners begin to empty their guns. Four bullets hit the target. The men do not slow their fire as their victim desperately flops back inside the bar. He tries to rise to his feet and get to some sort of cover, but it's useless; he slips hard and slams down on the floor. The assassins close the door behind them, plunging every man inside into a state of trembling fear. While they scatter, seeking cover, sneaking into the dining area, the larger of the gunmen stands directly over the bleeding body of Frankie "Shots" Abbatemarco to examine him. Frankie tries lamely to stop the blood which is leaking from his neck. He can't focus his eyes, but he does not grovel in his last moments. He takes deep breaths and offers his own revolver to the angel of death above him. His executioner reaches down and removes the cold steel from Frankie's hand, places the barrel to his forehead and blasts a final shot. Having completed the job, the two men open the bar door and duck out into the cold November air, then vanish back down Carroll Street.

***

Frank Abbatemarco was a well-known and well-liked Brooklyn man. His dealings in death may have earned him the moniker "Shots" many decades prior, but at fifty-nine years old, his life in the rackets was confined to loan sharking, policy games, and bookmaking operations. It was rumored, that Abbatemarco owed Giuseppe Profaci fifty thousand dollars in back "taxes" that he either could not, or would not come up with.

The men appointed to kill Abbatemarco were believed to be Joe "Jelly" Gioielli and one of the Gallo brothers. As a reward for the success of their assignment, the assassins were expecting to inherit part of Abbatemarco's lucrative gambling operation. After the blood dried, however, they were outraged when Profaci failed to offer them any of the spoils. Instead, he'd intended to hand over the business to older members of the gang. Jelly and the Gallos revolted. They began by placing Anthony Abbatemarco, Frankie's son, into "protective custody." Profaci was rumored to have ordered his execution next. They refused to release Abbatemarco's son, and demanded what they believed was their fair share of the Red Hook gambling rackets. A violent standoff ensued between the fractious young hoodlums, the Gallos and Profaci's cadre. The pawns wanted to kill their king.

This battle of succession bore an uncanny resemblance to the Castellamarese Wars. Power struggles of this nature were now receiving increasing attention from the media, and the press coverage was ideal for law enforcement. It was only a few years prior that the government-appointed Kefauver Committee broadcast their investigations into organized crime on national television, interviewing powerful men like Meyer Lansky, Tony Accardo and Frank Costello. The hearings were designed to prove the existence of a vast Italian/Sicilian organized crime conspiracy in the United States. This most recent revolt in Red Hook provided the substantiation they sought.

While the gangsters on President Street were devising a plan to ouster their current leader, Joe Colombo was watching his oldest son play his first season of high school football. Anthony was attending Saint Francis Preparatory, an esteemed, private high school in the Williamsburg section of Brooklyn. It was a bigger responsibility for his son, who now traveled to school by subway each day, but one that helped to build the independence he felt Anthony needed. Joe and his son grew closer during this first year of high school, but this was a bittersweet time for Joe, whose own opportunity for education had been stripped away with the murder of his father.

On Friday nights when Jo-Jo had already taken Joe Junior and Vinny upstate for the weekend, Anthony would stick around Brooklyn and wait to ride up with his father. Anthony took the

West End line to meet his father at his social club on New Utrecht Avenue. Some nights they would stop in Manhattan for a pizza before their drive up north together to the estate. Other times they would stay at the club and Fat Steve, the club chef, would prepare dinner for them and some of the regulars. If the club was very busy, the two might spend the evening together in the apartment upstairs. Anthony relished such excursions with his father. Joe never missed an occasion to impress upon his son the importance of hard work, discipline and, above all, education.

***

"When I was a freshman I attended school at St. Francis Prep on Bedford and North 6th Street in Williamsburg. It was a very strict school, run by all brothers from the church. I tried out for the football team and made it with ease. The coach for the freshman team was so impressed by me and a few other freshmen they moved us up to the Junior Varsity team. My father was very proud. He would come to most of the games to watch me play. The coach used to really work us during our practices after school. I remember a few times I was so tired coming home on the train that I fell asleep and woke up at the last stop in Coney Island: the custodian would wake me up as they began cleaning the trains. I loved football, it was my favorite part of school. I was a hard-hitting middle linebacker who loved tackling. A bunch of the older kids would call me fireplug, based on my short and solid size. There was a kid a few grades older than me that never took a liking to me. His name was Dan Henning and he was the quarterback on the varsity team. Nothing specific ever happened between Dan and me, but he made it clear he didn't like me. While I made a name for myself on the field, unfortunately, I didn't fare so well with my Latin class. It didn't interest me at all so I was having a real hard time learning it. By the end of the school year I had failed Latin. I figured they were going to give me summer school, but I had already been expelled.

When my father found out, he blew his top. I remember being out in the front of the house playing when he came home. At this point I had no idea I had even been kicked out of school. It was my Uncle, Joe LaRosa that told my father. His cousin, Brother Brendan, who was a teacher at the school, had originally helped get me into the school. My father didn't even pull into the driveway before he hopped out of the car and started yelling at me. I didn't even know what the hell I'd done. Once he started in about me getting thrown out of the school, I knew I was in for it. School was the most important thing in the world to him. He would ask us about it constantly. I guess he wanted better for us considering he never had the chance to finish high school after his father died.

He screamed and yelled and whacked me in the yard, and then booted me in the ass from the front of the house all the way up the driveway, down the steps into the house, and gave me some more in the basement. And then he gave me the belt. I wasn't allowed to cry when he disciplined me, you had to take the beating like a man, even when it hurt like hell. I don't know what hurt more, the belittling from him or the welts across my ass. I tried desperately to tell him that I wasn't supposed to be kicked out. When you fail two subjects it is grounds for expulsion, but one subject and they would have you make it up in summer school. I should have been given that chance. He didn't try to hear a word I said, he just kept shouting at me expressing his disgust and disbelief. Just when I thought he had calmed down a bit, he had a new way to punish me…At that time, my hair was coiffed into an 'Elvis' style pompadour. It wasn't long in the back or on the sides, only in the front. My father asked my mother for a scissors so he could get rid of my top hair. My mother handed my father a dull pair of scissors so he could not get much cutting done. I could see my Mother and Aunt Ray Ray, wishing they could somehow stop him, watching, dismayed, as my father removed my pompadour like the mad hatter.

A few days later when my father came home from work he got out of the car and I was standing on the porch and he said 'Come here, I wanna talk to you.' I thought to myself, 'Holy Shit, here we go again,' except when he approached me this time he had an entirely different stance. He pointed to the steps and said, 'Sit down, Anthony.' My ass hurt, but I did it anyway. He told me, 'You didn't get thrown out of that school because you failed Latin. You got thrown out of that school because of something that has to do with me.' I was completely confused by what he'd just said. 'You have a kid in your school named Dan Henning?' I said, 'Yeah, he is the quarterback for the football team.' 'Well he's got a father who's up there in the NYPD, and he's been down at that school getting in the administration's ear for a long time about you being in that school. They've been looking for a way to get you out of there.' He never discussed why this police officer would have a problem with him. I knew my father gambled. I'd seen him shoot craps before with his friends and I knew he bet on the horses. I never thought anything bad about that kind of stuff. It just didn't seem to be such a big deal to me, still doesn't. When the cops came to the house asking my father questions he would send us somewhere before he would let them speak to him. It was never open for discussion what was being asked. Whatever my father was doing at the time didn't seem comparable to the gangsters I was reading about in the paper, after all his name wasn't in the papers, and the papers print the truth about everything, or at least as a kid, that's what you believe."

∗∗∗

On January 15, 1960, The Italian-American League Against Discrimination announced that it would launch a publicity campaign to counteract the media's pervasive depiction of Italians as criminals.[vi] It was only a year prior that Joe was reading about the Order of the Sons of Italy condemning movies and TV shows based on the alleged existence of the "Mafia." They began to combat defamation by contacting the sponsors of the shows and engaging in lawful boycotting.[vii] Joe had disdain for groups of people attacking a smaller weaker group. He was not just a proponent of the Italian-American League in New York, but an organizer as well. However, at this time in his life, Joe felt his gambling activities and some of his relationships might compromise the efforts of the League if he were a more vocal member, so he refrained from being in the forefront and instead offered financial backing and advice from the backseat.

Joe also belonged to another order in New York for many years: the Freemasons. He drafted his son Anthony for membership with them in the late sixties. Joe attended meetings in Manhattan, at the Columbus Lodge in the tenth district of the Masonic order. This group of men was separate from the tough crew of pals he'd grown up with on the streets of Brooklyn. These men were businessmen; many of them were elites, living in Manhattan and Queens. The group, which was known for its mystery was steeped in oaths and rituals. The privilege of membership appealed to him, and the rhetoric espoused was intriguing and often compelling. Much of it was reminiscent of conversations Joe's father would have with his coterie about events in the city involving politics, work strikes and various injustices the working class endured during the Roaring Twenties and through the Great Depression. Many hostile stereotypes forced Italians and Italian-Americans out of work and out of the country during the World Wars. At various phases in his life, Joe sought to uncloak his father's past and discover more about his family lineage and his personal declivity.

Joe's father, Anthony Colombo was born in Brazil on February 16, 1898. He was the second born of five children, and the only son. His parents, Giuseppe, and Olivera were temporary residents of Brazil originally from Calabria, the southern-most, and poorest region in Italy. His oldest sibling, Grasia, was born there in a small town called Acri. Shortly after she was born Giuseppe took his pregnant wife and daughter on a long journey across the Atlantic. Instead of heading to New York City, they took a passenger ship to South America and settled in São Paulo, Brazil, a destination sought by many Italians during the years of heavy immigration.

Eight months and eight years after he was born, Anthony and his sisters would set sail on the *Verdi*, leaving from Buenos Aires and arriving in New York City. When passing through the medical check at customs on Ellis Island, officers sent Anthony's sisters to the hospital. Grasia and Anthony managed to stay healthy during the passage, but Angelina, Teresina, and Nicolina did not pass the inspection. They had contracted influenza and were kept at the hospital for further observation. After ten days in the care of the hospital staff they were declined entry into the country. They were deported back to Argentina to be met by their mother. Sadly, at nine years of age, Anthony had seen his three sisters for the last time.

Anthony Colombo went to prison for the first time when he was eighteen years old. After a few previous arrests in his mid-teens, he was convicted of robbery and sentenced to two years. He served this sentence in upstate New York at the Elmira Correctional Facility. It was on the ride up to prison that Anthony got his first glimpse at the rolling hills and pastures that sit at the base of the Catskill Mountains. In spite of his grim destination, Anthony was captivated by the beauty of the passing landscape. He returned to this area only a few years later, under very different circumstances. In his mid twenties, as a free man, he enjoyed this picturesque country with his new family. That tradition would continue with Joe and his own family. In fact, all of Joe's children would eventually settle in Orange County, not far from the road that their grandfather first traveled almost a century before.

After his release from Elmira, Anthony returned to Bensonhurst to make up for lost time. In the next few years he was arrested a few times for vagrancy and disorderly conduct, most charges stemming from illegal crap games around the neighborhood. At the age of twenty-two he was convicted of burglary. He found himself again riding with law men upstate, this time along the east side of the Hudson River to one of New York State's most infamous prisons, Sing Sing. During this period of incarceration, he would cross paths with some of the most notorious figures in the New York underworld; there would be no reforming or 'correcting' during their stay. Sing Sing was a breeding ground for master criminals and a convention center for aspiring gangsters during the era of Prohibition.

***

In the spring of 1960, Joe decided he would move his family out of the city to live full time in rural Blooming Grove. He had a number of reasons for making the move. He was alarmed by the circumstances of Anthony's expulsion from school. It was through a friend in the NYPD that he'd gathered the information about Dan Henning's father. Joe had been tipped off that the Central Intelligence Bureau (CIB) and the FBI were building files on every member of the Profaci organization, and this included Joe. The CIB had placed wiretaps in one of the President Street haunts frequented by members of the Gallo crew, and they were recording all sorts of interesting dialogue. While the intelligence gathered wasn't sufficient to make any arrests, it implicated dozens of men and confirmed suspicions of a national syndicate.

It was around this time the director of the FBI, J. Edgar Hoover, created his clandestine Counter Intelligence Program

(COINTELPRO). While the group was established specifically to sabotage and destroy dissident political groups, it was believed that the FBI used many of the same "black bag" operations and disinformation campaigns against men suspected of involvement in organized crime. These tactics were adopted by men at the state level as well. While they found it difficult to penetrate into criminal circles to gather information, they found that by exploiting the weakest links in the chain they could create stress cracks within the organizations' walls. With counterintelligence, officers did not need to sit and wait for a crime to occur; they could incite one with a specific target in mind and then make a firm collar. In many instances their objective was not to end organized crime, but to disrupt it and exploit its dark side. New York CIB Detective Ralph Salerno wrote:

> INSTEAD OF TRYING TO CATCH AND CONVICT INDIVIDUAL GANGSTERS WE OUGHT TO CONSIDER HOW THE TIGHT KNIT FABRIC OF ORGANIZED CRIME ITSELF CAN BE RIPPED APART. ONE OF THE MOST EFFECTIVE WAYS TO DO THIS WOULD BE TO ENCOURAGE THE DISSATISFACTION OF YOUNGER MEMBERS TO THE POINT OF OPEN REVOLT.[viii]

Joe was just trying to avoid another gambling charge and keep his distance from a possible gang conflict in Brooklyn. He was wise in moving his family to Blooming Grove, for reasons unbeknownst to him at the time. Law enforcement was developing a sophisticated plot involving a paper trail which led back to some of the highest-ranking members of the Mafia. These counterintelligence methods would result in a bloodbath. With the targets including a greedy ferocious despot from Sicily, and an implacable hoodlum from Red Hook, the feds would get the sensational stories, front page headlines, and the body count they were seeking.

***

The tall grass blows for miles in every direction as the Colombo boys follow their father across the open fields behind the Blooming Grove ranch. Anthony and Joe Junior follow in quiet formation; they look at each other in anticipation. Today they are going to get a special treat. They keep walking farther away from the horses and stables. They have never been out this far before with their father. Joe is leading the way with his serious grin. He has on his best country gear, a pair of rounded cowboy boots, pants and sweater, and his hunting cap. The boys aren't looking at their father's attire, although they always find it odd to see him without his suit. Today they are focused on the Browning shotgun he has resting on his shoulder. Their eyes widen with the mere thought of firing this weapon. They have both held his World War 2- bolt action Enfield, but neither has shot a gun before.

They approach the small brook and Joe stops to look around. There is nothing in sight for miles, just open fields and sparse trees. The boys stand and wait as Joe turns to kneel. He looks down at the grass momentarily and balances the shotgun on his leg. "I want to tell you something." Joe's brusque delivery has the boys at attention. "There're a few things in life that you're not going to do and I'm not going to tolerate." Joe makes sure his sons are focused. "You know you can never fool around with drugs." He pauses and looks at both of them, "You know that, right? You can't sell drugs. You can't use drugs." The boys know this. They do their best to express silent understanding. "You also can never become cops. You know that, right?" His questions were not to be answered; just heard and understood. "You know you can never rat on anybody, for any reason." Joe fixes his position, shifting the gun between his hands and repeats, "You don't rat on anybody for any reason. Something happens to you, you take care of it yourself." He fiddles with the gun's moving parts. "You don't go to the law for nothing." He concludes, "And you can't marry outside of your race." He holds the shogun vertically and begins to load the shells into the chamber. He does not break eye contact with them as he does this. "Because if you do any of these things... you see this shotgun?" They nod. "Let me tell you why I bought it. Before anybody else kills you for doing any of those things, I'll kill you and bury you myself on this property right here." He motions to the infinite locations of burial space surrounding them in every direction. He looks back at them severely. They know this warning is not for effect, but meant with complete sincerity.

A few moments later, Jo-Jo stepped outside on the patio to start preparing an outdoor lunch. She fired up the grill, something Joe would usually do. The lighter fluid always made her nervous and as she held the metal can in her hand, a powerful blast from the fields behind her gave her a jolt. Her heart raced for a moment as she'd forgotten what was going on out there with her boys. Then she remembered Joe was giving them their first lesson with the new gun. She had absolute trust in Joe when it came to the boys. He was a great father. She turned to try and see them, shielding her eyes as she looked out into the fields past the pond. She knew it was during these lessons that their father would forge her sons into men.

***

Joe became increasingly jovial around Christmas time. He loved the holiday spirit and took great joy in decorating the interior and exterior of the home. The larger house gave him new real estate for decorations in the yard and on the roof, and Joe covered every inch. He owned all the right tools and had ample passion, but his family chuckled when he would fumble, as he wasn't as skillful as he wanted to believe. On Christmas Eve, Jo-Jo's sisters came up from Brooklyn, along with Joe's mother and younger sister, to help prepare the traditional Italian Feast of the Seven Fishes. On Christmas Day they would serve lasagna and baked ham. Joe did everything he could to encourage everyone's spirits and prolong the holidays as much as possible. After Christmas, he would host a family New Year's Eve party. The boys were allowed to stay up late to watch Guy Lombardo and the Royal Canadians and the ball dropping ceremony in Times Square. Champagne was served for the toast, but Joe was not much of a drinker. On special occasions he would have a glass of wine, but he never drank alcohol socially. At midnight, he would take a sip from a glass of champagne, and then share a kiss with his wife, wishing his family continued harmony and prosperity.

Just as their first holiday in Blooming Grove had been a success, the first semester of school also went smoothly for the boys and the family. At Washingtonville High, there were no preconceived notions about the Colombo boys. As far as the teachers and faculty were concerned, they were a nice Italian family who had moved up from Brooklyn. The Colombo boys fit in comfortably with their fellow classmates, since Anthony and Joe Junior had already made a number of friends during their summer vacations. Anthony became even more popular after insisting his way into the Jeep Willys his father had purchased that year. He had diligently practiced his driving on the family tractor and this was his father's reward to him for his efforts.

***

"Once I got the keys to my Jeep I drove around constantly with my friends. If my father was in the city for business on the weekends, my mother would let me stay out past curfew. I had no idea of the type of stress my father was under during that time and I honestly didn't care much. I was a teenager with a new car, a new set of friends, and no responsibilities. One night I went out, and though my curfew was at eleven o'clock, I stayed out way past that. I wasn't doing much, just hanging out with a bunch of my friends, drinking. Most nights my father stayed in the city, but this night something must have happened and he came home unexpectedly. When he didn't see all of his children in bed he got angry pretty fast. My mother didn't know where I was and told him that I'd never called to say I would be late.

He left the house in a fury and started to search for me. I was dating my wife, Carol at that time so he went right to her house and woke her and her father up. Neither of them had any idea where I was. At that point in our relationship, Carol was only fourteen and deathly afraid of my father. She told him everything she knew, that we had gone to dinner, and then to the movies, and that I had dropped her off by nine o'clock. She told him to check the Countryside Inn, a little pub restaurant that used to serve us beer. He went there and didn't find me, drove to a few different parks, still didn't find me. He drove around hunting for me all night. I can only assume that what was going on in Brooklyn had gotten serious that day and maybe he feared I had been kidnapped or something.

I got home about two o'clock in the morning and he wasn't home. My mother was wide awake and very calmly said, 'Your father is going to kill you.' I definitely didn't expect him to be home. The first thing I thought about was how he would be able to tell I was drunk. I had only had a few beers but at that age in didn't take much to get me drunk. My mother knew I was drunk and said, 'Come on in the bathroom,' and put my head under the cold water in the sink and tried to sober me up. She made me brush my teeth and made sure I looked presentable for when my father came home. The phone rang and she went to grab it; he had been calling about every fifteen minutes or so to see if I was home. She answered it and told him, 'Yeah, he's home Joey. Don't worry about it, he's home, everything's fine and he's going to bed now.' I could hear my father's voice commanding through the phone, 'Don't let him go to sleep! I'm on my way home!'

Our house upstate had a pretty big living room. I sat for about twenty-five minutes, alone on the couch, buzzed and panicked, waiting for him to walk through the door. I'd seen my father in a fit of rage before. He would get so angry sometimes he would actually jump up and down or even spit. I had way too many thoughts going through my head at this time and I'm sure my eyes were still glazed from the beer. He walked into the house and came into the living room and said, 'I don't want you to lie to me!' My father didn't hate much in life, but he vehemently despised lying. He asked, 'Where were you?' I couldn't think of what to say without telling on my friends so I told him I was out "jack-lighting" deer. Enraged he said, 'Don't lie to me. I want you to tell me the truth.' I think by this point, the sight of him had completely sobered me up. I gave him the same answer and he said again, 'Anthony, I am telling you I want the truth and you're lying to me.' I would have preferred it if he were yelling and screaming and jumping up and down. But he was so serious, just standing there, looking dead into my eyes, calm and controlled, asking me over and over, 'Where were you?' I told him the same story and he finally said, 'One more lie from you and I'm going to knock you out!' and he clenched his hand by his side and made a fist for me to see. He knew I had won a few fights at school so he invited me into my worst nightmare, 'You think you're a tough guy?' I answered in my softest tone, 'No, Dad, I don't think I'm a tough guy.' He snapped at me, 'Then don't lie to me. Now I'm going to ask you again, where were you tonight?' I said, 'Dad we were jack-lighting deer.' 'Oh yeah? You want to keep being a tough guy, then why don't you pick your hands up to me?' Now, that thought had never occurred to me, there wasn't a chance in hell I would pick my hands up to my father. Belligerent, he said, 'This is the last time, tough guy. Tell me the truth, or pick up your hands!' He stared fiercely into my eyes and I froze. He went to grab my hands to raise them so I could defend myself, but I didn't know what was going on. He was so tense that when he grabbed my arm with his right hand I got scared and jerked, thinking that hand was going to smack me. He didn't even flinch when he saw I was actually going to put my hands up, and from out of nowhere his left arm jabbed me in the face. Now when I say my father was strong, I mean he had the most pure form of strength, like a bull. I got knocked out so badly that I didn't remember anything from the moment after he touched my hand. He probably had to pick me up and put me in my bed.

The next thing I knew, my mother was waking me up for breakfast. Now on the weekends my family didn't eat breakfast until around eleven o'clock. I didn't open my eyes for close to nine hours after that punch. I remembered what happened and told her I didn't want to eat. She said my father had already demanded that I get up to eat, but I was stubborn and refused. She went into the kitchen and told him and he yelled from his chair, 'You better get in this kitchen right now, or I'll come in there and drag you out by your hair!' I got up, frustrated and bitter and went into the kitchen and sat down. The table was quiet, I didn't attempt to eat a bite off my plate, and I just sat in my chair sulking. He said to me, 'Eat your breakfast!' Now I really wasn't in the mood to eat. I was hurt and as mad at him as I could ever be. I told him, 'I'm not hungry.' 'You eat your breakfast on your own right now or I'm going to come over there and stuff that food down your throat. You're going to eat it one way or another so what will it be, tough guy?' I wanted to say I wasn't hungry again but a little angel in my head warned me that if I did he was really going to do exactly what he just said he was going to do. So I said, 'Okay, Dad.' And I started picking things off of the plate, swallowing humiliation with every bite I took. While I ate he said, 'Let me tell you something, everything that happened last night is done and over and you're not going to be mad at me one minute more. Do you understand? You don't get mad at me, I'm your father.' I looked at him and said, 'Dad, I'm okay.' He said, 'I want to see a smile on your face.' I was sixteen years old, he had scolded me, knocked me out cold, forced me to sit at the table and eat my breakfast, and now wanted me to forget everything and smile. What was next? I looked at him and he told me, 'You better smile to let me know you're not holding a grudge.' I answered him with a phony smile. He knew it wasn't sincere, but he said, 'That's better!' Afterwards it was really like it never happened. But I had learned that my father was a man who would make good on his threats. When he said he was going to do something, he was going to do it."

***

While the Colombo's were enjoying an idyllic life in the country, rumors arose that members of the Gallo crew in Brooklyn had successfully managed to snatch up a few of Profaci's trusted supporters. The men who were kidnapped were not the type to run to the law, so it wasn't until years later that police would learn of the abductions. But the popular belief was that the Gallo's had taken Profaci's brother Frank as well as his bodyguard, John Scimone, the "Underboss" Joe Magliocco, and Sally "The Sheik" Mussachio.

Perhaps the Gallo's had underestimated Profaci's ruthlessness, or overestimated his willingness to negotiate.

Without kidnapping Profaci himself, the rebel group had nothing with which to bargain. Instead, animosity between the factions intensified, and reprisal seemed imminent. It was assumed that Joey Gallo wanted to shake down Profaci by showing him some blood. "Ya kill one, ya tell 'em ya want a hundred G's in cash as a good faith token, then we sit down and talk."[ix] This type of action was not sanctioned by Joey Gallo's older brother Larry or by Joe Gioielli. Rumors circulated that they had their own internal struggles about the direction of the negotiations. When Joey couldn't be convinced to calm down and think logically he was sent to California to cool off and spend some time with his fiancé, while Larry Gallo and Joe Gioielli made negotiations on behalf of the group. During the next few months, peace in Brooklyn's gangland rested on a thin sheet of ice.

Shortly after the "jack-lighting" incident, Anthony began to pick up bits and pieces of the Gallo/Profaci conflict from the city newspapers his father brought home. He learned about some of the men associated with his father and the things they were being arrested for and accused of. He thought it odd that his family wasn't taking as many trips to Brooklyn as they had in the past. Now he viewed his father's angry and erratic behavior from a new perspective. It must derive from his fears that if one world boiled over, it could spill into another.

By the summer of 1961, more stories about Brooklyn gangsters were appearing on the front pages. On August 20th Larry Gallo was escorted out of the Sahara Lounge after a few men allegedly tried to kill him with a sash cord. He recovered from the attack with a burn around his neck and a vendetta in his heart. After the attack on Larry, the Gallo crew received a message alluding to the whereabouts of their heavyset leader, Joe "Jelly" Gioielli. Gioelli had left for a fishing trip a few days prior and never returned. It was rumored that an article of his clothing was found wrapped around a fish, and tossed in front of a candy store on Avenue U in Bath Beach.

In October of 1961, while living upstate, Jo-Jo gave birth to a fourth Colombo boy, Christopher. Joe was still commuting to the city for work. He would stay a few days during the week at his apartment on New Utrecht and then spend weekends with the family. Joe began to see Brooklyn as an undesirable place to raise his children during the conflict; and in the next few months his intuition proved right.

In November, John Guriglia, a Profaci associate, was shot just around the corner from Joe's new social club. Each act of violence was followed by a reprisal. The Gallo crew took a loss when Joseph Magnasco was shot to death on the corner of 4th Avenue and Union Street in Brooklyn. Charles "Ruby" Stein, a moneyman in a Profaci policy and loan-sharking business, purportedly took a severe beating in midtown Manhattan. A month later, on the Gallo's block, shots from a moving vehicle injured Larry Carna. While Profaci loyalists Nicholas "Jiggs" Forlano, "Donny Shacks" Montemarano, and Carmine Persico were in the Copacabana in January they ran into Sidney Slater, a Gallo loyalist who, unbeknownst to them, was a paid informant for the CIB. Forlano assaulted Slater and cut his face open with a newspaper hook in an attempt to take his eye out. A few days later Forlano would survive a barrage of gunfire without taking one bullet. More bullets would fly in the upcoming months, most missing. Years later, writer Jimmy Breslin dubbed the Gallo crew *"The Gang That Couldn't Shoot Straight."*

This conflict that split the organization was referred to in the papers as "The Gallo/Profaci War." The incessant fighting had the NYPD keeping a close watch over the Gallo camp as they holed up in two apartment buildings at 49 and 51 President Street. Not only did the CIB have wiretaps feeding them information, they had also obtained an informant from the crew. Sidney Slater had been arrested with Joey Gallo in May after Joey's attempt to shake down a wealthy bar owner in Little Italy. Joey was convicted, but his co-defendant was released. Slater didn't hesitate to turn against Joey, and since then, he regularly reported to the CIB. Over the next few years, Joey was frustrated into fits of rage as his hangouts were raided continuously, always with impeccable timing.

During the middle of the Brooklyn battle between the Gallos and Profacis, Joe received a call from his mother that she would be moving back to California. Catherine expressed her fear that she felt something bad might happen to Joe and she did not want to be around if it did. Angered, Joe argued with his mother reminding her, "So if something ever happened to me, you'd rather be across the country instead of here with my family, your family? The times in my life I needed you the most you pack your bags and leave me alone." There was no reasoning with his mother; her mind was already made up and to Joe's dismay, she left for the west coast again.

The Gallo/Profaci war only intensified. When a group of thirteen was brought before Judge Barshay for arraignment, he was privy to what was happening in the once mysterious Profaci clan; "It is quite obvious to the court that this is an incipient gang war, (being fought) either for supremacy or revenge."[x] While it seemed that negotiations would be impossible, the arrests were mounting on the Gallo side and the insurgents seemed to be losing in all other phases of conflict as well. But Profaci's days were numbered; no bullets, no kidnapping, no car bomb or sash cord. The Boss would succumb to a killer that took more lives in the Italian-American community than any Mob war ever could; Profaci died of cancer on June 7, 1962. Even this news did not end the feud and neither did Joe Gallo's fifteen-year prison sentence, which he received after failing to appear in court for his extortion trial.

While the Profaci organization was fractured and now in the shaky hands of Joe Magliocco, an ambitious plan was being contrived by a cool, smooth talking gang leader with the distinguished looks of a politician. His name was Joe Bonanno, leader of his own crime organization, which he'd inherited after the death of Salvatore Maranzano in 1931. The popular belief was that Bonanno became fearful after the death of Profaci, who was his closest ally in the Commission. He was already out of favor with Commission men like Gaetano "Tommy" Lucchese, and Carl Gambino. His plan, according to the majority of true crime experts, was a preemptive strike in which he would kill three Dons: Tommy Lucchese, Carl Gambino and his cousin Stefano Magaddino.

Bonanno denies ever plotting to take over the Commission. Long after all the great Dons of that era had vanished, he wrote in his 1983 autobiography *Man of Honor* about the attempted takeover, claiming that Colombo left the organization after Magliocco asked him to carry out a plot to kill Gambino and

Lucchese. This information took Magliocco out of power. Bonanno went on to claim that Stefano Magaddino spread rumors about a Bonanno "Coup" to kill Gambino, Lucchese, and Magaddino and take over the Comission.[xi]

When the contract was issued to execute these three bosses, it purportedly went to Joseph Colombo. To the FBI he was relatively unknown at the time. His name had come up in charges a number of times, and he had been interviewed during other investigations. At the time of Profaci's death, however, he only had a couple of local misdemeanor convictions, and was listed only as suspected ringleader in a few gambling operations. The FBI didn't even have a recent photo or mug shot of Colombo on file.

According to most true crime writers, Joe had more Mob stature than the FBI gave him credit for. Magliocco knew him to be very loyal. Joe's father, Anthony, was a close friend of the deceased Don's. Colombo was well-liked by the Profaci's. He attended parties and dinners at the Don's home. Throughout the entire Gallo struggle he had respected boundaries and protocol. His movements reflected caution and insight, but he was somewhat mysterious. During his entire suspected tenure in organized crime he was never arrested for a violent crime. Nonetheless, popular legend placed him alongside Carmine Persico, Larry Gallo, Joey Gallo and Joe Gioielli, as a member of Profaci's infamous five-man hit team. Years later, Mob historians assessed him as "experienced and wise enough to comprehend the futility of devising a double or triple execution of godfathers."[xii] If Joe was actually a killer of killers, he had no desire for credit. He spoke quietly and little, hallmarks of a true tough guy.

***

It was a warm August day as Joe drove his '63 Cadillac through the streets of South Brooklyn to the home of his mentor, the man who had been guiding him and pulling strings for him since his father's death in 1938. He enjoyed the company of the old Don who'd known his father. Today, they would have a private lunch to celebrate the Don's sixty-first birthday. It was just after two when he arrived at 2230 Ocean Parkway; the home of Carl Gambino, or as Joe's sons called him, Uncle Carl. Carl's wife, Catherine, a delicate Sicilian woman of about sixty, opened the door and invited him in. She had an immediately stern look, but her bright personality created a sense of warmth around her. As they walked through the modestly decorated home, she told them that Carl was waiting for him in the dining room off the kitchen.

In his chair at the dining room table was the man law enforcement and the media believed was the head of the largest criminal organization in the United States, and possibly the world. The success of Gambino's gang, unlike Profaci's, was due in large part to its covert existence. Gambino did not rise when he saw Joe, and Joe did not expect him to. He had been suffering from various ailments in recent years. His eyes were dark but sympathetic, his cheeks hung with wrinkles around his exaggerated nose. Carl was always polite and composed; his every move was slow and precise. He spoke carefully, but always with passion. After lunch the men retired for espressos in the small living room next to the dining area. After Carl got comfortable in his chair Joe presented him with a gift for his birthday. Carl was touched by the gesture. He had adored Joe since he was a boy. Carl opened it and was pleased to see a new fedora. Joe had impeccable taste and a knack for style. As a separate offering, Joe presented a card to Carl with peculiar care. Carl noticed the change in Joe's demeanor. Joe paused and said to Carl, "This card was given to me. It is something I need you to see. Something I do not know how to approach." Carl seemed unperturbed, despite Joe's oddly grave tone. He opened the envelope and positioned a pair of horn-rimmed glasses as he read. What he saw next needed no explanation. The sympathy card was in honor of three men: Carl, Tommy and Stefano.

Chapter 4.

"From This Moment On"

(1963-1966)

The children peek out from behind the steps and whisper "Il Gigante," as he passes them on the sidewalk. He is the largest man they have ever seen. As he turns the corner onto the street, the entire sidewalk seems to tremble from his steps. He is so massive that men and women step into the gutter to allow him ample space to pass. His labored, offensive breathing is audible, and he sometimes snarls or grunts when presented with a familiar face. Donning his custom tailored brown suit, he is the epitome of a "Black Hander." His swollen hand resembles a glove as he raises it and tips his hat a bit more sideways. He is a gangster through and through.

 Across Sackett Street, tucked behind the door of an apartment building, two men clock the giant's steps as he approaches. The men are dressed in all black, top hats and shiny shoes. Both men are well-built, their backs and chests powerful from years of manual labor. They tightly secure kerchiefs across their faces. The first man holds two revolvers, and once he inspects them, he replaces them under his topcoat into his vest pockets. It is mid afternoon and Sackett Street is filled with people. The two men watch as their mark begins to cross to their side of the street. The first man places his hand on the doorknob and nods to his partner. He opens it and they move swiftly out of the building.

Like ghosts they glide down the stairs of the apartment house. Piraino sees the approaching men, the first one with two guns poised at his chest. In the broad daylight the hammers clap back from the assassin's twin pistols. There is no time to maneuver; within five seconds enough bullets are buried in Piraino's chest to ensure his death. As the giant falls dramatically off the curb, a few extra shots make their way into his torso, thigh and a piece of wood across the street. No matter, the first few have sealed the deal. The assassins walk briskly down Sackett Street. They pass dozens of people, all of whom avert their eyes. Behind them, lying still and soaked with blood is "The Clutching Hand." Piraino's brown hat skips down Sackett Street, carried by a light breeze, freed from its owner for good.

***

Joe's father first met Carl Gambino when both men were in their early twenties and living in the Gravesend section of Brooklyn. Gambino was a chubby young immigrant who focused mostly on the business side of racketeering. Colombo or Durante as he was known among gangsters, was a robust man with a formidable reputation as a brawler. He was known for his impressive skill on the golf course, and in smaller circles, for his precision as a marksman. His talents for sharpshooting and fist-fighting, as well as his cool charm with the ladies, made Colombo a legend in South Brooklyn. Gambino admired Colombo not only for his talents and charisma, but most notably for a very specific feat he performed in 1930 on Sackett Street. The mark was a colossal but elusive man—"The Clutching Hand" Piraino—well-known for surviving murder attempts. There was no room for error. His murder was crucial for the elimination of Uale's remaining loyalists, and allowed for Brooklyn's "Five Famlies" ascent to power.

***

In 1930, homicides rose in Brooklyn to a record total of 144, most of which were attributable to gang warfare.[xiii] Most of the subsequent investigations would not produce any concrete evidence. The day of the Piraino shooting, everyone on the street claimed they had heard the gunshots, but not a single person would admit to having seen anything. For the NYPD detectives, it was a long day of shoulder shrugging from the forty-plus witnesses on Sackett Street. The medical report would conclude that a professional shooter was behind the killing. The first three slugs pierced Piraino's heart in a space that could be covered by a half-dollar.[xiv] A few days later Piraino was buried in full "gaudy pomp." The casket alone was valued at over seven thousand dollars. The streets of Brooklyn were lined with spectators as the cortege of over seventy cars made its way to Greenwood Cemetery.[xv] Soon the terror wrought by "The Clutching Hand" would subside and

Brooklyn's gang wars would cease as new leaders emerged. Giuseppe Profaci and Joe Bonanno would rule Brooklyn uncontested and relatively peaceably for close to thirty years.

***

In 1963, once the plan to kill Gambino, Lucchese, and Magaddino was exposed, the Commission was forced to take action against Bonanno and Magliocco. Bonanno went into hiding, and it was rumored that Magliocco, who retired early, was ordered to pay back what he'd earned as a boss. Even with Magliocco out of the picture there was still plentiful bloodshed in Brooklyn. Carmine Persico was wounded by gunfire, but successfully cheated death several times during the conflict. Gallo loyalists Emile Colontuono, Alfred Modello, Louis Mariani, and Ali Hassan Waffa, were not as fortunate. They were all killed within a few weeks during that hot summer. But then, in September, something strange happened. After three years of turmoil and revenge murders, both sides ceased fire.

Sources would later reveal that Bonanno's plot to assassinate the three bosses had not only been foiled by young Colombo, but that Joe had also successfully executed Gambino's plan to restore harmony within the Profaci clan. The Commission praised Colombo for his peacemaking ability and leadership qualities, and within the organization he gained respect in the way he was taught by his father, by giving it. The peace deal resulted in Nick Bianco and Carmine Persico becoming made men. The request for territory in Red Hook would be granted to Larry Gallo, and the reorganization of the Profaci gang would continue throughout the fall of 1963.

Shortly after the violence abated in Brooklyn, shots were fired on Elm Street in Dallas, 1,500 miles away from New York. The President of the United States, John F. Kennedy was assassinated while riding in the presidential limousine alongside his wife, surrounded by a fleet of secret service. Police arrested Lee Harvey Oswald, the suspected sniper, and charged him with the murder. Two days later, before any investigation could begin, Jack Ruby murdered Oswald while he was in police custody. The Warren commission and the FBI released official reports that Lee Harvey Oswald had acted alone. The results of this investigation are still being disputed today. Almost every theory about the assassination links the president's death to some of the highest-ranking men within the military, CIA, and FBI.

A few days before the New Year, Joe Magliocco suffered a fatal heart attack. Years later, new evidence emerged suggesting that Magliocco may have been the victim of murder. In 1969, his body was exhumed and tested for poisons. Law enforcement's awakening of the dead failed to reveal any signs of murder.[xvi] This was one of a myriad of instances of the government responding to unreliable sources and erroneous intelligence.

In their offices at 201 East Sixty-Ninth Street, federal agents worked on the Profaci gang's chart, trying to accurately determine the organization's structure. After Magliocco's death, they could only assume the underboss; Salvatore "The Sheik" Mussachio was now in command. They were confused, however, by reports from street informers who told them "The Sheik" was not running the group. It would take more money and manpower to correctly detail the Profaci family hierarchy. The bulletin boards at their offices were filled with names such as Anthony "Shatz" Abbattemarco, Salvatore "Sally D" D'Ambrosio, Lawrence "Larry" Gallo, Joseph "Crazy Joey" Gallo, Joseph "Joe Ship" Schipani, Bartolo "Barioco Bartulucia" Ferrigno, Gaetano "Toddo" Marino, and Giuseppe "Joseph Tifa" Tipa, which comprised some of the lower half of the board under the title of "Soldiers – Buttons." The upper level was reserved for the administrative section of the gang. Across the top of the chart was written CAPOREGIME; "capo" meaning "head" or "boss", and "regime" meaning "system." The names and photos under this heading included Sebastian "Buster" Aloi, Salvatore Badalamenti, Simone Andolino, Leo "Big Leo" Carlino, Harry Fontana, Ambrose Magliocco, Nicholas "Jiggs" Forlano, John "Johnny Bath Beach" Oddo, and Joseph Colombo. The mug shot of Salvatore "The Sheik" was fitted in the underboss position and the two photos of Joe Magliocco and Joseph Profaci had the label "deceased" underneath their FBI numbers. While there were plenty of other names listed along with mug shots on the board, it was the identification of the upper echelon of this organization that was most important for detectives.

The FBI's impression of the gang was gathered from both news writers and informants at the state level. The FBI worked aggressively to add more informants to the payroll. The pay scale ran from two hundred dollars a month to as high as eight hundred dollars a month.[xvii] The advantages of being a stool pigeon extended much further than a paycheck, however. Although it wasn't an official practice by the FBI, informants were warned of raids and given notice if they were under any other type of investigation. Agents turned a blind eye to the criminal activities of these men, allowing them to "earn" provided they continued to supply information. The informants were also awarded lump sums of cash for various pieces of intelligence. This could include anything from learning the identity of a new member or giving the location of a new gambling spot. While the agents maintained close contact with all paid informants, they were also supposed to keep careful accounts of the monies being paid out, but they inevitably failed to do so.

After about a year of investigations, many of the FBI sources were pointing their fingers at Joe Colombo as the new boss of the Profaci organization. It was puzzling to the agents that Colombo, who up until then was a relatively quiet and unknown man, could have leapt suddenly to head of the organization. The sources the FBI used for their intelligence were not "made men" or sanctioned members of La Cosa Nostra. They relied upon men on the outskirts of the organization. Their information came from bits and pieces told to them second, third and fourth hand. According to the FBI's Anti-Racketeering report, a confidential informant was defined as:

> -A PERSON WHO IS FAMILIAR WITH HOODLUM ACTIVITIES IN THE NEW YORK CITY AREA.

-AN INDIVIDUAL WHO IS IN THE POSITION TO FURNISH INFORMATION REGARDING CERTAIN HOODLUMS ON A CONTINUING BASIS.

The FBI did not have any hard evidence to establish Colombo as the boss. As they continued to gather new information from wiretaps or witness testimony, they obtained a series of unsigned statements from their paid informants. Agents learned that the organization was being renamed and restructured. New men were to be inducted as captains, along with new disbursements of the rackets.

This new batch of information was being fed to the FBI from a source closely connected to two soldiers in the Profaci organization. The soldiers were James Rubertone and Charles LoCicero and the rat was a recently jailed racketeer named Greg Scarpa.[xviii] At this time, Scarpa's information was of the highest intelligence the FBI had ever received on La Cosa Nostra. He gave them information about the size of the crew and the inner workings of the crime groups including indoctrination rituals. In 1963 Scarpa reported that there were 114 made members within the Colombo/Profaci group and each paid dues of $50 per month.[xix] He reported rumors to the FBI that Colombo was given financial support from Gambino for gambling rackets. He also reported that Colombo was paying off local police to the tune of 1,500 per month as hush money for his neighborhood gambling operations.[xx] He was confident in reporting that Colombo had succeeded Magliocco as leader of the Profaci clan stating that there was a ceremony held on April 4, 1964 in Celebration of Colombo's new position.[xxi] Scarpa was not in attendance and could not give the location of the event but FBI agents recorded it as factual information.

The FBI was confident with Scarpa's information and began gathering as much on Joe Colombo as possible. Agents began amassing information about Colombo's banking, tax records, schooling, and both family and criminal history. They identified his legitimate businesses at the time as Prospero Funeral Home in Brooklyn, Catania Clothes, a cutting company in Manhattan, and the Como Lounge on 86th Street in Bensonhurst. Spot checks occurred frequently at Joe's home and businesses in an attempt to identify Joe's associates and possible illicit activities. Colombo had been employed full time for a few years as a real estate salesman at Cantalupo Realty, also on 86th Street.

The agency's owner, Anthony Cantalupo was an old friend of Joe's from childhood. Cantalupo was a tall, well built man whose appearance didn't fit the mold of a stereotypical Brooklyn Italian. He dressed like a Hollywood producer in flashy clothes with vibrant colors, and always had a large mustache. While the two men did not share the same taste in style or indulge in the same vices, they did share a love for the game of golf. As teenagers, both had caddied for their fathers at the course across the street. Anthony's father, Joseph Cantalupo had started the real estate company in 1928 and passed it on to his son. When agents were sent in to question Cantalupo, they discovered no pertinent information about Joe or his suspected criminal empire. Cantalupo and Colombo weren't the best of friends their entire lives, but they certainly got along well, and respected each other tremendously. Cantalupo explained to the agents that Joe Colombo was an extremely successful real estate broker and would probably earn close to $20,000 that year. The numbers were accurate and

Cantalupo knew the information he was revealing would not injure Joe. Anthony was questioned about Joe's personal real estate holdings in Blooming Grove, and about the fire that had destroyed the knotty pine home. They inquired about Colombo's suspected associates and rackets. Cantalupo had no knowledge of Joe's involvement in any illegal activities; he knew him simply as a broker who worked on commission and contributed substantially to the agency.

Colombo was indeed an exceedingly effective salesman. He was a striking figure in Bensonhurst, always driving a shiny new Cadillac and wearing impeccably tailored suits with custom made shoes. His beautiful fedoras always coordinated perfectly with his shirt and socks. Joe Colombo more resembled a Wall Street executive than a Mob boss. FBI agents didn't observe a man who displayed the arrogant swagger of a Don, rather a warm and approachable man people gravitated towards. Locals who were questioned by the police consistently described Colombo as a gentleman who was polite and generous.

Agents learned Joe's full routine within a few weeks. This was not difficult as Joe was a creature of habit. He frequented all of the same places in a familiar rotation. He arrived at work every morning around ten. He got his haircut and a manicure once a week at the same salons. He visited his apartment on New Utrecht Avenue once a day. And at least twice a week he was followed into Manhattan to his tailor Catania's and then seen having a coffee on Mulberry Street. Every week on Friday, he would leave the city to spend the entire weekend with his wife and children. The agents made a few trips upstate to Blooming Grove as well, but at the time, the FBI did not believe his activities extended further than the city. At this time Anthony was attending Valley Forge military school a few hours away in Pennsylvania, so Joe would sometimes take his wife and Anthony's girlfriend, Carol, to visit him for football games and school events.

***

Investigations into Colombo's life eventually led the FBI to his home in Orange County, New York. Agents would drive up from the city and introduce their version of Joe Colombo to local law enforcement. They made their rounds at local schools and businesses, asking questions about Joe's activities, trying to obtain information about his associates or personal life. If Joe bought a lawn mower, they wanted to speak to the sales person; if he purchased lumber, they wanted to know what type and what it was for. By the mid-sixties if a person had any type of encounter with Joe Colombo there was a good chance he would be questioned by the FBI.

Federal agents showed up at Cantalupo Realty to question Joe about their recent reports. Colombo was invariably cordial; he invited them into his office and offered to help them in any way he could. They continuously asked him about his position within the Profaci organization. Joe stated firmly he had no involvement in anything called "La Cosa Nostra." He pointed out to agents that things had been quiet in Brooklyn lately, and he wondered why the FBI had such an interest in him. They replied that it was the FBI's responsibility to identify every member of La Cosa Nostra, as well as their known associates. Joe answered, "I can give you any information you guys need when it comes to real estate. As far as that other business is concerned, there is nothing I can tell ya." The Agents then asked, "Joe, the gentlemen that just left here, he drives the blue Buick, you were with him at lunch yesterday, who is that? He looks just like you." The agents were referring to Rocky Miraglia, and indeed, Miraglia looked so much like Joe that agents were getting the slip on many occasions while trying to tail Colombo. They knew who he was, and Joe knew this as well. "That's my friend Rocky. He is a great man, a father of five and currently out of work. I'm trying to find him a job. Maybe you gentlemen can help?" The agents laughed. Joe put them on ice with ease. He was an easy man to interview, affable, courteous, and confusingly sincere. Joe apologized that he could not be of further assistance. He let the agents know that his door was always open, but regarding La Cosa Nostra, he could be of no help.

Despite what Joe said during the interview, the FBI kept receiving reports that Colombo was head of the Profaci organization. One FBI source reported that a ceremony was held where Colombo was announced as the Boss of the Brooklyn gang, and that a special meeting took place between Colombo and Larry Gallo at Renato's restaurant in Brooklyn. They purportedly spoke about the future of the organization and decided that, in an effort to avoid bad blood, the gang would no longer be referred to as the Profacis. From this day forward it would be called the Colombo organization. The agents also learned that Joe Bonanno was on the lam, but that since the fall of 1963 no more blood had been spilled from the Gallo feud.

***

As the FBI's gang board began to change shape again for the Colombo organization structure, new information about the leadership of the Bonanno gang began to come in. Apparently, the Commission no longer recognized Joe Bonanno as the head of his group, and wanted to name his successor for him. While Joe Bonanno wanted his son Bill to take over the gang's administrative duties, the Commission instead appointed a leader for him, choosing, Gaspar DiGregorio, who was Bill's godfather and best man at Joe Bonanno's wedding. This decision was not favorable to Joe Bonanno who kept pushing for his Son Bill to lead the many men still loyal to him. For the henchmen and Captains within the organization, loyalties became confusing and the gang seemed to be falling apart. The Commission would make a move to confirm that Joe Bonanno was no longer in control of his organization.

On October 21, 1964, Joe Bonanno was to appear before a Grand Jury in Manhattan. As a result of Bobby Kennedy's campaign against organized crime, Attorney Robert Morgenthau began the crackdown on suspected leaders, and sought out Bonanno. After dining uptown with his lawyer, Bonanno was planning to spend the night at his lawyer's Park Avenue home. Upon arriving at their destination, Bonanno was kidnapped. During a midnight downpour on Park Avenue, two men locked their arms with Bonanno's and rushed him towards an idling car on 36th Street. His lawyer yelled, possibly in hopes of startling the kidnappers. He was met with a warning shot and fell silent. In his book, *A Man of Honor,* Bonanno asserts that the two kidnappers were Nino and Peter Magaddino; Joe Bonanno's cousin and arch nemesis from Buffalo, Stefano Magaddino's brother and son.[xxii]

***

While the FBI was busy keeping tabs on the crime organization structures, Joe Colombo was keeping tabs on his son Anthony, who was enrolled in Valley Forge military school in Pennsylvania. Anthony's first year was miserable. Under the school's "plebe" system, he was subjected to ceaseless harsh discipline. Wake-up was at 6:00 a.m., and before students could eat breakfast they had physical fitness. Everywhere they went they had to travel in double time. Anthony complained to Joe about the mandatory study hall and rigid 10:30 p.m. curfew. Regardless of Anthony's complaints, Joe was very proud of him for persisting. Anthony had never experienced this type of structured environment before, and Joe felt that it was necessary for the development of his character.

By his second year, Joe noticed Anthony's attitude towards the school had changed dramatically. He managed to maintain good grades and became a leader in many of the school's extracurricular activities. He was promoted to Staff Sergeant in charge of the athletic program and was also inducted into the Anthony Wayne Legion Guard, a very prestigious honor. The academy began to deeply influence Anthony and by the time of his graduation, he had developed a great admiration for the armed forces. During his last semester of school, he was spit shining his shoes and belt buckle and singing military calls whenever he walked the campus. He graduated in 1965, along with many of his classmates, who were going to fight in Vietnam that fall. Anthony also wanted to join the war effort and recalls what happened when he attempted to do so.

"I went down to Whitehall Street in Manhattan and volunteered to join the army. I already had two years of officer's training school at Valley Forge so I would have entered as a second Lieutenant. I wanted to go fight for my country. I went home and told my mother. She just looked at me and said, 'Your father's going to kill you.' I asked her why. 'Mom, I want to go fight for my country.' She said, 'How do you go and do that without telling him?' 'Mom, I volunteered.' She said, 'Okay, I'll tell your father, and we'll see what he says.' After she told him he had a fit. We were living in Blooming Grove and he came home from work that night and asked me in a pretty calm tone, 'What did you do?' I told him I volunteered. He asked if I had taken the oath already. I said no; I'd just gone down there and given them all my information. They wanted me to go back and get a physical. He said, 'Well that's not happening. You're not going anywhere.' I said, 'Dad, what do you mean? You fought in the war, now I want to!' He said, 'Anthony, I fought in a real war. Our country needed to get into that war. This war they have over there is all bullshit. It's all political. This isn't a war you go and fight in. We're not there to win, and I won't let you go somewhere to fight a war we don't want to win.' I said, 'What do you mean we're not there to win?' He told me I didn't understand now, but that one day I would. I never went to Vietnam. My father and I watched the news and saw how horribly our soldiers suffered for going over there. The protests were meant for the administration I'm sure, but many of those young men took the brunt of the anger.

My dad was saddened by the way the soldiers were treated when they returned. He felt they were duped by our government and had no chance to succeed. Over fifty thousand boys died over in Vietnam. I lost a few of my friends from Valley Forge. My father assured me I wasn't being unpatriotic, he just didn't want me fighting in that war. In hindsight, with the way it was handled I have to say he was right. He was always very in tune with politics at every level, from the guys on the street corner to foreign policies and governing structures."

***

On Labor Day weekend in 1965, Joe spent an evening with his wife Jo-Jo at a resort at the base of the Catskill Mountains. Among the guests at the Concord Hotel that weekend were two very high-profile suspected mobsters, Carmine Lombardozzi and Larry Gallo. NYPD detectives were at the hotel and reported seeing Joe sitting at a table in the Night Owl Lounge with Sonny, Larry, and their brother Albert Gallo. Joe's anonymity had disappeared even in his sanctuary outside of the city.

On October 14, 1965, Joe Colombo, Larry Gallo, Johnny "Bath Beach" Oddo, Joseph "The Minx" Livoti, Albert Gallo, and Salvatore "Sally the Assassin" Perritore were brought before a Grand Jury to be questioned about the infiltration of legitimate businesses by racketeers. On December 7th each member of the group was fined $250 and sentenced to a 30-day jail term for judicial contempt, as they refused to answer any of the Grand Jury's questions. Aaron E. Koota, the Brooklyn District Attorney, called the sentence, "a breakthrough for law enforcement and investigative bodies against the facade behind which the Mafia is trying to legitimize the proceeds of loan sharking, narcotics and other criminal enterprises."[xxiii] Koota, along with other state and government attorneys would use these contempt cases as a tool to continually lock up suspected racketeers again and again for the same charge of criminal contempt.

Colombo and his associates were called back by Koota on December 15th and again refused to answer any questions. The men would be dubbed the "Silent Six" after refusing to speak to the panel. During the Grand Jury proceedings Joe met a young lawyer named Barry Slotnick. Slotnick suggested to Colombo to speak to the panel. This action contradicted every piece of advice ever offered to a man in Joe's position. "Talk to them," Barry stated, "Answer a few questions. They can't hold you in contempt if you are cooperating with them. Answer the easy questions for them and tell them what you know is true. They are granting you immunity, so offer them information that could potentially save you from a jail sentence." Colombo liked Slotnick; he presented himself as a fearless fighter who employed unconventional tactics in the criminal courts. What the young defense attorney lacked in experience he made up for in tenacity. Slotnick had Colombo convinced that he should speak to the grand jury, even if it was only to answer a few questions. Joe's friends and colleagues strongly disagreed with Slotnick's advice. Their lawyers snubbed Slotnick's idea calling it reckless and advised their clients to continue to accept the contempt charges and do the time in jail.

In May of 1966, taking the advice of his lawyer, Joe Colombo offered to appear before the grand jury to answer questions. Colombo sat down and when asked a simple question, "how did you arrive here today?" he answered. Then he answered a few more; his name, occupation etc. With great surprise the DA ran out of the room and up to Barry Slotnick saying, "He's answering questions!" Slotnick said, "Of course he is, you're granting him immunity. Now go ahead and ask him about crimes, ask him about gambling." The DA knew what Slotnick and Colombo were up to. With immunity, Colombo couldn't be charged with any crimes he might be questioned about. They dismissed Colombo and never allowed him to testify again.

On October 10, 1966, The Silent Six would receive new indictments for criminal contempt for their refusal to speak in December after their convictions. The DA would not permit Colombo to testify but made an offer for the "Silent Six" if they pled guilty to receive lighter sentences. Slotnick advised Colombo and his co-defendants to refuse the offer and fight the case on grounds of Double Jeopardy. None of Joe's co-defendants or their lawyers wanted to fight the charges. Slotnick admitted the fight could go all the way to the Supreme Court, but he was certain the charges were unconstitutional. Joe took Slotnick's advice though his associates were very vocal about being against it. They complained, "no one wins in the Supreme Court." Joe replied, "If anyone can win in the Supreme Court it's Barry Slotnick."

Slotnick battled the indictment back and forth for many years. During that time, only about one half of one percent of the petitions filed received the writ of certiorari—a requirement for lower courts to turn over their case record for higher court review. Slotnick won his motion for dismissal from the Kings County

Supreme Court only to have it overturned in the Court of Appeals. Slotnick would not give up the fight and Colombo supported him in his decision to keep battling. Colombo was unsure of how Slotnick was going to win this case but trusted the young Attorney. He asked Barry, "You think you can win this case?" Barry responded, "What they are doing is unconstitutional and I can prove it." Slotnick took the case all the way to the United States Supreme Court and filed a petition for a writ of certiorari. In October 1970, Slotnick was granted the writ and Justice Black sent the case back to the court of appeals saying the charges should be reversed on the grounds of Double Jeopardy.[xxiv]

When the case was sent back to the court of appeals it was again overruled. They refused to consider the opinion of the Supreme Court and adhered to their original decision. Slotnick would have to fight again in the Supreme Court. This time he would finally win. The Supreme Court not only granted the writ of certiorari, but also ordered the court of appeals to vacate the judgment. Slotnick and Colombo made history. Their Double Jeopardy case would go into the law books and the Court of Appeals was forced to reverse the charges and dismiss the indictment.[xxv]

During the appeals when Joe was brought before the State Division of Licensing, he explained he was at the Concord to eat dinner and see a show with some friends. "I was in and out."[xxvi] He obligingly answered what questions he could. District Attorney Koota spoke to Justice Hyman Barshay about Colombo's real estate endeavors, speculating that they were "a way of siphoning off illegal money and getting illegal gains in that fashion."[xxvii]

Prosecutors continued to ask questions about Carmine Lombardozzi's suspected plan to purchase large amounts of real estate in Sheepshead Bay. The District Attorney alleged he had evidence that linked Colombo to the operation and demanded to know where Lombardozzi was getting the money. Colombo could not answer. As much as Slotnick argued that Joe was a real estate man with no criminal record and should not be subjected to this line of questioning, the contempt conviction would remain. The court would also grant the New York City Police Department a search warrant for Colombo's home.

By this time, Joe had purchased a house and was living again full-time in Brooklyn. The day after his appeals, a search warrant was granted. NYPD detectives and FBI agents arrived at 1161 83rd Street in the heart of Dyker Heights, in hopes of finding any evidence that could be used against Colombo. The resulting FBI report stated,

> THE SEARCH REVEALED NO WEAPON AND NO INFORMATION OF VALUE WAS OBTAINED AS A RESULT OF THE SEARCH.

During Colombo's many court appearances the New York Police began to run round the clock surveillance on him. They learned he was back on New Utrecht Avenue running a new social club called The Club Under The L. They followed him to Coney Island where he dined at Shoal's Restaurant and made stops at a few of the local hotels. They questioned owners but found no evidence of gang involvement within the management. The Suffolk County Police did bust a numbers headquarters in Long Island and the press released information that Joe was behind the operation. Informants were cashing in with reports about suspected Colombo operations that ranged from restaurant ownership to cigarette imports.

In March after he returned from a vacation in Miami, Colombo's conviction was upheld by the New York State Court of Appeals. His lawyer, Barry Slotnick applied for a stay, keeping Joe free on bail, waiting another court date and sentencing in May. He would serve the thirty-day sentence for contempt in May of 1966. With the help of Slotnick's counsel, this would be the only criminal prison sentence he ever served.

***

While Joe Colombo and Larry Gallo were in jail together, Joe Bonanno resurfaced after his disappearance two years prior. Since his failed coup attempt in 1963 and his subsequent kidnapping, Joe Bonanno had lost control of his Brooklyn fiefdom. In early 1966, while Joe was still missing, his son Bill Bonanno and his partner and uncle, Frank Labruzzo, set up a meeting in an attempt to resolve the power struggle within the gang. While Bill still had the support of many of his father's loyalists, Gaspar DiGregorio and Paul Sciacca had assumed control of the other half of the gang with the blessing of the Commission.

The meeting was to take place on a quiet street in Brooklyn. Bill was in the meetinghouse awaiting the arrival of Gaspar and his men when they received a call cancelling the meeting. Gaspar was ill and needed to reschedule. Suspecting a set up, the men waited a few hours before reemerging into the Brooklyn night. When they finally exited the building, a slight pause of inspection prompted Carl Simari to shove Bill Bonanno to the ground as they were ambushed by machine gun fire.

Although there were no casualties, the shooting on Troutman Street decisively ruptured the Bonanno gang. The newspapers would get wind of the incident and the ensuing war was dubbed "The Banana Split." It was purported that many of the men in the Bonanno organization were defecting to Colombo's crew. The FBI also received reports from informants that a new war over Brooklyn territory was brewing between Joe Colombo and Joe Bonanno. The agents' reports to their superiors read:

> INFORMANT STATED THAT JOE COLOMBO AND LARRY GALLO ARE DUE TO BE RELEASED FROM JAIL ON 6/7 OR 6/8/66? INFORMANT SAID THAT IF THEY ARE RELEASED AND NOT RESENTENCED UNDER THE NEW YORK STATE IMMUNITY STATUE, THEN THE SHOOTING WAR IS TO START IMMEDIATELY.

That summer Joe Colombo and Larry and Albert Gallo were released from jail. No shooting war occurred between the Bonannos and Colombos. It was a peaceful summer in Brooklyn. Joe and his family travelled back to their summer home in Blooming Grove.

***

Anthony recalls, "In 1966, my brother Joey and I attended college together up in Vermont. It was a completely different experience for me after attending Valley Forge. When the summer came I was back in Blooming Grove with the family. The fact that my father worked so much and my being away at school kept me uninformed about his legal problems. We spent the summer together just like every other summer. We went to the movies, out to dinner, and now that I was a little older he would take us all to the racetrack. He turned that gambling vice of his into a family tradition. It was about a forty-five minute ride up Route 17 to the Monticello Raceway. He would bring a large group, including my Aunt Ray Ray and Uncle Do-Do, Aunt Sugar and Uncle Banjo. I was very serious with Carol at the time so she was always with me. We would get a table and eat a big dinner while we watched the trotters. He loved to watch the horses and he loved to gamble, but when it came to winning he was hapless. We were at the track religiously for years, but he never won. I'm not sure if it was the FBI having fun with the media or if they just wanted to write a story about him, but they printed a piece that my father was up there fixing races at the track. I knew it was complete bullshit. If my father were fixing the races at Monticello, he wouldn't come home from the track all the time so worked up about losing. I'm not saying that races weren't being fixed; I just know my father didn't have anything to do with it.

Right around the time that the article had run, our family was up at the track enjoying a nice day. My father would always give Carol money to bet, but she never spent it all. She would only place a few dollars on the horses and then save the rest. He noticed that she never had to ask for more money to bet. 'Carol, you're winning a lot today, I see.' She answered 'If I don't bet the money, I've got to be a winner.' 'You're not betting?' he asked her. She replied, 'Only once in awhile when I like a certain horse.' He really began to pay attention to her when she placed a bet. She just kept winning. After yet another successful pick, he finally leaned over to her and asked, 'Carol, how did you choose this horse?' She answered sincerely, 'I liked his name.' With his usual dry humor that might have been mistaken for cynicism if you didn't know him well, he said, 'That's one hell of a system.'

So we all bet on another race. It was a little after dinnertime and we were all having a really nice time. The ponies came out of the gates and of course my father's horse was dead last. He had that same look on his face. He knew that he had again picked a loser and he let out a big sigh and shook his head at Carol, whose horse was in the lead. But as they came around that turn her horse stumbled and fell down on the sulky. Then it was a disaster, about four or five horses went down in the race, one right on top of the next. Now at this point, my father's horse was so far behind the pack, he had enough time and space to negotiate around the mayhem. The horse hooked far right, avoided the entire pile up, and ended up winning the race. When the ticket taker came around to our group, my father said, 'I fix all the races here. Look at how good I fixed this race. Only six horses had to come tumbling down so I could win this race. Can you believe that?' Everyone was laughing with him. We had all read the article. But he found humor in it. He could care less about the media at that moment. He had finally won a race."

***

On a regular Thursday afternoon in September 1966, the FBI caught a big break while following a New Orleans gangster under suspicion of having ties to the JFK assassination. They were tailing Carlos Marcello and his brother as they entered an Italian Restaurant on Queens Boulevard. With round the clock surveillance on other suspected bosses of the New York Families, Marcello's agents would have bumped into the agents tailing Joe Colombo, and Carl Gambino that same afternoon.

The big break came around 2:00 p.m. when several suspected organized crime leaders entered the restaurant. Without having any just cause to detain the men under federal violations, the FBI would have to phone in for help from the local authorities. Police and detectives from the 112 precinct arrived at about 2:30 p.m. and entered the restaurant. They were preparing to break up a large group of gangsters, but instead were baffled at the almost empty main dining room. After several minutes of searching the premises, they reached the downstairs private dining area and encountered a large party of men sitting quietly, about to break bread for an afternoon lunch. There was no escape effort and no words were exchanged; in fact when the police entered the men didn't even flinch. The detectives operated according to the strictest of orders from the FBI. None of the suspects were to move until FBI Agents snapped photos of their current seating arrangement. It was their belief that this would reveal the power structure of Organized Crime on a national level. This was exactly the type of intelligence Hoover coveted; hierarchy.

On September 22, 1966, Joe was arrested along with twelve other men in the secluded dining room at La Stella's restaurant in Queens. The twelve included Carlos Marcello, Joseph Marcello, Anthony Carolla, Frank Gagliano, Thomas "Tommy Ryan" Eboli, Dominick Alongi, Anthony Cirillo, Mike Miranda, Aniello Delcroce, Carlo Gambino, Joseph N. Gallo, and Santo Trafficante. All the diners and the restaurant's owner were charged with "consorting with criminals." This charge was more a tool used by law enforcement to make arrests than it was a punishable offense. After the photos were taken in an effort to establish the leadership structure, the men were escorted to the Maspeth station house, in a quiet residential neighborhood in Queens. The press arrived at the station, along with a flock of curious neighbors. The men were led into the station house without handcuffs. They behaved with great decorum and compliance. Police mentioned to the press that the booking process was a bit complicated, as they were uncertain of the names, ages, and addresses of the men in custody.[xxviii]

If Joe Colombo and Carl Gambino dining together were a punishable offense, the courts would stay in business as long as the two men were alive. They met weekly for dinner and lunch, both at restaurants and at family functions. It was only a few weeks after the La Stella arrest that Joe's fifth child was born; his first daughter named Catherine, after his mother. Colombo chose Carl and Catherine Gambino as the godparents.

Like Joe, Carl had been beset by legal woes, but the FBI was never able to come up with anything substantial. Gambino mostly stayed at home with his wife. The few times he was detained by police were based on frivolous arrests and trumped up charges that didn't stick. In December, however, the government handed him a deportation order. Gambino managed to evade deportation hearings as doctors declared him unfit to stand trial due to his ailing health.

The raid at La Stella's became known as "Little Appalachian," and served as the launching point for a new plan in the FBI's counterintelligence division. The FBI sought to pit two of its targeted organizations against each other. The New York Offices authorized an operation that would attempt to create a war between the Communist Party—a group Hoover had detested his entire life—and suspected La Cosa Nostra figures. Agents were instructed to send anonymous letters to the men arrested at La Stella's restaurant. The purpose of these letters was stated by the FBI in their internal security report:

> THIS ANONYMOUS LETTER IS DESIGNED TO HELP PROVOKE A DISPUTE BETWEEN LA COSA NOSTRA AND THE COMMUNIST PARTY, USA. MEMORANDUM OF F.J. BAUMGARDNER TO MR. W. C. SULLIVAN, CAPTIONED AS ABOVE, DATED 10/4/66 AND APPROVED BY THE DIRECTOR, OUTLINED A LONG-RANGE PROGRAM FOR THIS PURPOSE UNDER THE CODE NAME HOODWINK.[xxix]

The letters were handwritten and agents were instructed to purchase cheap paper. They were sent from the Communist party to Gambino, Colombo, Trafficante, Marcello and others. These fabricated letters accused the leaders of being behind the recent bombing of a Communist party building. They claimed that the Mob bosses had all been named as culprits in the national Communist newsletter "The Worker." The letters also stated that the party was planning to "RID THE COUNTRY" of them… "WITH BOMBS AND GUNS WE'LL COME IN THE DAYTIME – NOT SNEAK AROUND IN THE DARK LIKE THE SHINY COCKROACHES YOU ARE."[xxx]

Another letter drafted by the FBI was sent to the editor of "The Worker". It concerned the recent death of Thomas "Three Finger Brown" Lucchese. Lucchese was the leader of the New York crime organization bearing his surname and his successor would weigh in heavy on the balance of the Commission and criminal alliances within New York's underworld. The letter was intended to seem as if written by an old Jewish member of the party, signed, "T. Cohen." It spoke provocatively about Lucchese's death and the candidates vying to be his successor. It compared members of La Cosa Nostra to capitalists like Carnegie, Rockefeller, and Ford; some of the men most hated by the Communist party. The letter claimed that La Cosa Nostra was responsible for most of the damage done to the working and middle class of America. After two pages of ranting, the FBI's decoy letter was cleverly signed with a postscript:

YOU HAVE MY PERMISSION TO PUBLISH THIS LETTER BUT PLEASE WITHHOLD MY NAME IF YOU DO.[xxxi]

ALL PRECAUTIONS WILL BE TAKEN TO PROTECT THE BUREAU'S IDENTITY IN THIS MATTER.[xxxii]

The FBI was banking on it making it into the papers and igniting a dispute between La Cosa Nostra and The Communist Party. At the end of the internal security memorandum for this operation was the following message:

***

In 1967, Life Magazine ran a two-part series on organized crime that included an account of Joe Bonanno's failed attempt to take over the New York crime families. It described Joe as "an ambitious young torpedo" who was more strategic than he was vicious.[xxxiii] The magazine also featured Joe Colombo's photo as well as Bonanno, Angelo Bruno and twenty-two other of the nation's most powerful suspected crime leaders.

The barrage of grand jury investigations, search warrants, and counterintelligence operations was crippling to men like Joe Colombo. They had no public platform from which to refute allegations. The papers could print rumors and accusations with impunity, and no one would ever sue or demand proof. So long as the articles were peppered with words like "allegedly" "purportedly" and "reputed," the media didn't need to provide evidence in its depiction of an evil empire, replete with murders, kidnappings, and other illicit activities. The stories printed by the papers served as a reference for the organized crime task force of the FBI. They helped convince lawmakers to appropriate millions of tax dollars to expand departments and conduct investigations. Working together, law enforcement and the press constructed the story of a national threat from a small group of Italian men known as the "Mafia."

Chapter 5.

"Me and My Shadow"

(1966-1969)

Bernie Welsh towers over every man on 86th Street. He wears a cool smile for several reasons; he is genuinely affable, has a good sense of humor, and is not ashamed of his profession. His partner Boland, who stands beside him, does not have a trace of kindness in his face. The timing of these two federal agents is impeccable. Joe Colombo is walking across the street to his office at Cantalupo Realty. The agents approach him and, as usual, Boland is morosely silent while Welsh speaks. "Joe, we would like to ask you a few questions." Joe pauses for a moment, looking up at the agent who stands a full foot above him. He glances around. "Let's take it inside." Joe steps into the office with the two agents in tow. As they pass a few of the desks none of the employees dare meet Joe with their eyes. They know these men are not his friends or associates. Joe leads them down the hall and into his office.

"What can I do for you gentlemen?" Bernie pulls closer to Joe's desk and whips out a piece of paper. "Joe, I'm Bernie Welsh. This is my partner Martin Boland. We are special agents with the Organized Crime Task Force. This paper is a waiver for your rights; if you would please sign this it'll help protect you." Joe cuts him off. "I'm not signing anything. You have questions, I'll do my best to answer them." Joe leans back in his chair. Bernie continues to hold the paper out. "You can put that thing away, I'm not signing it." Bernie continues, "Joe you were with a few persons of interest to the FBI at La Stella's last fall, Santo Trafficante and Carlos Marcello. Can you tell us how you know these two gentlemen?" Joe answers honestly. "I don't know them. I met them for the first time that day. I would be glad to get to know them better, but I doubt they'll be returning to New York anytime soon." Bernie sounds excited to hear anything Joe has to say. His tone is almost buoyant. "Well what went on there that day? What were you guys all meeting about?" Joe seems slightly tired by the question. "I was there to have lunch and I didn't even get that. All I can tell you is that since that day my life as a real estate salesman has been very difficult. I haven't sold a house in six months due to all the negative publicity. I didn't even commit a crime that day and I received more media attention than a murderer." Welsh notes, "Well you were charged with something, no?" "I was charged with consorting. I have to appear before Judge Thompson to see if it will be dropped." Welsh presses forward. "What about Carl Gambino? Is he the leader of La Cosa Nostra?" Joe answers, "Carl is a very sick man, sicker than you people think. This excitement alone is enough to kill him. They should consider the man's health before they make these phony arrests." Welsh nods his head, "We will make a note of your concerns." Boland rolls his eyes in his silent corner. Joe continues, "You know, all this unfavorable publicity that I have been receiving is not only destroying me, it's destroying the Italian-American people. You men should know that Italians are very patriotic people. Anytime this country has had a conflict the Italian-Americans came to its aid. I remember during the occupation of Italy when Charlie Luciano helped the American *troops. Twenty-two and a half million Italian-Americans feel very hurt by the way the press portrays them. Mark my words, there will come a day when the Italian-American people will come together in order to stop this stigmatizing of their people. I belong to an organization called A.I.D. We have been working on putting an end to the drug problem that is plaguing our younger generation."* Welsh looks over at Boland. Boland doesn't believe a word of it. He knows this man is a mobster and there is nothing Colombo can say or do to change it. *"Joe, sorry to cut you off, but what about the Colombo organization? Are you the head of that crime family?"* Joe leans forward on his desk and folds his hands. He looks at the two agents with a mask of sincerity, *"Listen gentlemen, I've heard all the stories. Some guy died and now I'm the boss. They're just rumors."* Bernie isn't satisfied, *"Are they true?"* Joe looks at Bernie and tilts his head a bit. His eyes send a mysterious message to the agent. He does not answer Bernie's question. He does not say anything at all.

✼✼✼

The investigation of the Mafia was not only important for the FBI, but politicians discovered it to be a mobilizing issue as well. Where Hoover had once denied the very existence of a "Mafia", by the late sixties, the FBI was in full pursuit of Italian criminal organizations within the U.S. The media was also finding it very profitable to nourish the public's fascination with crime families.

Joe watched anxiously from the sidelines as the FBI marched with impunity into the homes and businesses of citizens throughout the boroughs, in an effort to arrest or simply gather information about anyone rumored to be associated with the rackets. What agents couldn't accomplish through intelligence they would try to achieve through intimidation. They threatened foreclosures, loss of livelihood, deportation and imprisonment. Local merchants and family members alike were coerced into providing evidence against suspected members. And during this witch-hunt Colombo learned the FBI was suspending his real estate license application.

The organization A.I.D. (Americans of Italian Descent) was established by Joe and a few friends in an attempt to combat the negative stereotyping of Italian-Americans and to stop the harassment and violation of their civil liberties. Many of the Italian-Americans who had served their country in battle and contributed financially and culturally to the nation felt they were still second-class citizens. Ultimately, the organization fell short of its goals and failed to reach its full potential. While its objectives were well conceived, it never effectively harnessed the power of the people it sought to help. This was largely a consequence of the administration chosen to lead the group. At the time, Joe and his close friend Larry Gallo, knowing their reputations might undermine the organization's credibility, felt they couldn't assume prominent positions. Instead, they appointed esteemed men from the community, including wealthy doctors, lawyers and businessmen, as leaders. This decision came at a price. Behind closed doors, these men all agreed that Italian-Americans were facing severe discrimination and infringements on their civil liberties, but they would only go so far in making their grievances public. They were concerned that if they were too vocal, they might jeopardize their businesses or professional reputations. In the New York Times alone, references to the Mafia increased from 2 in 1962, to 67 in 1963, to 359 in 1969.[xxxiv] This progression was for no reason other than the fact that the word itself bolstered sales. So while TV shows continued their unbalanced and prejudicial depictions of Italian-Americans, and the newspapers cashed in on the image of the Mafia, A.I.D., along with other related organizations remained relatively silent.

In 1967 A.I.D. attempted to make some changes. They appointed Frank Sinatra as the new chairman. The selection was met with a wave of criticism. Ralph Salerno, an NYPD CIB detective, condemned the decision, arguing that Sinatra lacked credibility due to his relationships with known organized crime figures.[xxxv] Sinatra received full support from the organization, which vehemently defended its choice, calling Salerno's attack unjustified. Spokesmen for A.I.D. cited Sinatra's many relationships with the most powerful leaders not only in the US, but around the globe. For Joe Colombo and Larry Gallo, there was hope in having someone like Sinatra at the forefront of their campaign.

✻✻✻

FBI investigations into Joe Colombo's life had now extended to his immediate family members as well. In December of 1967 the FBI learned of Anthony's upcoming marriage to longtime girlfriend Carol O'Brien. A few weeks before the wedding, the FBI paid a visit to a place most would think was off limits, and made a request. They approached Monsignor Williams at Saint Agnes

Cathedral and asked to install cameras in the church so they could film the wedding. Unbeknownst to the federal agents, the monsignor was a distant relative of Carol's father. Monsignor Williams told the agents with some disgust, "Absolutely not. This is not a place for that kind of business." The agents, a bit embarrassed by the man of the cloth, tried vainly to plead their case. "We just want to be able view people at the event, and we don't want our presence known. This way we don't disturb anyone." The Monsignor stood fast. "This is a private event for the family. You can film from across the street but you do not have permission to come on the church's property."

The young couple was married in Rockville Center, Long Island. It was standing-room only as Anthony waited for Carol to walk down the aisle. Across the street, FBI agents worked like Hollywood paparazzi, snapping photos from the tops of their vans. A team walked around on foot recording the license plates of every vehicle within five blocks of the Cathedral. The men never entered the church but did set up a small station across the street, preparing to get their best photos as the guests made their exit.

***

"As we stood in the back room waiting for the services to begin, my father wore a proud grin as he looked over all of his sons, donning our tuxedos, looking sharper than we ever had. The room fell silent and he and I got into a kind of staring match for a second or two. He told everyone but me to leave the room for a minute. My father was an eloquent speaker, a man who never had any trouble getting his point across. Once everyone left, the mood got real serious and I didn't know where this was going. He put his hand on my shoulder and asked me, 'Anthony, are you all right?' I paused and thought about my answer. 'Yeah, Dad, I'm fine. I'm about to get married, I'm happy.' I didn't know what he was going to say. He gave me a friendly look and said with an unusual pause between his words, 'No, are you all right? Do you know everything?' I looked at him, and quickly figured out where this was going. He wanted to know if I had any questions about what was going to happen in the honeymoon suite later that night. My father and I were very close, but we had never had the 'sex' talk. Now I had the rare opportunity to toy with him a little. I wish I'd had a bit more time to prepare a better prank, but the moment was short. I looked at him with a serious face and said, 'Oh, you mean, that!' I looked away, took a beat, and said to him, 'Dad, I'm a virgin.' His eye squinted a bit and he nodded slowly and meaningfully, but before he began to explain the birds and the bees, I stopped him and said, 'Dad, I'm only kidding, I know everything.' He looked at me with a playful mug and I said, 'Why, is there something you want to know?' He chuckled a bit and said, 'Don't be a wise guy.' I let him off the hook easy. My father and I were never buddies in this way, our relationship of father to son was always clear, even though he let me in a few times to joke.

The wedding party arrived at the Queens Terrace in eight Cadillac limousines. I was in a car with my wife, my brother Joey and his fiancé. The catering hall was very large; I worked there full-time with my Cousin Sabbie. It was right underneath the L on Roosevelt Ave. We all walked through the long lobby and headed straight upstairs into a special room for the bridal party. We took pictures and did all the normal stuff as we waited for everyone to arrive. Our guests that night numbered more than a thousand people. The guests walked through the lobby and down a set of winding steps that led into three reception rooms, which then opened up into the main dining hall and dance floor. I remember my father grabbed me a few minutes before everyone piled in and walked me through the hall to look over everything. The set up was extraordinary. I worked there, so I saw weddings all the time, but this was really something special. Custom silverware and dishware were brought in. There were wall-to-wall tables with hot dishes, shrimp boards, giant lobsters for decoration behind the seafood platters. Beautiful bowls of fresh fruit, everything done in unique designs. All of the displays and dressings were first class, a real sight to see. Tom Mano, who was a close friend of my father's and owned the Huntington Town House, helped with the reception. The Huntington Town House at that time was the nicest catering hall in New York. Tom sent over his team of people to handle the wedding, including his gourmet chef and maître d'.

While I was going back to my wife and the wedding party, I walked through the Starlight Room and saw several men; two of them had their arms hooked around a third man, supporting him. The gentlemen approached me, and as they got closer I recognized the one in the middle from the newspapers. It was Larry Gallo. He called me over and one of the men put a chair out for us to sit. He said to me, 'Do you know who I am?' I said, 'Yes.' He said, 'Yeah, who am I?' I replied humbly, 'You're Larry Gallo.' 'Okay, let me tell you something, Anthony. I am a very sick man. And I came here today to personally congratulate you on your wedding day. Anthony, don't believe all that bullshit you read in the papers

117

about your father and me. There is and never was nothing between us. Your father is one of my dearest friends, and I mean that. He is a good man, one of the fairest men I have ever come to know. I have a lot of respect for your father and he has a lot of respect for me. I am dying of cancer, and wouldn't leave my bed for anyone in this condition. But I came here for you.' It was a very humbling experience. I didn't say too much. I thanked him earnestly for coming to my wedding. Then he handed me an envelope with my gift and said, 'This is for you and your bride. I want you to have the best wedding day and many years of good fortune.' I shook hands with him, gave him a hug and a kiss and said, 'Thank you very much for coming today. I am honored that you came, especially under your circumstances, it really means a lot to me.' He nodded his head to me, and then his friends helped him to his table.

The rest of the guests were piling into the three reception rooms, the Starlight Room, the Emerald Room, and the Duchess Room. These three rooms were set up for the cocktail hour and afterwards we were served dinner in the great room. Our table was in the center of the dance floor, set up just like a dais so the entire room was facing us. At the tables in the front of the room closest to us were some of my father's most important guests. I recognized many of his regular pals, Mimi Scialo, Rocky Miraglia, Joe Notch, Joey Smash and Frankie 'The Beast.' Of course Carl was there with his wife, as well as Peter Castellano. Carmine Persico and Hugh McIntosh were there with their dates.

My father pulled out all the stops for this wedding. The entertainment at my wedding included some of the best acts in New York during that era. The comedians were Morty Storm, London Lee and Pat Henry. And the musical performances featured Jimmy Roselli, as well as the Del Vikings, Fran Warren, and Silvia Sims. It was a dream wedding for sure. My father went around to all his friends and family making sure everyone was having a good time. My wife and I were in heaven that day. It's been over forty-five years since we tied the knot. The event was like nothing I had ever experienced before, and I've never seen anything like it since."

***

Shortly after the wedding, Carol's father began to receive visits from the FBI on a regular basis. They had now begun to pursue any individual who was separated from Joe Colombo by four degrees. Timothy O'Brien, owned and operated a fillet house in the Fulton Fish Market, a job that had kept him working seven days a week since he was kid. He had developed an extraordinary work ethic and learned young how hard it was to earn a decent living. He didn't understand how the FBI could justify using taxpayers' money to take photographs of him as he filleted his fish and helped unload packages at the docks. He would tell his daughter what was going on but the stories stayed between them. Carol knew Anthony was no criminal, and as for the rumors surrounding her father-in-law, she refused to believe they were true. After she and Anthony moved into their new home in Dyker Heights, she began noticing agents following her on her daily trips to the grocery store or laundromat. They shadowed her as if her own husband were a Mob boss. These experiences were bewildering and at times frightening. She would often be followed by a van or car. The agents progressed from tailing her to striking up conversations with her. As she walked down 86th Street one afternoon, Agents Boland and Welsh rolled up alongside her and hopped out of their van to ask her some questions.

"What's a nice Irish girl like you doing with a guy like Anthony Colombo? We're Irish, you should talk to us. Us 'micks', we all got to stick together." Carol stood still and stared coldly at them as they continued. "We're going to go and talk to your dad. He'll understand, because he's from the old Irish school, the east side." She told them, "My father may come from the same place as you two but he is nothing like you!"

They continued to visit Carol's father at his job, trying to embarrass him in front of his coworkers. But these men didn't intimidate O'Brien and he definitely wasn't embarrassed. While they questioned him he stayed calm and kept about his business. The agents tried to press O'Brien for information and offered him cash for anything he could tell them about Joe Colombo. He just puffed his cigar and took a deep breath and said, "I've got nothing to say to you people." But they followed him more and more. They snapped photos of him and his employees, and hung around long enough to tail him home at the end of the workday. As a result of these experiences, O'Brien developed a strong bond with Joe Colombo. O'Brien saw how these agents would waste their days following innocent people in order to collect useless bits of information on their suspects. He was Irish from the east side of New York. They had their own gangs running around and this was a part of life. Criminals committed a crime and they were arrested. It was natural, but now citizens were being investigated before they committed a crime and people who weren't even criminals were being subjected to the stress and harassment of the FBI. His whole life Timothy O'Brien had been a man who took things like government and politics seriously. But once he started to see these abuses he became disillusioned and mistrustful. He and Joe began to talk for hours at family functions about the growing rift between the working class of this nation and its political leaders. O'Brien respected Joe and thought that even if this man did some of the things police said he did, he sided with him anyway. O'Brien believed that Joe was a man of integrity, yet he saw agents relentlessly trying to fabricate reasons to arrest him. He was asked repeatedly if he had participated in or seen Colombo participate in any type of crime. He responded, "You think that's all I got to do. I work all hours a day and this is what we're paying you to do. People think the FBI is a respectable job, that you're protecting the greater good of the country. If they only knew you drive around in a car all day long, taking pictures of people at work or watching my daughter pick out vegetables at the market. You men should be ashamed of your positions." Carol was nervous when her father spoke his peace. He was always inclined to say something to them when she was with him and they were being followed, but she asked him to refrain. She was fearful that these men might do something to hurt him. She implored, "You don't know what they are capable of."

***

While the FBI was busy collecting information and taking photos of Joe Colombo's new relatives, the Bonanno gang was trying to recover from its recent rupture. Since Bonanno's ejection from the

Commission, the group could not find a way to move forward in solidarity, which affected everything from their rackets to their relationships. The faction against Bonanno was led by acting boss Paul Sciacca and underboss Frank Mari. It was rumored that those wanting to end the conflict had defected from the Bonannos and moved their rackets over to the Colombo crew, swelling Joe's clan with new business. This only served to further poison the already bad blood between Colombo and Bonanno. The FBI knew that the bulk of Joe Colombo's profits came from "service crimes." Unlike labor rackets, extortion and stolen goods, the service crime was an accepted business practice in the underworld which provided goods and "services" that were deemed illegal by the government. Since prohibition was no longer a problem, men focused on other vices like cigarettes, gambling and loan sharking.

Loan sharking was a very interesting racket for gangsters. While many people held the belief that loans were only sought by unlucky gamblers, junkies and failed businessmen, there was a different side to the business that did not receive a lot of focus from the media. Most Italian-American immigrants were ineligible for loans in the U.S. They either had no line of credit or were unable to complete the complicated paperwork. They often lacked the resources to outline a comprehensive business plan or show collateral, so they were routinely rejected by banks for any loan application, even when the ability to pay was not a concern. Many of them turned to the neighborhood loan sharks for a more unconventional style of lending. The government would call the loans usury, but for many of the people receiving the cash it was the only way to escape from poverty or free them from a lifetime of hard labor. Throughout New York City, new business owners of Italian descent brought their ideas to life with money from loan sharks. Everything from bakeries to trucking companies surfaced and flourished. The old tale of the loan default leading to broken kneecaps was a bit dated by the sixties. Newer and wiser loan sharks knew that there would be no way to recover the loan if they injured their "clients." They would either take a larger piece of the business or go in for a complete buyout if borrowers could not keep up with the payments. The days of murder and brutal reprisals of the "Mustache Petes" were long gone. A new era of Mob bosses had arrived, and the suspected leader of the pack in the 1960's was the youngest boss in the history of the Mob, an underdog with progressive ideas; Joe Colombo.

In one case where FBI informants obtained the name of a business owner to whom Colombo had loaned monies, agents applied great pressure to force him into disclosing information about the deal. When the agents could not coerce him into talking they placed him before a grand jury. As a result of his refusal to answer their questions, the state awarded him a six-month sentence for contempt of court. [xxxvi] It was rumored that for his show of good faith and loyalty, Colombo relieved the gentleman of his loan obligations.

While the burgeoning business of organized crime gave rise to a smarter and less brutal generation of gangsters, the rackets were still controlled by men who were obliged to protect and enforce certain codes of conduct. Most of them were family men, many of them religious, who attempted to reconcile their faith in god with the requirements of survival in their line of work. These gangsters were almost invariably treated as outsiders and second class citizens; as a consequence, they did not trust strangers, and placed no confidence in law enforcement. This sense of alienation served to strengthen their adherence to their own laws. Transgressions such as ratting, drug sales, kidnapping, adultery, or striking a "made member" were punishable by death.

As Colombo's organization flourished, Bonanno's was embroiled in conflict. The battle for succession resulted in numerous murders. All of the men killed during this period claimed allegiance to either of the two factions vying for control of the gang. There were five casualties, however, that puzzled investigators. Although they were eventually chalked up as casualties of the Bonanno war, police were never able to establish a connection. In truth, their deaths were unrelated to the conflict. These five men were slain for their participation in a double homicide committed in 1938. The murder of Anthony "Tony Durante" Colombo and Christine Oliveri. They were the victims of a revenge killing thirty years in the making.

***

He sits on the third stool at the empty service counter of Calisi's soda shop. It is a few minutes after nine on a Friday morning. He has his customary strawberry malted in front of him and he flicks his manicured fingernails against the flutes of the Anchor Hocking soda glass. He does not read the paper or attempt conversation with the clerk. At 64, his face is carved with deep lines, but beneath his top hat he still sports a full head of salt and pepper hair. He motions to the clerk, "Get me a pack of Lucky's." The clerk reaches for the cigarettes and places them next to the malted. The clerk does not ask for money for the malted or the cigarettes. The old man, nicknamed "The Sidge", short for Sicilian, is a retired gangster recently paroled from prison. Formerly a racketeer with the Profaci organization, his street credibility dates back to the mid twenties. Today, he sits comfortably and quietly, enjoying the peace of his morning routine. He seems entirely removed from the bustling traffic of the street outside.

As he takes his last sip of the malted, he hears the small ringing of the front door bell. He looks up to see the Raven in the doorway, whose eyes glow like diamonds through the narrow cutouts of his makeshift hood. The Sidge's eyes widen and for a moment he freezes. He draws a deep breath and raises himself from the stool in a futile attempt to flee. Machinegun bullets fly immediately, hitting his face, arm, shoulder, and neck. He crumples onto the linoleum. More bullets blast from the doorway and bury themselves in his body, as well as in the floor and wall behind him. The clip is exhausted. The gunman observes the heavy stillness of his victim. He turns out into the street and the wooden door slams closed with the jingling of the entry bell. The clerk is tucked away behind the counter, trembling in his white smock. He prays the bell will not ring again.

***

Chief of Detectives Albert Seedman called Joe Colombo down to the 66th Street Precinct House to question him about the recent murder of Cologero "Charlie the Sidge" LoCicero. The Sidge was well known by lawmen as a policy maker in South Brooklyn and his operation was alleged to be a part of Joe Colombo's crew. Before Seedman even called Colombo he had his own theory worked out in his head. He was only calling Joe in to "confirm or deny the connection between the killings."[xxxvii] Seedman had chosen the most obvious link in the murder case, creating a connection between the Sidge's murder and the murder of his Grandnephew a year prior. Seedman was unprepared for the meet with Colombo having already believed he had all the answers. Seedman did nothing during the interview but try and characterize Joe Colombo, judging everything from his clothes to his Italian-American pride. It never crossed Seedman's mind that he might have be sitting four feet away from the culprit and that the shooting was part of a thirty year vendetta that young Colombo may have been patiently waiting to execute. Seedman's gut instinct would lead him down the wrong path leaving him with another unsolved murder, the case closing due to exhaustion.

What Albert Seedman, or even Joe's mother did not realize about Joe was his incredible patience and determination. He only refused to leave for California as a teen because he knew if he stayed, one day he would find his father's killers and possibly avenge his death. It may have been the main motivation for him to get involved in the rackets, and most certainly the reason why he would have entered into the Profaci group as opposed to the easier choice in coming up under the wing of his mentor Carl Gambino.

In May of 1968, at the age of 41, Lawrence Gallo died in his sleep. The media did not recount the events of Gallo's life favorably. News articles focused on his purported loan sharking, his attempted assassination in the Sahara lounge, and his suspected plot to overthrow the Profaci gang with his brother Joey and longtime friend Joe Gioielli. The papers failed to mention his extraordinary act of heroism in 1962, when he ran into a burning building and saved the lives of six children, the first of whom emerged with her hair ablaze. Nor did they mention the brewing race riots Larry helped avert in East New York. While Gallo had successfully brokered a truce between warring teenage gangs, city officials or the media never credited him. Instead, officials called the event a "civic disgrace," and condemned the City Youth Board's decision to enlist "gangsters" to do police work.[xxxviii] It was never mentioned that Gallo's help was enlisted after the city police force failed completely to quell the conflict. In his obituary in the Times, one of Gallo's surviving brothers, Albert, was omitted, but the paper did not neglect to mention that his brother Joey was currently in prison for extortion.[xxxix]

Joe Colombo, however, was well acquainted with Larry Gallo's loyalty and virtues, and he mourned greatly the loss of his old friend from President's Street. Colombo and his family attended the funeral, which embraced the lavish style of the Prohibition Era gangsters. Gallo's hearse was driven to Greenwood Cemetery, followed by five floral cars and twenty-seven limousines.[xl] Police detectives and FBI agents stood with cameras along the trees on Flatbush Avenue.

While Joey Gallo grieved the loss of his older brother from prison, Carmine Persico was joyfully reunited with his older brother Alphonse, who had just completed a seventeen-year jail sentence. Alphonse "Allie Boy" Persico was convicted in 1951 of the murder of a longshoreman named Steve Bove. Many sources in the

127

underworld, however, reported that in fact, Carmine had been the killer. When the police interviewed the witness who was in the car beside the victim, he told them "Persico" was the shooter. Wishing to protect his younger brother, Allie Boy stepped up and confessed to the murder. The brothers believed the judge might deliver a merciful sentence as a reward for his acceptance of responsibility, but they were aghast when Allie Boy received the maximum of 20 years. The witness, known as Blue Beetle, pointed Allie Boy out from the stand in front of Carmine and a gang of his friends. There were stares and hand signals made during the trial that even the judge noticed. He addressed the entire courtroom during Persico's sentencing, warning, "If anything happens to this witness while you are serving this sentence I will see you finish the rest of your life in prison." After the trial, Blue Beetle went into hiding anyway. Evidently, he was not adequately reassured by the judge's speech. He didn't return to south Brooklyn until 1968, 17 years later, supposedly to visit his ailing mother.

Once he was back in Brooklyn, Blue Beetle spent a number of afternoons in a social club off Sackett Street, playing cards with some old friends. Underworld sources reported that Blue Beetle was in the club one day when the door opened and two men entered. In front of about twenty people, with no masks concealing their identities, the men walked right up to Blue Beetle. He was ripped from his chair and slammed to the floor by the larger of the two men. The man kneeled down on Blue Beetle's chest, pinning his arms to the floor, then pointed a revolver over his face and blasted every bullet into his skull, screaming, "You rat-cock-sucking-mother-fucker! You piece of filthy shit! How do you like that, you filthy fuck?" After he emptied the revolver of bullets, he continued to pull the trigger. He finally stood up, looked briefly around the room with his partner, and both walked out casually. The police couldn't get a single description of the murder.

***

In 1968, in the months following the assassinations of Martin Luther King, Jr. and Bobby Kennedy, the FBI was still searching for intelligence on the man who had become the youngest Mob boss in U.S. history. Joe was picked up by the NYPD in July while dining at the House of Chan's Chinese Restaurant in Manhattan with Carlo Gambino, Angelo Bruno, John Scimone, Thomas Massotta and Vincent Aloi. The diners were officially charged with violating section 240 of the New York penal law, otherwise known as "loitering." Here was another example of the police's ability to detain suspected gangsters at anytime with impunity. Once the men were taken to the station house, the FBI stepped in and instructed the police to place Bruno, Gambino, and Colombo into a separate holding cell with a single chair in the center. They watched, believing that the Boss would be revealed when offered the seat. Instead, Gambino was given the chair since he was the eldest of the group and suffering from poor health. Men like Colombo and Bruno were raised to respect their elders. No matter who was the official head of the "commission", Gambino would have been given the seat out of respect in any situation. The police tried to detain the men without giving them a chance to see the judge, but Joe's lawyer, Barry Slotnick filed a habeas corpus petition, and succeeded in obtaining an arraignment that evening. Once the judge heard them, the case was dismissed.

The FBI sought every opportunity to question Colombo after the House of Chan's arrest. Joe was invariably affable and never refused to engage the agents in a brief conversation. Colombo spoke frequently about his contempt for the sale and use of narcotics, and indeed he had the reputation even in law enforcement as one of the few Mob bosses in the country who opposed drugs. Joe expressed his position both to the FBI and to the men in his crew. In reference to the use of cocaine or marijuana, Duke Santoro, purportedly a member of Junior Persico's crew, a sect within the Colombo organization, told men, "The boss ain't having it. We're done chasing guys for that shit."

Although outspoken, Joe was always diplomatic when expressing his opinions, particularly to federal agents. He did, however, discuss his concerns about discrimination and the denial of civil liberties by the government. He complained to Boland and Welsh specifically about his experiences with crooked politicians and rampant corruption at the municipal level. He was deeply upset, over the denial of the liquor license his son Joseph had applied for. He could not understand why a person with a clean record and a promising future should be denied the opportunity to open a legitimate business. The wellbeing and success of his children were paramount to Joe. He was enraged that they suffered as consequence of the investigations into his own affairs. He did whatever he could to try to both insulate and provide them with opportunities to flourish. His sons, in turn, loved and admired him unconditionally, and never once doubted his virtue or integrity.

※※※

"My father would travel often with my mother. They took trips to Vegas, Puerto Rico, Miami, and the Bahamas. He loved to gamble so he picked destinations where gambling was legal. I remember my mother telling me about the first time she met Sinatra. They stayed as Frank's guests at the Sands Hotel back in 1960. My father introduced her to Dean Martin, Peter Lawford, Sammy Davis, Jr., Angie Dickinson, Joey Bishop, and Cesar Romero. She met the whole crew over dinner and got to see them during the filming of the "Rat Pack" debut, 'Ocean's Eleven.' My father was a friend of Sinatra's for many years, but it was Sammy Davis that he was closest to. The two of them really enjoyed each other's company, and they both shared the same passion for golf. Sammy was an exceptional golfer. My father was a very competitive person when it came to sports and from what I was told, Sammy used to get the best of him on the course. Years after my father passed, Sammy told me a story about a game he and my father played. They must have had a pretty good wager going on it. Now, Sammy lost his eye in a car accident in the 50's and wore a glass replacement. This one game he was beating my father really badly. When it was clear my father didn't have a chance to win, my father stopped him before an eagle putt. 'Sammy hold on a second,' he told him. He walked over and got behind Sammy. Sammy was confused and got a little nervous. He asked him if everything was okay. My father handed the club to his caddy and said, 'I just want to make this game fair.' He placed his hand over Sammy's good eye and said, 'Now, let me see you make the shot.'

While my father was on vacation in the spring of 1969, my wife was expecting. International calling was a real pain back then so we had a system set up. Every night at seven they would call my

Aunt Loretta's house from the hotel. The day my son was born I went over to my aunt's house and got the call. My mother said, 'Anthony, did Carol have the baby?' 'Yeah, Mom.' She said, 'Oh that's wonderful!' followed by lots of oh's and ah's. My father must have been right next to her because he grabbed the phone. 'Ant, congratulations! Is it a boy or a girl?' 'It's a boy, Dad.' 'Oh, that's just wonderful. How many pounds? What does he look like?' I knew all these questions were just a warm up, though. He was avoiding the one question he really wanted to ask. He wanted to know what I'd named my son. It was a tradition to name your first-born son after your father, but I didn't say anything and he didn't ask. And he made sure he kept talking. He asked, 'Did you check the toes and fingers? How is Dr. Goldstein? He did an excellent job, right?' 'Yes, Dad.' I enjoyed the little game. Then he says, 'So everything is okay?' I said, 'Everything is great, Dad. The baby is perfect, Carol is perfect.' Then he says, 'Anthony, what did you name your son?' Quickly I answered, 'Oh, I named him Rob. Robert Colombo.' The phone went silent. And I mean silent. It was so quiet I couldn't contain myself. I went from feeling thrilled to feeling horrible, knowing I'd just hurt his feelings. I quickly said, 'Dad, what do you think I would name my son?' He said in a somber tone, 'I don't know.' 'I named him Joseph, Dad. Your grandson's name is Joseph.' He was happy, he didn't go crazy because I'd just stuck it to him, but he was really happy anyway. He gave me another genuine, 'Congratulations,' and then put my mother on. She said, 'So you named him Joseph. You're a good son, Anthony. I said, 'Mom what do you think I would name my son?' She said, 'I know, your Father's crazy.' And she started laughing. My father was traditional, and I would definitely carry on the tradition like he wanted.

Family was the most important thing in my father's life and he kept us all together just as much in our twenties as he did when we were kids. My father and mother would take Carol and me with them out to all of the clubs and restaurants in the city. We used to see all the big acts at the best places. We saw Rodney Dangerfield and Engelbert Humperdinck, Henny Youngman and Don Rickles. Before he was the biggest act around, we saw Wayne Newton at the Royal Box, which was located in the Americano Hotel. I remember going there with big parties of at least twenty people, mostly my family, my aunts and uncles, my brother Joey and his fiancée Diane. And for years he took us to the Copacabana. These occasions were something we all looked forward to. Everyone was dressed in his or her best. We would roll up with our entire entourage to the front of the club. Every night there was a line reaching down the block. We just walked up to the front of the crowd where Big Junior was standing by the steps. We walked downstairs and right into the club where they had a bunch of tables waiting for us. We would sit right on the floor next to the entertainers or performers, just like they showed in *Goodfellas*. Now in that movie, Henry Hill tried taking an awful lot of credit. I highly doubt he was getting that kind of treatment in there. Maybe he had good relationships with the bus boys and waiters and that's why he went in the back entrance like that. He definitely wasn't getting bottles purchased for him by wise guys. I think he was talking a lot of self-gratifying bullshit. He was only a legend in his own mind. His biggest claim to fame was that he knew Jimmy Burke. Besides that he was a drug pusher, a junkie, and a rat.

There were definitely a lot of big names at the Copa. Guys would always come over to the table to say hello to my father. We'd get all of the entertainers to come sit with us for a bit to have a drink and say hello. Sammy, Sinatra, Tom Jones, Bobby Darren, they all sat with us when they were there. My dad would order a drink but he never finished it. Some nights we would eat dinner there. They served good food, but that wasn't really their strength. The menu was always simple, steaks, and chops and seafood; nothing extraordinary. People went there for the live acts and the atmosphere. Any night you would see Jules Podell at the far end of the bar, watching the entire club, making sure the place was running smoothly. If he saw a fork coming out of the kitchen that didn't shine enough, he would grab it off the tray and replace it with a freshly polished one. The place was always at capacity. They had a separate room upstairs with a full bar and smaller drawing acts for people who arrived after the downstairs was at capacity. Between these big nights out at the clubs and our continued Sunday dinners and trips to the movies, my father kept our unit as close as any family could be."

***

Colombo had a prodigious work ethic, and he expected his men to adopt one as well. He encouraged them to become more involved with legitimate businesses, knowing it could help save them from federal heat. At the same time, he was also rumored to be pressuring his men into taking a new approach to the rackets, expanding past policymaking and loan sharking into small profits on everything from fraudulent car loans to invisible stocks. This new style of non-violent crime kept a once wild gangland empire relatively quiet. Newspapers were embarrassing law enforcement as they printed bold stories about luxurious criminal enterprises built by Italian men, claiming that they'd converted dirty money into legitimate businesses. Articles described concealed interests in motels, cocktail lounges, restaurants, and funeral homes.[xli]

With the reduction of New York City's murder rate and scarcity of high profile crimes splashed across the front page of the paper, the FBI needed to find a new way to combat organized crime and its new rackets. Mob operations had become so clandestine that it would require the introduction of new legislation to catch them in the federal web. Criminal bosses were protected and somewhat unassailable, since they rarely took part in the actual crimes. The government would need to devise new conspiracy laws in which large groups could be prosecuted based on patterns of criminal activity or illegal enterprises. These laws, which only require the testimony of a witness for conviction, became the most powerful crime-fighting tool in the government's arsenal: R.I.C.O.

Some of the tactics used by the FBI against organized-crime figures were suspicious at best and, at worst, criminal. This might be attributable in part to the nature of their training at Quantico. An FBI agent assigned to the Colombo organization described how recruits studied everything from bank robberies to kidnappings and hijackings. They were taught how to gather evidence, interrogate suspects, pay informants and use weapons. However, in his experience, "There was almost no instruction on civil rights violations or the activities of organized crime."[xlii]

It was around the time of Joe's arrest at the House of Chan's that Joe Bonanno's house in Tucson was bombed, along with the ranch of his associate, Peter Licavoli. While the newspapers pumped out stories of a "gang war" after Arizona was hit with over 15 bombings, no one in the world of organized crime took credit for the bombings and no one could imagine who would have executed an assassination attempt in that fashion. The Bonanno war was coming to a close and Bonanno himself had never been a target. Moreover, bombings were not characteristic of organized crime; the New York underworld was baffled. A year later, the two men arrested for the bombing, William J. Dunbar Jr. and Paul M. Stevens told police that they were working with the FBI. They said they had been hired by an agent named Dave. Upon hearing this, Bill Bonanno knew immediately that they were referring to David Hale, a harassing agent in charge of organized crime in Arizona. After the men testified in court and identified Hale as their employer, he promptly resigned from the FBI. Frances Angleman, a student and friend of Hale's boasted to her friends that she took part in trying to bomb Joe Bonanno's car with Hale. On May 14, 1969, before Police had the chance to question Angleman, she was found dead in her apartment. She died from a gunshot wound to the head from a .22 caliber pistol found in her hand. The Tucson police ruled her death a suicide.[xliii] J. Edgar Hoover ran the media and state investigators in circles as they attempted to look further into Hale's misconduct.[xliv] Hale fled to Florida before answering a single question. He was never charged with a crime.

✳✳✳

In the fall of 1968, Joe Colombo suffered an episode of Bells Palsy. The nerve damage on the right side of his face resulted in swelling and a sluggish droop below his eyebrow. The muscles were paralyzed, and even under the care of the best doctors Colombo could not recover fully. It is more than likely that this was one of the adverse effects of the mounting pressure in Joe's life. Colombo's doctor suggested to him that an ear infection had damaged his facial nerve, since the paralysis occurred after a three-day bout with the flu. The condition persisted for almost two months and only began to subside around Christmas time.

FBI agents continued to monitor suspected La Cosa Nostra members who visited Colombo's offices at Cantalupo Realty. They made positive I.D.'s on men like Mimi Scialo, John Cutrone, Modesto Santoro, and Joe Notch. But when it came to identifying Colombo they had surprising difficulty. With Rocky Miraglia in the picture and the cold winter requiring the men to dress in layers, there were many occasions when agents found it impossible to accurately discern Colombo. One detective was quoted, "It's impossible to tell them apart. If I was a gangster and I wanted to hit Joe, I'd have to take them both to be sure I got the right man."[xlv]

What was no longer confusing to law enforcement, however, was the current hierarchy of the Colombo crime group. According to FBI reports, Joe not only had the full support of the Commission, but he had also achieved uncontested supremacy in an organization which five years prior had been on the brink of destruction. The FBI tried to foster discord in the organization by releasing sound bites to the press from a series of illegal wiretaps known as the "Goodfella Tapes." The tapes amounted to 2220 pages of verbal assaults and criticisms of various mobsters like the top-ranking New Jersey boss, Sam "The Plumber" DeCavalcante. The FBI was not permitted to introduce the tapes in court, so instead they became a piece of counterintelligence. At one point in his invective, DeCavalcante discredits Joe's status in the Commission. The line, "He was nothing but a bust out man,"[xlvi] made it to hundreds of publications with the help of the FBI. Its release was designed to cause friction between DeCavalcante and Colombo, and potentially foment a war. The press only ran a small part of DeCavalcante's tirade. In truth, the tapes contained condemnations of almost every major crime figure in the nation. DeCavalcante wasn't only taking a shot at Joe Colombo, he was insulting every man on the Commission, from Sam Giancana to Angelo Bruno. An excerpt of the recording is as follows:

> YOU TAKE ANGE BRUNO. WHAT THE HELL DOES HE KNOW? HE DON'T SAY TWO WORDS.... JERRY CATENA WETS HIS PANTS WHEN THEY TALK.... NOW, WHERE'S A GUY EVEN LIKE CHICAGO (SAMUEL GIANCANA), WHERE DOES HE FIT ON THE COMMISSION? YOU HEAR THIS GUY TALK AND HE'S A NICE GUY. YOU CAN ENJOY HIS COMPANY. BUT HE'S A JOKESTER. "HIT HIM, HIT HIM!"– THAT'S ALL YOU HEAR FROM THE GUY.... JOE COLOMBO SITS LIKE A BABY NEXT TO CARL (GAMBINO) ALL THE TIME. HE'LL DO ANYTHING CARL WANTS HIM TO DO.[xlvii]

DeCavalcante was a known curmudgeon, and while the leaked tapes did not get him into any legal trouble, he fell out of favor with the Commission for his disrespect and his persistent loyalty to Joe Bonanno. During the Bonanno war, DeCavalcante took control of a social club off Sackett Street that had belonged to a relative of his. Although DeCavalcante owned the club, it was in Colombo's territory. It was also the location of Blue Beetle's vicious afternoon murder. The retaliation slaying drew considerable and unwanted attention from law enforcement, and as a consequence, DeCavalcante lost members, money and respect. The rumor is that

DeCavalcante was granted a sit-down with Colombo in order to address the issue. The men had a friendly relationship before the release of the "Goodfella Tapes." In fact, it was only one year prior that DeCavalcante was sitting in the Queens Terrace celebrating Anthony Colombo's marriage. DeCavalcante was a bold and pretentious man, and he believed he was entitled to a generous amount of restitution from Colombo.

***

DeCavalcante exits his Cadillac from the passenger side onto the slushy Manhattan curbside. He and his associate trudge through the snow and walk up to the building entrance. His hat perches haphazardly on his head, and a cigarette hangs from his lips like an afterthought. He wears a haughty expression, with a thick, narrow mustache framing his frowning mouth. He takes a final drag from his cigarette and flicks it into the snow.

The two men walk into the building's front lounge and take in the surroundings. The large sitting room is adorned with gold trim and carved wooden furniture. Seated at a table are Rocky Miraglia and Joe Colombo. Joe wears an even smile and nods to his guests. Rockys takes DeCavalcante's topcoat and hat and hangs them on a rack. DeCavalcante's associate, a much younger Italian with an expressionless face, indicates to Rocky that he will leave his coat on. Colombo stretches his hand towards an empty seat and offers it to his guest. "Please sit down, Sam." Joe watches as DeCavalcante adjusts himself in the chair. He asks cordially,

"Can I get you a cup of coffee or an espresso?" Rather brusquely, DeCavalcante replies, *"I just came from coffee. I don't mean to be rude but I want to beat the storm that's coming, so if we could just get down to business."* Joe leans back thoughtfully in his chair. *"Before we begin I think we should have a drink, a toast."* DeCavalcante is impatient, but accepts the proposal with a nod. *"Rocky, get us a round of bourbons, please."* As Rocky pours two generous glasses, Joe begins his impromptu toast. *"To the death of a rat cocksucker! A snitch that sent a stand-up guy to prison for half his life. May his flesh get eaten by worms in his grave and may his body rot in hell for the cowardly move he pulled."* DeCavalcante swallows deliberately before taking a sip of his drink. He realizes now there will be no recompense at all for the loss of business at his social club. Joe winks at DeCavalcante as he throws back his shot. He slams the empty glass on the table and asks invitingly, *"Now, what is it you wanted to talk about?"* Everything DeCavalcante planned to say slips back down his throat with the shot of bourbon. The meeting is over.

Chapter 6.

"Three Coins in the Fountain"

(1969-1970)

The blue Buick hooks a slow left-hand turn off of Brightwater Court in Coney Island. It crawls along the dead end street and pulls up to the boardwalk's entrance ramp. The driver's door opens and his hand emerges, shaking out an ashtray full of cigarette butts onto the pavement. He taps the tray against the base of the car. He steps out of the car and begins to make his way along the boardwalk, holding his fedora down against the strong beach winds. He looks out at the choppy white water crashing in the shallows. It is a cold day; he snickers at the scattered people foolishly playing on the shore. When he reaches the guard shack he picks up the phone, puts a dime in and dials a number from memory. He takes a pull from his cigarette almost every time he takes a breath.

His sagging, defeated eyes liven as someone picks up on the other end. "I'm calling to report. This is Scarpa." He listens for a moment and quickly grows impatient. "Look, I don't got a lot of time, so get ready. I need this to be short and sweet." He pauses for a brief moment and then begins. "So, there was a meeting and they announced Yacovelli is going to be the new underboss." He pauses to listen for a minute. "No one knows where Freddy No

Nose is, or Sally D. And now they're sayin' that Richie Zorzi is missing too." "It's hard to say. I've heard a million different stories. They're all over the place. But Colombo is really concerned about them being missing. I gotta say he and a lot of other guys think it was retribution from Adamo and Mari." He is asked a question. "Who knows? There may be a couple more guys missing already, or they could be hiding out. But I asked around and no one knows where Mimi Scialo is either." He guesses at the last question. "I don't know. Could be a war brewing with the Bonanno's. Who knows? If that's the case then 15 or 20 guys are going bye-bye." He pauses and listens, then says, "I can't get to him. There's no one getting to him right now. You guys got too much heat on the street. You're ruining my chances of giving you more." He gets frustrated quickly and answers, agitated. "Well you might as well lay off. Everyone's been instructed to plead the fifth so you're wasting your time. Listen, that's all I heard and that's all I'm going to tell you, so do me a favor and get my lump sum C.O.D. money Saturday. All right? It's too fucking cold for this bullshit so I'm cutting it short." He gives him a second to confirm. "Yup! Saturday morning. You know where to see me."
He hangs up the phone without saying goodbye and coughs up a good knot of phlegm. He spits to his left, glances around a little, and hurries back towards his car.

✱✱✱

Most of the roads leading law enforcement to Joe Colombo were paved by the FBI's paid informants. These were men who either operated small rackets in Bensonhurst, or had some relationship with suspected members of the Colombo organization. The majority of the intelligence the FBI gathered about Joe Colombo came from Gregory Scarpa. He was a relatively forgettable guy, which made him an ideal informant. Acquaintances described him as a somewhat socially anxious chain-smoker who lacked much personality. But Scarpa had been selling stories to the FBI since 1963 and was considered a "Top Echelon Criminal Informant."[xlviii] He used this rank as leverage to pull more funds from the government on top of his illicit gains as a racketeer. Letters were sent to the FBI's third in command, William C. Sullivan reciting Scarpa's work, noting his position of "extreme personal danger," then further stating he was "currently in dire need of financial assistance."[xlix] Additional monies were given to Scarpa as lump sum payments during these times without question.

In the early 1990's, just before dying from HIV, Scarpa had become an infamous killer during the violent Persico-Orena wars. It was most likely his lack of direct access to Joe Colombo during the late 1960's and early 1970's that kept Scarpa alive as long as he was. If Colombo were indeed the organized crime leader the FBI suspected him of being during that time, any suspicions of treachery would have been responded to with the most severe punishment. The opacity of the Colombo organization was the result both of Joe's evasiveness and the efficacy of his own team of informants who routinely apprised him of police activity. Gregory Scarpa provided the FBI with information about Colombo's daily routines and some of the people he associated with, but never enough for agents to build a solid case against him.

It wasn't until the late 1960's that Joe Colombo's name began to appear in the front-page headlines of the New York press. Since his alleged assumption of control of the newly-titled Colombo crime organization in 1964, Joe Colombo had maintained a relatively low profile, and his suspected criminal operations never drew much attention from police. He was known both in Mob circles and by the FBI as the man who had achieved the truce in the Gallo/Profaci wars. Indeed, he had a reputation for exhibiting decorum and restraint in his personal and professional interactions. He was noticed by police only when he appeared in public places with other suspected criminal leaders. Even under the intense scrutiny of the FBI, reports consistently confirmed that Colombo's gang was "quiet."

At the end of 1969, however, the relative quiet of Colombo's life would be disturbed when the FBI learned of the disappearance of two individuals they had been watching; Salvatore "Sally D D'Ambrosio and Fred "No Nose" De Lucio. Sally D. was a recent parolee and an alleged "wise guy" in the Colombo gang. He'd first caught the attention of police after being identified as one of two men involved in a botched attempt on Larry Gallo's life in the Sahara Lounge in 1961. His accomplice in that crime was Carmine "Junior" Persico. Sally D. was charged in the case but acquitted when witnesses, including Gallo himself, could not positively identify him. Gallo's failure to do so wasn't surprising given that Gallo was also an alleged "wise guy" in the Colombo gang. He insisted that he couldn't recognize his assailants, who had pulled a rope around his neck until he lost consciousness. Disbelieving this account, the agent interviewing him said exasperatedly, "Come on, Larry!" Larry laughed. "To tell the truth," he replied, "I didn't know where I was."[1] Larry Gallo honored the code of "Omerta", or the code of silence. Years later, the scene of Gallo's failed garroting would be depicted in *The Godfather: Part II*. It was art imitating life as the Rosato Brothers attempted to kill Frank Pentangeli.

Sally D. can be credited with the inspiration for another, more famous scene from the first *The Godfather*: He is believed to have led Joseph "Joe Jelly" Gioelli out for a fishing trip in Sheepshead Bay. At the end of the excursion, a fish wrapped in Joe Jelly's clothing was tossed in front of a garage in Bath Beach. Similarly, in *The Godfather*, when Sollozzo killed Luca Brasi, he wrapped Brasi's bulletproof vest around a fish. "It's a Sicilian message. It means Luca Brasi sleeps with the fishes."

Fred "No Nose" De Lucio, despite his colorful nickname, was not as infamous or influential as Sally D., but at the time of their disappearance, he was a prime suspect in a recent Brooklyn homicide investigation. The FBI had no leads on the apparent disappearances of Sally D., and No Nose De Lucio. Their informants did, however, offer a few of their own personal theories. One posited that they were killed for their involvement in a "smut operation" with a Staten Island gang that wasn't approved by the leaders. Another theory was possible retaliation for any number of "jobs" performed by Sally D. and De Lucio on behalf of the gang. Others speculated that the men were on the lam to avoid police harassment and possible arrest for the recent murder in Brooklyn. A particularly creative theory was the "power grab," which presumably began with Sally D. after his return from prison. After being released, Sally D. had apparently been acting "ambitious," and perhaps even desired to depose Colombo as the gang's boss.

With Sally D. and No Nose presumed dead, and without any leads, the New York offices of the FBI decided to capitalize on this "power grab" theory. The theory was useful to the FBI as it could potentially injure Colombo by creating dissension within his organization. Since, according to the agents in charge, the Colombo gang "had been relatively quiet for several years,"[li] it seemed like a good time to stir the pot. Within a few days, the FBI instructed agents to send word to their street informants that Colombo had ordered the execution of Sally D. and No Nose De Lucio in order to foil a power grab. Sources close to Colombo denied any internal strife and insisted that this wasn't a plausible explanation, the agents continued to enact this counterintelligence plan.

During the course of their investigation, the FBI happened upon a social club in the Bath Beach section of Brooklyn. The club served as a hangout for local kids in the neighborhood, some of whom were friends of Anthony Colombo's. While looking around the club, the agents discovered bloodstains in the bathroom, as well as on a shirt crumpled in the corner. Lacking authority to further investigate this discovery, the FBI called in the local police. The "power grab" theory, in conjunction with the bloodstained bathroom and shirt, created a hybrid of fact and fiction. An FBI report stated:

> AS THIS INFORMATION DID NOT CONSTITUTE A FEDERAL VIOLATION, IT WAS FURNISHED TO APPROPRIATE AUTHORITIES WHO IMMEDIATELY INSTITUTED A HOMICIDE INVESTIGATION. THIS ACTION CAUGHT THE FANCY OF THE NY PRESS WHICH IMMEDIATELY BLOSSOMED THE FACTUAL SITUATION INTO FANTASY. [lii]

The Daily News headline on January 20, 1970 read, "Torture Room Raid Stirs Mob-Cops Quiz."[liii] The same day the Post headline read, "Probe Murder in Mafia Club."[liv] The articles implicated Joe Colombo in the gruesome deaths of almost a dozen men. Without any evidence or further investigation by the police, the media released the story of a social club bathroom used by Joe Colombo's squad as a "torture chamber." This "torture chamber" was also the purported place of Sally D.'s murder at Colombo's behest.

This fiction inspired by the FBI and printed in the papers bore no resemblance to the truth. The bathroom was in fact the scene of a recent fight between two local kids. The press released its version of events even after learning the truth from the young man whose blood had spilled on the bathroom floor. The blood belonged to Joseph Tumola, a young wannabe thug who lived around the corner from the Bath Beach club. Tumola was a caretaker of sorts for the hangout, which was no "Mafia" club; it was more of a gathering place for teenagers. Anthony remembers the place. Although it wasn't a club he frequented, a few of his close pals did. His pals included Phillip "Fat Philly" Dioguardi and Caesar Vitale. Fat Philly and Caesar had a combined weight of around nine hundred pounds. Fat Philly was a slovenly fellow, but Caesar was meticulous about his clothing and appearance. A few days before the FBI arrived at the club, Fat Philly had an altercation with Tumola that resulted in the mysterious bloody bathroom. Anthony knew of the fight, but didn't know about the blood in the bathroom until the news stories ran. Anthony remembers plainly, "When two guys get into it you never really think of how the story can be stretched out, especially the way this one did." Caesar explained it was simply a fracas. Fat Philly and Tumola had some words and Fat Philly opened up Tumola good; he busted his lip and broke his nose. From what Caesar saw, Tumola's nose was leaking like a sieve all over the bathroom. The real problem though, just like the gulf coast spill, wasn't with the leak, but with the cleanup. Not only were Fat Philly and Caesar similarly unwieldy, they also shared an aversion to anything involving physical activity. They were both intensely stubborn and they considered cleaning up the mess a menial task. The two friends, with their matching thick heads, bulging waistlines, and non-existent work ethic, refused to clean up the blood. Neither could have imagined that their laziness would have such disastrous results for Joe Colombo and his organization. Afterwards, Anthony recalls Caesar withdrew from public. He "disappeared" into a hospital at the time for complications due to his weight problem. Anthony has always believed Cesar checked into the hospital just to delay a confrontation with Joe, of whom he was deathly afraid.

While the authorities knew that the story splashed across the headlines was false, they did not attempt to correct it. The FBI reports reflect that they were pleasantly surprised by the effect of the "fantasy" story. One report read:

> THIS ACTION, HOWEVER, HAS MATERIALLY AIDED THE NEW YORK'S COUNTERINTELLIGENCE ACTIVITIES. AT THIS JUNCTURE, THE NYO FELT THAT TIME WAS PROPITIOUS TO SUGGEST FEDERAL GRAND JURY ACTION CONCERNING THE COLOMBO "FAMILY" AND ITS ACTIVITIES, WHICH WERE DETAILED IN NEW YORK PAPERS, DATED 1/21/70.[lv]

The FBI's informants had turned up nothing. The Grand Jury hearing resulted in the perjury convictions of two unrelated men who were at the club during the police investigation. No further information was uncovered about the missing men, Sally D. and No Nose De Lucio. The FBI couldn't produce any evidence to substantiate the media's body count of ten from a supposed "Mob war." None of this mattered to law enforcement, however, because the ends justified the means. A follow-up report from the FBI read:

> NEW YORK OFFICE IS CONVINCED THAT THESE UNFOUNDED RUMORS ARE A DIRECT RESULT OF THE "HEAT" BEING AFFORDED THE COLOMBO "FAMILY" BY BUREAU AGENTS WHICH HAS CAUSED MANY MEMBERS TO AVOID THEIR USUAL HAUNTS WITH THE RESULTING EFFECT BEING THAT THEY HAVE DISAPPEARED. NEW YORK WILL CONTINUE INTENSIFICATION AGAINST COLOMBO AND WILL SEIZE ANY ACTION TO FAN DISHARMONY AMONG THE GROUP.[lvi]

***

While the FBI was reveling in the somewhat inadvertent success of its efforts to subvert Colombo, Anthony had the unenviable task of bringing the morning newspapers to his father:

"I remember reading the paper the night before. When you read these types of stories about your father, it's devastating. When you read something in the paper, the story is all you have to go by. You rely on them to report the truth. But then when you read an article that you know for a fact is not true, you have no choice but to get furious and frustrated.

At the time, my father was living in a house on 83rd Street in Dyker Heights, in Brooklyn. It was a modest two-level home with a porch stacked above the garage. I was living around the corner on 84th Street with my wife, Carol. I remember climbing the stairs sluggishly that morning to deliver the bad news. I knew my father would be angry. I walked through the living room to an open dining and kitchen area where my father was at the table having his morning coffee. I handed him the papers, and he could tell from my expression that something wasn't right. He opened the paper while I stood there silently, waiting for him to say something. He didn't need to say a word. The displeasure was written all over his face. I told him about the fight that had occurred between Fat Philly and Joe Tumola. I told him all about the bloody shirt used to stop Tumola's nose from bleeding and about Philly and Caesar's refusal to clean it up. He looked at me and said, 'You see what happens from nothing, what could be created by these people?' He proceeded to angrily lecture me for the next two hours. I pled my defense and maintained that I had nothing to do with the fight or the club. I knew he wasn't mad at me, but was venting built-up frustrations with the media and its ability to print lies with impunity. I stood there and took everything he had to say.

About two weeks later, after everything had calmed down a bit, I was about to go pick up Caesar from the hospital. Calmly and almost ominously, my father asked me, 'You're going to grab your friend from the hospital today?' I answered unsteadily, 'Yeah, Dad.' He instructed me, 'When you go get that fat bastard, you bring him here! Don't take him to eat. Don't take him home. Don't take him no place. You bring him here first!' Now after hearing that command, I was expecting my father to give Caesar a taste of the same medicine I had gotten a few weeks prior, if not more. I was actually looking forward to Caesar finally getting yelled at. After being scolded for two hours about something that wasn't my fault, I thought it was time that someone more deserving felt his wrath.

When we got back to my father's house, Caesar sat down, visibly shaking, right next to my father. It was kind of a comical scene because Caesar was around 450 pounds and my father didn't weigh more than 160. Caesar wore such a pathetic expression that I could tell my father felt sorry for him. In a surprisingly friendly voice, much different from the tone he'd addressed me with, he said, 'Now Caesar, you understand what you did wrong here, you see from a little fight what they've created?' He was so scared, you could hardly hear Caesar stuttering his apology, 'Joe, I'm sorry. I know better.' Then he retold the story of what had happened in the social club. He just kept apologizing, and my Dad patiently listened. After a few minutes more, my dad put his arm around him and calmed him right down and said, 'Come on Caesar, Jo-Jo made some meatballs. Let's go eat. You look terrific.' And that was that.

Later, after Caesar left, I turned to my father and said, 'Dad, I don't understand.' He said, 'What's the matter, you expected me to yell at Caesar?' 'Yes, you lectured me for two hours about this thing and I had nothing to do with it! I wasn't

151

there for the fight, I never hang out at the club, and I had nothing to do with this whole thing. Caesar comes here and you talk to him like nothing even happened. I don't understand!' He said to me, 'Anthony, the kid just got out of the hospital. He's trying so hard to lose weight. If I yell at him now, who knows, he could go on an eating frenzy and gain even more weight. I just can't do that to him.' I still thought he could have said more to him and I said, 'Ok Dad, but it was all right to do that to me?' He gave me a firm look and said, 'You're different from Caesar, Anthony you know that.' I knew from his tone that this was no longer open for discussion, and he said, 'Now let's go eat.'

I think back now about how well my father knew people, and how in a moment he could calculate exactly how much a person could withstand. He possessed an amazing intuition. He could really read people. My father knew I was as tough as he raised me to be. He knew what I was ready to handle before I did. He brought me up to endure everything and fear no one. Most of the lessons I learned came from watching how deftly he handled all the obstacles he encountered. For the major part of his life he was at war with the government. He couldn't have made a more daunting enemy. What could you possibly be scared of in life if you don't fear them?"

✳✳✳

For the FBI, the "power grab" theory was ultimately a big opening act with no finale. Despite the media frenzy surrounding the case, no one could produce any evidence linking Colombo to the two disappearances; all of the evidence they collected at the social club amounted to nothing. The blood was Tumola's, and Sally D. and Freddy No Nose were still unaccounted for. As far as police were concerned, Joe Colombo was irritatingly elusive. They would need to dig deeper in order to bury him.

On March 6, 1970, Joe was arrested on specious charges. Two of the five-count indictment stemmed from a 1967 grand jury hearing in which he testified about his 1961 appearance at the Night Owl Lounge in the Catskills with Sonny Franzese, Larry Gallo, and a few other reputed gangsters. The other three counts concerned Joe falsely reporting his criminal history on his real estate application in 1966. He was arraigned and released on $1,500 bail. His lawyer Barry Slotnick told reporters that the charges were nothing more than "harassment."[lvii] The FBI didn't confine their harassment to Joe Colombo alone. Anthony and his uncle Do-Do owned and operated Leading Dry Cleaners for a number of years. One of their employees was a deliveryman named John Marcasoto. Marcasoto was an old friend of the family whose wife Helen played cards with Anthony's mother, Jo-Jo. He was a very docile man who'd probably never engaged in an argument in his life. One day when Mr. Marcasoto was out making deliveries in the truck, Boland and Welsh pulled him over. Marcasoto's wife later told Jo-Jo that they threatened to put him in prison because he was working for the Mafia, and that they could prove it. He was collecting an illegal salary; they listed ten crimes they could indict him for that day. Marcasoto was so terrified that he left the truck there and immediately ran home. He called Anthony's uncle Do-Do at the store and told him "The truck is on 13th Avenue with the keys in it, and I can no longer work for you." He said he had to quit and could never be seen near the Colombos again.

***

"By 1970, the FBI was following me every day. When my wife gave birth to my daughter Lucille I was on my way to Community Hospital. I was doing the speed limit because these guys were tailing me, and I didn't want to give them a reason to mess with me. They were pushing me to go faster by riding right behind me. Right up on my bumper, they were so close they could have hitched their car onto mine. They finally forced me over by cutting in front of my vehicle. I had to swerve out of the way just to avoid hitting their car. It happened right in front of my dry cleaning store. Welsh jumped out of the car with his gun drawn. Boland was on the other side of the car with his gun out, too. Welsh said, 'Don't move! Pull down your window!' I rolled down the window slowly. I didn't want these idiots shooting me out of fear. I asked him, 'Am I under arrest? Did I do something wrong?' Welsh told me, 'No. But we found out you're a draft dodger.' Now, at the time of the Vietnam War this was taken very seriously. You had young men signing up and going overseas to fight for freedom and if you didn't go and you made a phony excuse to stay it was frowned upon. I defended myself right away. 'What are you talking about, draft dodger? Two years ago I tried enlisting in the army and they rejected me for my health.' He said, 'No, I know you're a draft dodger. You ain't got no draft card.' So I reached over to get my paperwork from the glove box and to grab my wallet. He put the gun right to my head as I reached to the glove box. 'Don't move another inch or I'll shoot you.' I said, Bernie, calm down. I'm going to get my wallet and identification from the glove box, my draft card is in there.' He said, 'You don't make a move until I say you can make a move.' He told me to remove the keys from the car, so I shut the ignition off. I handed him the keys. Then he said, 'Get your draft card out and get out of the car.' I pulled my wallet slowly from the glove box and carefully got out of the car. He walked me to the back of the car with his gun still drawn. I handed him the draft card. He said, 'Yeah, well, we got word that you were a draft dodger.' I said, 'Well there's my registration card, Bernie so I guess you heard wrong.' I was a "1 Y" because I had two kids by that point, so I wasn't first to go. This whole time my uncle Do-Do was watching from the front of the store. So after they put the guns away, they said, 'Anthony, we gotta talk.' But it was the same old conversation every time, so I just said, 'Bernie, we got nothing to talk about. Are you going to arrest me, do you have a warrant or a subpoena? If you do give it to me please and let me go. My wife just had a baby and I'm trying to make it to the hospital to see her.' Boland slaps me hard on my back and says, 'Congratulations!' And it was a hard slap. Boland was mean-spirited; there was nothing celebratory in that slap. He said, 'Anthony, you're a nice kid but you're in a lot of trouble.' Then Welsh started in with his good-cop routine, saying, 'Look we know you went to a military college, we know you work hard. You're a nice kid.' And as they were saying all of this Boland continued to slap me hard on my back, just repeating what Welsh was saying to me. I turned to him, 'Boland, what are you doing?' I squared up with him a little bit hoping he knew he was out of line. Then

Boland said, 'We know you're a nice kid, but we also heard you're a tough guy, huh, a real tough guy.' He just kept slapping me on the back harder and harder. I said, 'I'm not a tough guy, I don't know where you heard that, but you're wrong.' Ignoring me, 'If you're a tough guy, Anthony why don't you pick up your hands?' I thought about it and knew this guy was trying to get me to make a bad move, to give him the green light to do whatever he wanted to do to me. I kept my cool and left my hands in my pockets and just stared back at him. It continued for a while until Welsh made his proposition. 'Stop going to see your father. He's only going to get you in trouble. You're a good kid, and only bad things are going to happen to him and around him. This is good advice, Anthony. You should take your wife and kids and move away from New York and stay away from your father.' Finally, he handed me back my draft card and said, 'You're going to take my advice, right? I wouldn't steer you wrong, it's the best thing you can do.' I squeezed my wallet tightly and took a step away from Boland toward Bernie and said quietly, 'I see my father once a day, because I am his son and I love him. Now, because of what you just said, I'm going to see him twice a day, maybe three times.' Boland snapped loudly, 'What are you a wise guy?' I said, 'If you think you can tell me not to go and see my father or to move away, you're both crazy. It will never happen.' And I slammed my car door, started it up and drove away. Bernie couldn't believe I'd said that to him. These guys made these kinds of 'suggestions' to me all the time. They imagined that with the right offer or the right threat, they could sever the ties of a family. They operated totally without principles. No honor, no respect, nothing."

The ethics of the FBI were more than questionable. Anyone who knew Joe Colombo was fair game as far as the bureau was concerned. One evening, before Anthony returned home from work, his wife Carol received a mysterious visit. The kids were in bed and she was watching television in the living room when the doorbell rang. This was very odd to her because no one would come by the house at that hour without calling first. At first she thought it might be Anthony coming home, having forgotten his keys. She went downstairs and looked through the peephole, but didn't see anyone there. She waited a second and then went back upstairs. The bell rang again, and again, she looked through the peephole and saw no one. The bell continued to ring every few seconds. At last, summoning her courage, Carol opened the door and noticed a small pin stuck inside the bell, forcing it to ring. She removed the pin, looked around, and then went back into the house and secured the door. She was worried now that someone might be checking the house for occupancy so they could break in to burglarize it. She sat down to try and calm her nerves and the bell rang again. This time she went to the front door with a baseball bat. Again, no one was outside and again a little pin was stuck in the doorbell. She removed this pin and waited downstairs with the lights out. As she looked out of the peephole, she saw two men walking around the house. She began to panic. Then, as she struggled to compose herself, she heard banging on a window at the back of the house. As she crept towards the back of the house she got a good look at the two men as they passed under porch light. She recognized the tall one immediately. It was Bernie Welsh. He was stumbling around back to the front of the house. Welsh saw her move inside. He started knocking on the front door and calling her by her name. "Carol, we want to talk to you." He seemed drunk, stumbling and not able to stand still. She instantly called Barry Slotnick to tell him what was going on. Barry told her, "Tell the police what you saw and when they arrive, you run out of the house screaming." When the police arrived, Boland and Welsh were on her front stoop knocking on the door. She flipped the exterior lights in the driveway, opened a window and screamed for help. Welsh and Boland were startled and bolted around the side of the house. Welsh shouted, "Whoa, whoa, it's us, Carol."

As the police car pulled up into the driveway, the two detectives dashed around the back of the house. They ran through the backyard and hopped over the concrete brick planter separating the neighbor's yard. The police officers laid chase, and ended up catching Boland and Welsh before they could make it back to their car. A little while later the officers returned to the house to fill Carol in on what happened. They asked her, "Did you know that the two men were FBI agents?" She answered slightly defiantly, "No, I did not." She asked why they hadn't been arrested, and how any person could have the right to do what they did. One of the officers responded, "Well we got in a lot of trouble when we caught up with the two men. They are FBI agents and they said they know you and you knew it was them." Carol vehemently denied this, pointing out that if what they said were true, they'd have no reason to try to sneak around or escape. After a few more questions the two officers left. Boland and Welsh were never required to account for their behavior that night.

Joe had mostly ignored threats by the FBI, claiming to his face that they "would get him any way they could." Up until their next move, he'd felt equipped to manage the pressure of their incessant "interviews," the surveillance, the frivolous charges. But on April 4, 1970, Joe Colombo Jr. was brought in by the FBI on charges of conspiring with a group of men to melt silver coins into ingots. The charge was a stretch to begin with; it was based on a law that had only recently been written into the books, and which would be written out within a few months. But the charge was enough for Joe Junior to be indicted, so his father found himself in court again as well. Joe Junior's wife Diane told Joe that the FBI had pushed in the screen door on her and taken Joe Junior from the home. This event would result in a drastic shift in Colombo's relationship with law enforcement. In a striking departure from his usual composure, Colombo responded to his son's arrest without regard for consequences. That evening he collected his entire family and marched down to the FBI offices at 201 East 69th Street.

***

"Where were you? Your brother got arrested. I have been trying to get in touch with you for hours." Anthony says apologetically, "I was with Nat, we ran by the track. What happened?" Joe is moving in a million different directions. He is consumed by rage. Nat tries helplessly to offer some words of advice, but Joe can't settle down. He screams at Nat, "I have to do something now! They've been threatening me for years! They've threatened that they would get my children and me and now they have! What kind of people are they? What kind of father am I to let this happen?" Nat offers calmly, "Look, if we are going to go down there, let's do this the right way. We have to have a legal protest. This way we all don't get arrested." Joe yells, "I don't care if I get arrested! I want to

march down there and turn us all in. Me, Anthony, Jo-Jo, and Vinny." Nat looks at him and says, *"What good would that do, Joe? Please, let's do this my way first. Trust me, ok?"* Joe looks at Nat's face. He does trust him. He shakes his head, closing his eyes. *"Fine."*

Almost a dozen cars pull up to the FBI offices on Third Avenue and 69th Street. Nat turns to Joe and gently reminds him of their plan. "Joe, we're going to do this thing the right way. A peaceful, informational protest." Joe has his head down. He shakes it yes and says, "Yup. Now stop the car." Nat puts the car in park and Joe immediately flies out the passenger door and runs to the front doors of the building. His family and a group of about fifteen protesters watch him, stunned, realizing Joe has come with a different agenda. He starts kicking at the doors, screaming at the top of his lungs. "Here I am! You want me? You want my family? Come on down here and open the door!" He keeps kicking and smashing at the door. He tears at the handles savagely. "Here we are! My whole family. You want to arrest us? You want to put us all in prison, well we're all ready to go!" The armed guards and FBI personnel watching from the opposite side of the glass aren't sure how to respond. His group of supporters stands uncertainly on the sidewalk with their makeshift protest signs.

✵✵✵

Joe Junior made bail the next morning and was charged with conspiracy to melt down silver coins into ingots. Once he had regained his composure, Colombo began to mobilize a plan for his defense. He first sought out the leaders of A.I.D. for help, explaining that his son was innocent and mustn't fall victim to the FBI. He needed their participation in the protests. They refused. After failing to enlist the support of A.I.D., the organization he'd helped to build, Joe was compelled to create a new, more effective group of his own. His previous attempts to protect himself and his family had been too frail, too furtive. With the help of a close friend and former union organizer, Nat Marcone, he founded the IACRL (Italian-American Civil Rights League) in April 1970. The League announced itself by picketing the FBI offices every night. Sympathetic crowds accompanied them, and grew steadily. Within weeks, thousands were picketing. This flood of demonstrators was undeniable evidence of the FBI's harmful intrusions in the Italian-American community. The media and the Bureau, however, initially ignored the protesters. A spokesperson at the FBI remarked, "A lot of people on the line don't realize what's behind all this. They think it's a legitimate gripe. But Colombo's button men are the ones that got people there."[lviii]

Nevertheless, demonstrations continued into June, attracting protesters from all over the city. They were occasionally bused in, and the crowd numbered over five thousand on certain nights. The picketing was noisy at times with the thunderous chanting of "Hi-dee, hi-dee, hi-dee, ho-the FBI has got to go!"[lix] But the protesters were organized and restrained. They obeyed the boundaries of the barricades set up by the NYPD, and tended to be respectful towards the officers. In contrast, many of the FBI men inside the buildings mocked the protesters, and even pelted them with ice and eggs from the rooftops. Reporters took notice of the peacefulness of the crowds and the fairness of Colombo's message: "We march cold and warm; we've never stopped. We respect the FBI, it's the greatest organization in the country. But they're framing our children and harassing pregnant women, and we want them to stop."[lx] He continued, "If I do something, then I deserve to pay the penalty. But the FBI shouldn't harass my children and relatives because of what I do."[lxi]

The FBI began to challenge the picketing more actively. It was rumored that they encouraged neighbors who lived nearby to file complaints against the League, specifically Colombo and Marcone, and the protesters. Donald Goodwin, a local building manager, complained that the police could not control the picketers, and that the noise of the demonstration could be heard several blocks away.[lxii] The two leaders of the League were ordered to come into court and prove why they should be allowed to continue. Prior to the hearing, a Supreme Court judge visited the FBI demonstrations to see what all the commotion was about. When Colombo and other League members attended the first hearing, the judge seemed optimistic and said, "They impressed me with their reasonable conduct here."[lxiii] But once he learned that a suspected crime boss was behind the civil disobedience, he was aghast. He remarked to Barry Slotnick, "Colombo's the instigator. Suppose Colombo had come up to me and shaken hands with me? I had no idea he was in the courtroom."[lxiv]

The investigations into the legality of the protests were concluded a few days later. Judge Starke said the picketing could continue, but he wanted to establish rules to ensure that the rights of the protesters did not interfere with the rights of the local residents. In the case of noise, he revoked the League's right to use sound equipment, although they had previously obtained this with a five dollar permit from the police. The judge stated that while the League was entitled under an administrative code to be able to use the devices, further sections of the code bar the use of sound equipment within 500 feet of a hospital.[lxv] A few days later Judge Starke issued further guidelines to the defendants. They were not allowed to picket past 9 p.m.; they were not allowed to engage in "tactics designed to create excessive noise", exemplified by joining in unison in loud chanting, shouting, stamping of feet, clapping of hands, sounding of horns, banging of signs, etc."[lxvi] In short, protesters were barred from doing virtually everything that characterizes a public demonstration.

Joe knew the picketing would eventually die down. But he had already initiated a plan to expand his vision and mobilize support for his cause. He intended to organize a giant, peaceful rally in the city. While the IACRL had already won the support of thousands of New York residents, Joe's intention was to draw national attention to the event. League members began in their communities by asking storeowners to hang signs, stickers and plaque cards to promote the June 29th Unity Day Rally. Some storeowners did not want to hang signs and many did not want to honor the rally by closing their businesses that day. The media eagerly received reports of coercion and threats. When Thomas Guida, a spokesperson for the IACRL, was questioned about reports of Italian men intimidating and threatening storeowners, he responded, "They are not our people."[lxvii] Nat Marcone, the president of the IACRL, spoke to the press about the recent claims of threats. He said he was "sure there are people in the Justice department who are trying to create the idea that we are making threats."[lxviii] Joe gave members careful instructions as to how to treat the storeowners who did not want to support them. There were certainly no threats of harm or injury, but there may have been intimations of a drop in business. At a Park Sheraton meeting, Joe was informed about particular shop owners who didn't understand the event and why it meant they had to close. Joe left it up to the League officials to explain to the shopkeepers that they should respect their community and observe the day by shutting their doors, just as the majority of local stores had agreed to do. He told the captains frankly, "You go into these stores, and explain to them that the Italian-American community has been paying their bills and supporting their businesses without ever asking a favor for close to a hundred years in this city. They can close their stores for one day to show their support." Caesar Vitale asked Joe, "But what about the stores that aren't Italian-owned? The Chinese food place in Bensonhurst and the cleaners in Gravesend don't want to close." Joe replied, "Doesn't the Chinese food place have mostly Italian-American customers and the cleaners too? You let them know that if they close their doors for one day they will be remembered, and if they don't, that will also be remembered."

All the major unions in the city backed the IACRL for the day of the rally. It gained full support from District Council 37 and the Municipal Employees Union, which represented 8,000 city workers. The Longshoreman union vice president told the press, "I would assume that this port would be virtually wrapped up Monday."[lxix] The rally was also sanctioned by the mayor's office, and local politicians pledged to attend, some of who were scheduled to speak. The IACRL's members were arranging everything from transportation to entertainment, preparing for an unforgettable event in the city's history.

***

"I was with my father at some point almost every day of my life, with the exception of when I was away at Valley Forge in Pennsylvania. When I started working for the League our relationship changed. I went from being his son to becoming one of his associates. I started to see my father in a completely different light. I watched him negotiate, direct, and strategize. He was always the boss of our family and we had all given him the proper amount of respect, but once I started to see him interact with all of these other people with such composure and balance, that respect reached a whole new level. I never thought that was possible. Along with all of the business aspects that were added to our relationship and the political mentoring that I was receiving, we also just began spending a lot more time together. We were in the car together, driving around the city to different meetings and appointments, and in those hours I really got to see who my father was. I saw his reactions, his interests, his humor and his wit. I know during this time I became even fonder of my father, and I can only imagine that this was the case for him back in his youth, when he would spend time riding around Brooklyn with my grandfather.

I remember we would be driving along the city streets and he would just say suddenly, 'Anthony, pull over, pull over right here.' At first I didn't know what he wanted and I would get worried. But then he would hop out and grab a dirty water dog. He had little obsessions with certain foods. He loved chocolate, and hot dogs from the truck. After a few weeks, I started getting used to it. I would see one as we approached the corner by a light, and before I got jammed into it I would ask him, 'Dad, you want me to pull over at the hot dog truck?' He would just look at me and smile.

A few days before Unity Day we were driving underneath the West Side Highway, at that time it was still elevated below 59th Street. There was a traffic jam and an officer was redirecting cars away from where we needed to go. My father had to make a meeting with the police department and the detour would have definitely made us fifteen or twenty minutes late. My father was a very punctual person, no excuses; he would get there on time. We were stopped in the left lane, two lanes of cars were moving in the opposite lane and the cop was waving for us to go straight or turn right. I paused for a second, looking at the detour, and my father turned his head to me and said, 'Make the left.' I couldn't make the left until the opposite lane cleared, so I inched up and waited and the cop looked at me and waved me on and pointed for me to go right. He told me again, 'Make the left." I told him with no hint of an argument, 'You see, the cop wants me to go straight.' And he said, "And I'm telling you to make the left!' In a high, accepting tone, I said, 'All right, Dad" and I sat, waiting for the traffic to clear. Meanwhile we began blocking traffic behind us, and cars started to honk their horns. The cop walked right over to the car and said, 'Do you see me? I'm telling you that you have to go this way.' My father boldly replied, 'And I'm telling him he's going to make the left!' The cop thought he heard wrong and asked, 'What did you say?' He repeated it firmly, 'I said, he's making the left.' The cop said, 'You can't make the left.' My father told him, 'Well, we're making the left whether you like it or not.' The cop got so mad at my father I watched his face turn the color of a tomato. There were still cars honking away behind us and I still couldn't make the left even if I wanted to. The two had a few more words. And then finally my father had enough and he put his hand on the wheel and told me, 'All right, enough, just go!' The cop said, 'You can't move, stay right here. I want your license and registration.' My father gave me his look. 'I said go!' So I just pushed out into the traffic and made the left, almost getting hit by the oncoming cars, while the cop waved at us screaming, 'I wish you were driving that car! Get behind the wheel. Why don't you drive the car?' My father yelled out the window, 'If I was driving the car I'd make the left too!' The cop hadn't taken my plate down so I never got a ticket. The cop was pretty fair; I assume he never wrote a ticket because he knew I wasn't really driving the car, my father was driving, from the passenger seat. We arrived at our meeting on time. My father and I met up with Nat Marcone, Barry Slotnick and about twenty of the NYPD's top-ranking officers. The purpose of the meeting was to discuss the march which would follow the Unity Day Rally. All the men present at the meeting knew who my father was; there was no hiding his identity from anyone in the nation with access to a newspaper. The meeting was interesting for me to watch. The policemen argued in front of a giant map for a good half hour about different ways to route the protestors with the least amount of obstruction to the buses and traffic. My father sat back and waited patiently for the men to exhaust their ideas and then asked if he could offer some help. He walked up to the map and immediately showed how the march could be accomplished with minimal interference to the city and sure enough, he was absolutely correct. After we left the meeting and got into our car, I looked at my dad and asked him, 'Dad, how did you know the answers to the traffic questions those guys were throwing at you? And how did you plan that route?' He just looked at me with his half-smile and didn't reply. He really enjoyed those little accomplishments. He had a remarkable ability to identify solutions to problems without belittling those he was helping, even if it would have given him great satisfaction to do so."

***

Joe admired the grass roots movements of the black civil rights groups. He also admired their leaders. Most of them came from humble beginnings and had strong roots within their communities. Their political views were informed by the adversities and challenges they experienced with their people. Joe, too, wanted to help his people. It was important to him to teach people how to defend themselves. The League's initial purpose was to combat the FBI, but given its rapid growth and the zealousness of its participants, Joe saw the potential for a broader agenda. He wanted to achieve a nationwide coalescence of the Italian-American community.

The first annual Unity Day rally surpassed everyone's expectations. It had only been thirty days since Joe had introduced the idea at a meeting in the League's Park Sheraton offices. The crowd on June 29th numbered well over 100,000. The main event took place at the 59th Street rotunda, just below the statue of *Cristoforo Colombo*. Throngs of supporters stretched deep into Central Park and all the way up Central Park West to 61st Street. Broadway, too, was packed for blocks in both directions. As promised, the unions all took the day off, as did hundreds of shop owners. The atmosphere was mostly celebratory and harmonious, with children waving flags and eating ice cream. Many who attended simply watched and listened, curious about the League and its purpose. Some participants expressed their frustrations and chanted during the speeches made by honored guests on the platform. The overwhelming response of the New York community was vindicating for the League. One participant who was interviewed explained, "My parents came over here when they were about 14. I was born here, an American citizen. But I'm discriminated against, like all American Italians."

The speeches focused principally on issues of unity, freedom, equal rights and the power of the community. Vice President, Anthony Colombo stood over the crowd like the massive nose guard he'd been only a few years before on the football field. He gripped the podium with enough strength to hurl it if he chose to. He began yelling out at the crowd as if the microphone were only a prop. "Yesterday, thirty courageous Italian-American people started a fight against discrimination, harassment, and defamation at the hands of the FBI. The FBI laughed and called it a passing fancy. The news media ridiculed us and laughed at us in print. Today we are united. Today we are one!" The crowd chanted these words repeatedly, "We are one!" "We are one!", then hushed as Father Gigante arrived to introduce Joe Colombo. Colombo weaved his way slowly to the front of the platform. He was the shortest man on the stage, but he commanded more attention than anyone:

"I thank you for this honor, and again I say, I thank God I was born Italian. But today, this day belongs to you, the people. You are organized. You are one. Nobody can take you apart anymore. Your day starts today. You have a new opportunity. You have the ball and you have to carry it. You have to let no one, but no one, come between you. You've gotta fight for one another, you've gotta build yourselves strong. You've gotta overcome what no Italian has overcome in this country." He paused and looked over the mass of supporters and said, "God bless you, and thank you!" The crowd roared and chanted the word, "One!" again and again. As the rally came to a close, thousands of people marched to the FBI headquarters with the League leaders. Reporters grabbed random protesters for statements, always asking about one man in particular, Joe Colombo. One marcher demanded, "Who says Colombo is in the Mafia? Why isn't he under arrest if he is a Mafia man? Tell me that. Put up or shut up I say. I'll tell you who are the crooks, the FBI. They take his tax money and my tax money and your tax money and they don't do a proper job. They're bums. All of them."[lxx]

Over ten thousand people marched through Central Park out onto Third Avenue towards the FBI buildings, and despite the peacefulness of the crowd, the NYPD was nervous. They received reports of an injured policeman a few blocks north of the protest. There were officers throughout the rally, but they were not sufficient should the demonstrators get restless. The IACRL had promised them a peaceful demonstration. Officers sought out Joe Colombo to help them manage the crowd. They knew well the power Joe had in his community. They furnished him with a flatbed truck equipped with a sound system, and asked if he would get the crowd to disperse. With the police captain and Anthony riding alongside him, Joe admonished the crowd, "Be careful, you have your mothers here and your daughters here. Be respectful and go home. God bless you all. Now please, go home."

The League officials, including Marcone, Colombo and Cesar Vitale, held a press conference in the evening after the rally had ended. Reporters asked countless questions about Joe's involvement both in the Mafia and in the League. When asked why Joe's help was enlisted to disperse the crowd, Anthony answered, "Only because of their love for him, and the police knew most of the people who were there would listen to him. There stands the FBI, watching. I wonder what they're thinking, and how they are going to explain why a man they've condemned in every newspaper across the country is standing up and preaching peace. What are they going to say, now that this man that they've insisted is so violent is uniting people and trying to help people, including the police?"

***

On July 1st, two days after the rally, Joe Colombo was indicted and arrested. He was arraigned at the Mineola courthouse in Long Island again on a charge of criminal contempt. He did not arrive alone. He was met there by hundreds of supporters, all of whom believed this was a smear campaign to discredit Joe and undermine his surging popularity. Protesters aimed their attacks at D.A.

William Cahn, waving flags at him and cried, "Cahn is a tool of the FBI."[lxxi] Cahn responded to the press, addressing the issue of discrimination against Italian-Americans, stating, "I have never used a phrase or a word that would lend credence that crime is controlled by any ethnic group." He added, "I am convinced that Joseph Colombo is an important figure in organized crime and does operate a crime family."[lxxii] After being released by Judge Paul Kelly on $5,000 bail Colombo stopped before reporters and, after being asked about his arrest, said, "I can't believe it. I answered each and every question every time I was there. I never refused to answer any questions. I promise I will let the press see the minutes of the grand jury. You will see for yourselves." He continued, "If this isn't harassment, then I don't know what to call it."

Joe had recently been incensed by the absence of penalty for the former president of the New York City Tax Commission, Michael Freyberg. Freyberg was given an unconditional discharge after pleading guilty to perjury for lying to the Grand Jury during an investigation into bribery and extortion in the City Planning Commission. State and City officials, when facing the same charges as he, were gently reprimanded, freed, and welcomed back into the community. Joe wanted the League to not only give him a chance to combat defamation and promote the equality of Italian-Americans, but also to expose political corruption, and protest those agencies like the FBI, whose intrusions into citizens' lives were not only pernicious, but unlawful.

***

The backyard of Joe Colombo's Blooming Grove estate is filled with smiling faces during a summer family barbeque. Families are planted all over the manicured lawn and lounging alongside the pool. Kids play chase in the grass beside the patio. At the grill, Fat Philly smokes an abundance of sausage and peppers. Barry Slotnick sips a glass of lemonade at a table with Joe and his sons. "You know, Joe, as long as you stay visible with the League, they will keep coming at you with these frivolous arrests." Joe says coolly, "Their case is nonsense. There's nothing in it. They want to arrest me, they can arrest me. I'm not going to hide from them." Barry agrees, "The case has no merit; it's the same contempt you were convicted for in civil court. I will file an appeal and we will win. As your counsel, I just want to make sure you know what you're getting into before you move forward." Joe smiles and pats him on the shoulder, "Thank you, Barry." Barry looks down at his son Stuart, who's crawling between his legs, and he says to Anthony, "Anthony, tell me something. How is it that our kids are the same age, but yours can walk around like nothing and my son is still crawling?" Anthony answers, "I had nothing to do with it. That's my father's doing. He taught him how to walk in one day." Joe smiles. Barry chuckles and turns to Joe, "How about I give you my son for a day and you teach him how to walk?" Joe stands. "Give him to me for a minute right now. Look at him, he's dying to walk." Joe leans down to pick up Stuart. Barry is a little surprised. "You want him now?" Joe responds, "No better time than the present." He picks Stuart up and walks him past the party to the far side of the pool by the vegetable garden for some privacy.

About an hour passes and the men have all finished eating their meals. Barry can see Joe over the plants in the garden. Barry's wife Donna walks over to the group of men, "Barry, don't you think you should get Stuart back from Joe? He's been over there for almost two hours. He didn't even eat lunch." Anthony steps in, "Donna, trust me, he loves children way more than he likes to eat." The men laugh. "He's fine, besides one thing about my father, once he's on the job he won't finish until it's done." Barry thinks aloud, "We do have to head back to the city in a bit. There's no way he's going to teach him how to walk in a day." At this moment, Joe comes back from the far side of the pool walking slowly backwards, no baby in his arms. The entire party turns to see Stuart Slotnick emerge from the garden walking completely on his own, trying to catch up to Joe. His face is full of glee from his newly won freedom. Joe says to him affectionately, "That's right, Stuart, let's go see Daddy. What a strong boy you are." Stuart giggles and makes his way on two feet, swaying with each step. Donna is in awe. Barry nods his head, he should have known better. He laughs to himself, "Unbelievable!"

Chapter 7.

"It Was a Very Good Year"

(Summer 1970)

The offices of the Italian-American Civil Rights League are teeming with activity. Since Unity Day, the dozen or more daily workers have been inundated with phone calls and requests for aid from League chapters all over the city. Anthony Colombo stands in the center of the room, talking on the phone and looking overwhelmed. A young lady brushes past him, carrying a large box of copy paper to the back room. Anthony looks over at Caesar Vitale, who sits rather idly, examining a newspaper clipping. The girl passes with a second box and Anthony puts down the receiver for a moment. He says to her, "I'll get this, don't worry about it." He drops the box heavily onto Caesar's desk. "Are you really going to let her carry these boxes?" Without looking up, Caesar replies, "I'm researching." "Well, you can research later!" Caesar reluctantly picks up the box and heads to the back room. Anthony returns to his call. He appears troubled by what he's hearing, and he glances anxiously at his father, who is talking to Barry Slotnick. Joe feels Anthony's eyes on him and looks at him inquisitively. Anthony tells the caller, "Let me get back to you in a few minutes with an answer." He hangs up the phone and shuffles past some boxes over to his father and Barry. "I just got off the phone with Bill Federici from the Daily News. He wants to come down right now to do an interview. Says he wants to clear the air about what's going on here." Joe seems to like the idea and agrees immediately. Anthony adds, "There's one condition. He only wants to interview you." Joe sighs and looks up at Barry for a reaction. Barry is hesitant, knowing well the potential pitfalls of such an interview, but he is inclined to accept the terms. Anthony waits patiently for direction. Joe rubs his temple a bit and begins to nod, almost to himself. He looks at his son. "Alright. Send him down."

***

On July 3, 1970, the Daily News printed Bill Federici's historic interview with Joe Colombo. It was the first time a suspected member of organized crime spoke openly to the press and willingly answered any of their questions. The article included plenty of direct quotes from Colombo, as well as a number of candid photos. Up until that point, suspected gangsters' photographs were limited to mug shots or furtive courthouse exits. These men lived in the shadows and deflected the media at every opportunity. In contrast, Federici described Colombo as "sincere, expository, and selflessly philanthropic."[lxxiii] Joe hastened to repudiate his suspected title as head of the former Profaci crime organization. He dismissed repeated inquiries about his position, saying, "They gave me the title because Mr. Profaci is dead. And then Mr. Magliocco died and they needed a scapegoat."[lxxiv] Joe was referring to the deaths of Joe Profaci and Joe Magliocco that resulted in his alleged succession to the head of the Profaci crime organization. Regarding his association with other known gangsters, he insisted, "I've known many people like Carlo Gambino since I was this high (and he held his hand two feet off the ground)."[lxxv]

Joe disclosed his criminal history, which was public record, and pointed out that the media was more interested in speculating about his illicit ties and activities than it was in printing the truth. He denied any affiliation with the group known as "La Cosa Nostra," the term used to describe organized crime by the FBI, NYPD and news media, and pointed out the obvious contradiction between his membership in a secret criminal society and his willingness to talk to the press. He challenged the FBI to convict him of the crimes they were accusing him of; particularly since they were leaking their theories to the press. He discussed his profession as a real estate agent in Brooklyn, and described the incessant FBI harassment of his boss and childhood friend Anthony Cantalupo. Cantalupo told Joe after he started at the company, "The FBI was here and according to them, every morning when you wake up you push a button on your bed and gambling, hijacking, murder, robbery, and kidnapping begin in Las Vegas, Puerto Rico, Miami, and all over New York."[lxxvi] Joe laughed as he finished the story, "I went home and looked for the buttons."[lxxvii] He remained composed, even when discussing his son's arrest. "I was willing to suffer through the attacks made by authorities, but when they framed my boy Joey then I knew I had to do something. That's why I picketed the FBI."[lxxviii] This was the catalyst for his establishment of the Italian-American Civil Rights League, which, in contrast to the FBI's guerilla tactics and harassment, would organize peaceful protests to achieve its aims. "This is the way it must be done. They have to stop defaming

Italian-Americans. Guilt by association or ancestry is not the American way." Joe was asked about all the shop owners who were supposedly pressured into closing their stores on Unity Day. There were rumors that resistant business owners were threatened and coerced into closing by League members and sympathizers. Joe responded, "I'm sure these store owners thought it was going to hurt their business by shutting down for one day. But the truth is that most of their patrons were at the rally. In hindsight, they know better now, but I understood some would meet the favor with resistance. They did a noble thing and will be remembered for it. Those that didn't want to close were told they would probably lose business, and business in our communities has been good. As far as any threats, I know nothing about that. No one from this League would do anything other than refrain from shopping there, or telling their family and friends to do the same." The reporter asked, "What about reports of men breaking shop windows?" Joe asked, "You're a reporter, how many windows were broken last month? Don't you think the media would have put the photos on the front page if that happened? Do some investigating yourself. I don't think you'll find much evidence with these stories. They're just rumors."

***

The attention that the IACRL received subsequent to Unity Day posed a great threat to the credibility and reputation of the FBI. Not only was the FBI under constant fire by the League, but the media was now closely following the IACRL and making serious inquiries into its claims. A producer from the Huntley Brinkley show on NBC contacted the New York FBI offices, asking about recent allegations of FBI harassment against Italian-Americans. The caller informed the FBI that they had conducted interviews with members of the League who had provided specific instances of harassment. They wanted to interview someone from the FBI to either substantiate or disprove these allegations. The producer was told by the FBI that "this could not be done" and advised that if anyone had any complaints "they can bring them directly to the attention of the FBI."[lxxix]

During this time, street informants were providing reports to FBI agents of a great harmony within the New York crime groups. When FBI agents asked their informers about other crime leaders' and captains' perceptions of Colombo's public and political presence, FBI agents were told, "Colombo had the complete blessing of Carlo Gambino" as well as "moral support from other 'families', some of whom sent some of their people to march."[lxxx] There were rumors that Joe was using the league for political purposes and many people thought that by staying close to and supporting Colombo they could use this as a "political springboard." This city-wide support from the underworld must have been discouraging to the FBI, as they had hoped Colombo's high-profile public protests would anger the other bosses and create internal discord. In spite of the tacit support he'd received from the other organizations, as well as his favorable reputation in the community, it would require great efforts and lots of campaigning to change people's perception of Colombo. And that bothered Joe. The media had painted a vivid criminal portrait of Colombo in a series of articles describing his purported illicit activities and leadership of Brooklyn's largest gang. Joe saw an opportunity to not only expose the operation that falsely indicted his son Joe Junior, but also as a chance to improve his image in the public eye. He knew it would prove an arduous task since the media always showed loyal support to law enforcement of any kind. What he did not know was how entwined the two entities actually were.

In 1949, CIA agent Frank Wisner created a program called the Office of Policy Coordination (OPC), a covert action division within the CIA designed to influence the media. It was rumored that by the 1950's Wisner "owned" members of media groups ranging from the New York Times to CBS.[lxxxi] It was a strategic infiltration of the corporate media that sometimes involved a complete takeover of major news companies. J. Edgar Hoover, a jealous and power-hungry leader designed COINTELPRO shortly after learning of OPC. The two operations were very similar in origin, but operated under different jurisdictions. The OPC focused on disinformation and media campaigns usually involving foreign affairs, while the FBI's targets with COINTELPRO were solely citizens of the United Sates. Hoover's tactics included not only the censorship of news media and the spreading of false stories, but also planting information and spying on citizens. Its operations were coined "black bag jobs."[1] Because of the illegal nature of its maneuvers, most of the g-men who were involved in these operations kept no paper trail, thus giving their superiors "plausible deniability" in case the agents were caught committing a crime.[lxxxii]

---

[1] ***Clandestine operations agents were involved in. Many of the missions were illegal in nature forcing agents to perform them without the knowledge of superiors.

FBI Assistant Director William Sullivan described the filing procedure for these operation in a memo in 1966 and stated:

> THE FACTS ARE INCORPORATED IN A MEMORANDUM, WHICH, IN ACCORDANCE WITH THE DIRECTORS INSTRUCTIONS, IS SENT TO MR. [CLYDE] TOLSON OR TO THE DIRECTOR FOR APPROVAL. SUBSEQUENTLY THIS MEMORANDUM IS FILED IN THE ASSISTANT DIRECTORS OFFICE UNDER A "DO NOT FILE" PROCEDURE.
>
> IN THE FIELD THE SPECIAL AGENT IN CHARGE PREPARES AN INFORMAL MEMORANDUM SHOWING THAT HE OBTAINED BUREAU AUTHORITY AND THIS MEMORANDUM IS FILED IN HIS SAFE UNTIL THE NEXT INSPECTION BY BUREAU INSPECTORS, AT WHICH TIME IT IS DESTROYED.[lxxxiii]

Some of the counterintelligence practices were simply smoke and mirrors. The FBI would leak 'information' about suspects to various sympathetic publications, and then include the articles as evidence in their criminal records. In a seven-page report to FBI Deputy Director Cartha "Deke" DeLoach, Special Agent J.H. Gale wrote, as planned, unrevealed sources at the Daily News would be running articles "concerning Colombo and his associates, which will show just what a 'bum' he is and [expose] his past criminal activities."[lxxxiv] If DeLoach approved, they would provide the Daily News with information "without any attribution whatsoever to the FBI."[lxxxv] DeLoach was not only the number-three man in the FBI, he was also the FBI's liaison to the CIA and a very close associate of Frank Wisner, head of counterintelligence at the agency.

During the summer of 1970, Joe, Barry Slotnick and a number of others suspected the illegal bugging and spying on the League offices and members. They were vocal about this to news reporters, begging them to investigate further, but none did; thus giving the FBI the confidence to continue and progress.

Until the spring of 1971, Hoover could deny the existence of these practices. Then, in March 1971, members of a citizen's committee to investigate the FBI broke into some FBI offices in Pennsylvania and stole thousands of classified documents that became hard evidence of Hoover's COINTELPRO operations. Soon after, Hoover formally terminated the taxpayer-funded, illegal program. Many of the COINTELPRO documents, including illegal and immoral activities were leaked after Joe's shooting. There would be no way of learning the entire scope of the program as only a portion of their operations was found.

***

"Our fight against the FBI was very organized. The League had amazing discipline considering some of the men that were involved in it. My father was very demanding about the way people were to conduct themselves. The last thing you wanted was it getting back to him that someone was mistreated or threatened. He insisted that everyone demonstrate respect and decorum at all times. After that first night when he'd lost his composure, our protests at the FBI building always ran smoothly. We had incidents with the agents throwing eggs and ice at us, and sometimes they would flash their guns or invite men to fight, but nothing ever came of it. Protestors knew they were to be on their best behavior.

I'm not sure what the reason for it was, but one night the TPF (Tactical Police Force) showed up to the protests. These men weren't like the regular officers that worked the pickets. They were wearing helmets and had shields, and they all looked like they were anticipating a fight. Every night, hundreds of people were bused in from all over the city. While one of the buses was unloading passengers from the front, some young kids opened the back door and jumped out on to the picket line. As they were scrambling out, a flagpole one of the kid's was carrying accidentally hit one of the officers. The cop became enraged and went chasing after the kid, and threw him onto the ground. When League members saw this, they rushed over to try to break it up, then the other cops tried to hold them back and chaos ensued. It turned into a real brawl. You saw fists flying everywhere and the cops were swinging their nightsticks freely. I was exchanging blows with an officer when I saw my father run right into the middle of everything. I don't know what came over me, but when I saw him I was afraid for his life. In that moment, I imagined someone really trying to hurt him. I thought about the random arrival of the TPF, and the possibility that they'd use this pandemonium as an excuse to harm him. I ran over and I locked my arms under his lifting him off the ground, and I started pulling him from the mayhem. He was mad as hell. He screamed at me,

'Put me down now, Anthony!' He even started cursing, and my father never swore. He was booting me in the shins with the heel of his shoe, and elbowing me in the stomach, screaming for me to let him go. I said, 'No, Dad. Now's not the time! They're gonna try and hurt you!' He continued to scream, 'Let go of me!' But I just held him with all my might, taking every shot he was giving me, physically and verbally. Eventually the melee stopped and everyone started to calm down, including my father.

Soon, this little lieutenant from the TPF started going around trying to arrest people. Meanwhile, a bus filled with more TPF officers arrived and started unloading. They lined up against the barricades like an army. My father called Caesar and me over and said, "Anthony, I want you two to grab a pen and paper and write down the badge number of every cop that just lined up against that barricade.' I grabbed a pad and got right to work. The cops were staring daggers at me as I wrote down their names. One of the cops asked me what I was doing. I answered politely, 'We are taking your badge numbers down, because you're all a bunch of tough guys with guns, bats, helmets and shields, and you're messing with kids. We want your badge numbers; so on those days when you're walking the beat by yourself, people will know who you are. Maybe that way you'll behave a little bit better, because right now it seems you don't mind taking advantage of the situation.' He snapped, 'Are you threatening me?' I replied, 'No, I'm just telling you the reason I'm taking your badge number down. That's why you wear a badge, so in situations like this we can identify you and call you out for your behavior.' He didn't like what I had to say one bit. He walked straight over to the TPF lieutenant and started to tell him what I was doing. The lieutenant went berserk. He started jumping up and down and yelling and then headed directly over to me. My father immediately got right in the middle of us and faced him. The lieutenant said, 'I want to talk to him! Who is he?' My father answered, 'You can talk to me.' He started yelling at my father and while he was yelling, a group of white shirts came over to see what all the commotion was about. The highest-ranking one was a tall, distinguished-looking man much older than my father. I think he was a Chief Inspector. Noticing that my father was standing there calm and poised, he asked the lieutenant, 'What's all the yelling about?' The lieutenant told him I was taking down badge numbers and he demanded I be locked up. The Chief Inspector asked why I was doing that and my father cut in and said, 'Because I told him to.' The Inspector asked, 'Why do you want their badge numbers?' My father said, 'The question is not why he's taking down badge numbers, the question is why any of these men are even here tonight. What was the purpose?' The Inspector answered, "I really don't know. It wasn't me that called them in. I have no idea why this was done.' My father continued, 'We are peaceful protestors. We've been here for a few months every night without a problem. We don't bother the officers that are here and now all of a sudden we got new men here that want to fight and they start by hitting kids.' The Inspector didn't reply. 'You want a battleground? Fine. Tomorrow I'm gonna bring four hundred of the biggest men I can find. No more women or children on this line, just men. Men that can fight. You want to make it a battle ground then let's make it a fair one.' The inspector tried to calm Joe. 'Joe, why are you talking like that?' 'These men hit women and children. They came here to fight us tonight. What did we do? We've been here months and months and never seen any action like this until these bums showed up. I wanna know who brought them here.' While the little lieutenant stormed and raged and tried to intervene, the Inspector didn't want

185

things to escalate. In front of everyone, he ordered the lieutenant to shut up. He acknowledged my father's grievances, and right away you could perceive a mutual respect between my father and the Inspector. After that night the TPF was never at our picket lines again."

***

While the FBI, in conjunction with the media tried to enfeeble the Italian-American Civil Rights League with rumors, speculation about why the League began, and what its purpose was, became a popular activity. Italians had never organized at such a level before the League's inception and they have never done it since. One of the League's major campaigns was against stereotyping and defamation. Disdain for Italian-Americans was evidenced daily by the use of certain words in the media and by law enforcement. The liberal use of words such as "Mafia" and "La Cosa Nostra" created the perception that the only organized crime in the United States was conducted by Italians; and further, that most Italian-Americans were criminals. There were no front-page headlines about the black gangs, Jewish shylocks, or Irish gambling rings that existed at the same time. This was one of the topics emphasized at the Unity Day rally, and, remarkably, the media was receptive. Almost overnight, the IACRL went from being a spurious group of "Mob owned" protestors, to an intrepid civil rights organization that deserved respect. Confirmation of this change came in the form of press release from the nation's Attorney General. In July of 1970, a few weeks after the Unity

Day Rally, Attorney General John Mitchell called for all government departments to stop using the words, "Mafia" and "La Cosa Nostra" in their communications. Joe was happy about the victory and publicity that came with Mitchell's press release, but bothered deeply by a news article written soon after. The same organizations he had sought aid from after Joe Junior's arrest were now taking credit for the attention Italians were receiving after Unity Day. An editorial written in the 'Golden Lion', the official publication of The Order Sons Of Italy took full credit for the Attorney General's announcement. The editorial read, "This can only be made possible though the Order Sons of Italy in America, the only nationally recognized "grass roots" organization representing Italian-Americans."[lxxxvi] Joe was beside himself. He could not believe the audacity of this paper, not only in taking credit for something the IACRL had clearly accomplished, but also for claiming they were a grass roots organization. He was immensely proud of the fact that the IACRL was a group built by hard-working Italian-Americans. He made sure these people were the foundation of his organization after witnessing the failed models that had come before. Groups like C.I.A.O., The Order Sons of Italy, and A.I.D. were largely composed of well-to-do businessmen and women. These groups avoided the fights of the common people. Joe knew they were preying on their members with fees that went to trips, dinners and ceremonies for the officers and leaders.

Soon after the press release by the Attorney General, Governor Rockefeller issued a similar injunction to the press to avoid the use of the banned words. He said the words did in fact hurt the Italian-American community, noting, "Organized crime includes members of virtually every ethnic group." He continued by saying, "The insistence of foreign labels to lend a Hollywood aura of sensationalism to this criminality undeniably damages the good name of millions of Italian-Americans to whom hard work, self- reliance, solid family upbringing and respect for the law are a tradition and the rule." He advised that, "When speaking out on organized crime to call it just that and to forsake the easy, vivid catchwords that unjustly slander Americans of Italian or any other descent. [lxxxvii] But the League was also met by a small group of cynics; the most vocal member of the opposition was an Italian-American himself, New York State Senator John Marchi. He was a Staten Island resident who took every opportunity with his media contacts to try and damage the group with his contemptuous rhetoric. He even went as far as condemning his colleagues for supporting the massively growing grass roots organization saying, "For public officials to lend prestige and enhance [this] preposterous gathering with their presence is a very sad commentary."[lxxxviii]

Regardless of the cynics and critics, the League's burgeoning could not be slowed. Once its victories within the government were witnessed, more supporters emerged to join the fight in eliminating discrimination against Italian-Americans. A supporter stated, "My father came to this country and worked with his hands. He helped build the Empire State Building and the Chrysler Building. Yet, when people talk about Italians, they talk about criminals and the underworld. How come they don't talk about Botticelli or Enrico Fermi or Pirandello? Yes, I belong to the Mafia. Mothers and Fathers of Italian Ancestry."[lxxxix]

Joe Colombo's vision of joining the Italian-American community together for a fight was becoming a reality. There were 20 million Italian-Americans in the nation at that time, the majority were hard working taxpayers, and many of them were angry that the media was defining their culture with stereotypes by exploiting the few thousand of them that were criminals.[xc]

***

After the successes with the State Governor and the Attorney General, the League went to work on the second giant; the Media. Anthony Colombo teamed up with League officer Steve Aiello in mailing letters and making phone calls to as many news and media companies as possible. After months of mailing letters, protesting, and calling their offices, the League was finally invited to discuss its accusations concerning harassment of the Italian-American community, with New York FBI director John Malone. While Malone offered no immediate resolution and basically mollified the IACRL, the group did see other results. Many newspapers began adopting the words "Mob" or "underworld" in their reports, but there were others that showed resistance. When the written protests failed, they reverted to their strength in numbers and began demonstrating.

As vice president of the League, Anthony Colombo was placed in charge of all protests. Protests ranged from the physical ones that occurred in the streets of New York City to the massive letter-writing campaigns directed at politicians and corporations across the country. Steve Aiello usually assisted Anthony, as he was already a political activist. Steve had spent time in the 1960's as a part of the civil rights movement and was also involved in the anti-war movement. Aiello grew up the son of Sicilian immigrants and felt proud of the many contributions Italian-Americans made to the country. During his time with the League he was employed as a full time schoolteacher in Brooklyn,. Aiello would later go on to twice become the president of the board of education in New York City. He resigned his position in 1980 to work as an assistant to President Jimmy Carter. Aiello was an eloquent speaker and prolific writer for the IACRL with a remarkable ability to re-interpret and express Anthony's passionate and sometimes overbearing prose.

The League also hired a newspaper clipping service to follow up on media exposure and document the progress of its various campaigns. It was noted that the New York Times was not only unresponsive to letters from the League, it was also continuing to print the words 'Mafia' and 'La Cosa Nostra' in its publications.[xci] When Barry Slotnick contacted Times Managing Editor Abe Rosenthal in hopes of addressing the League's concerns, he was met by a scornful refusal that the Times would never work with the League. In a few words Rosenthal let Slotnick know that the paper would "use whatever words we want." Slotnick then warned Rosenthal that the IACRL would exercise its right to protest and that the Times could have trouble getting its papers out if it continued to resist the League's demands. Rosenthal replied, "Watch me."

Barry immediately told Joe about the call with Rosenthal. Wanting to take immediate action, but knowing he couldn't be the one to lead the fight, he discussed his plan of attack with Anthony. Joe knew that if this league were to grow and operate independently, he needed to have his son take on as much responsibility as he could and fast. Abe Rosenthal was one of the most powerful men in the country, in charge of the most influential publication. It was widely accepted that the views espoused in the Time's editorials profoundly affected public opinion. For instance, an editorial had run a few years earlier about a small, rather lightweight militant group in Harlem called the "Blood Brothers." The depiction transformed this relatively innocuous group into a formidable force that posed a serious threat to public safety in New York City. Subsequently the city's Chief of Police held a small press conference at which he explained, "The Blood Brothers were not quite what they were made out to be."[xcii] Once the Times ran misleading stories, other periodicals followed suit. Sensationalism and propaganda had consistently proven effective, which was precisely the problem Joe wanted to address.

In July, buses filled with supporters unloaded at the West Side plant of the New York Times. The protestors formed a human chain to block the trucks from exiting the buildings. The League had already discussed the protest with the Times Union truck drivers. The drivers were sympathetic to the League and did not try to cross the picket lines. This worked for one full day, depriving the New York Times newspaper of its largest means of delivery. It would be the first and only time in the paper's history that delivery was halted as the result of a peaceful protest. The following day, the police set up barricades and threatened mass arrests of the demonstrators. The barricades created a safe passage for the trucks and gave the union drivers a clear path to enter the truck garage. The League's attorney, Barry Slotnick persuaded the protesters not to bar distribution and the police not to arrest the demonstrators. Both sides refrained from such actions and a peaceful, legal protest continued.[xciii]

Abe Rosenthal realized he had to take a meeting with the IACRL. Arriving on the League's behalf were President Nat Marcone, Treasurer Caesar Vitale, legal counsel Barry Slotnick, Vice President Anthony Colombo and distinguished officer, Dr. Sinatra*. They sat in a sprawling boardroom facing the entire New York Times managing group. At a large conference table with Rosenthal and Anthony at either end, the IACRL officials complained about the paper's discrimination and the defaming use of the words "La Cosa Nostra" and "Mafia." Rosenthal was well known in editing circles as a controlling and rigid despot. He appeared largely unsympathetic to their objections, and addressed most of his comments exclusively to Dr. Sinatra. He did, however, tell the League officials that he would review the papers to see if their claims were true. He rather grudgingly agreed to discuss the terms in question with his editors and reporters but insisted, "that under no circumstances would the Times respond to pressure tactics."[xciv] Anthony grew frustrated during the meeting, as he realized that they were being pacified and that nothing would be done about their demands. He argued that the Times was unsympathetic to the discrimination that Italian-Americans suffered and that it was ignoring the new axioms adopted by government officials. He looked across to Abe and told him firmly, "Unless you do something to solve this, your trucks will not roll." Abe was not accustomed to this type of challenge. Anthony stood fast and was backed by his group. After a few more minutes, Abe Rosenthal relented. He agreed he would examine the reports in detail and told the League officers that he would implement a policy that required writers to refrain from using the words unless they were taken from a direct quote.

---

* A doctor from Brooklyn, no relation to Frank Sinatra the actor/singer.

The success at the New York Times was monumental for the League. When the story of Anthony's performance was relayed to Joe he was elated. That Sunday, when the family got together for dinner Joe praised Anthony for his nerve and tenacity. Anthony was only 25 years old at the time of the meeting. He had initially been overwhelmed by the amount of responsibility his father had asked him to assume. Only a month prior Joe pushed Anthony into his public speaking debut. One night on the picket line he handed Anthony the megaphone and said, "Speak." Anthony asked his father anxiously, "Dad, what do you want me to say?" Joe told him, "Say what's on your mind. Tell the people how you feel." Anthony's fears evaporated as he discovered that he was an effective public speaker who easily commanded his audience's attention. Joe modeled much of his instruction to Anthony on what he had learned years earlier from his mentor Carl Gambino. Gambino knew young Joe was already a seasoned fighter, so he sought instead to build his strengths in the areas of negotiation and management. He convinced Joe that violence and anger were weapons of the weak and that good leaders did not need to exert force to get desired results. Over the years Joe witnessed the amount of respect Carl received from people without ever having to display his temper. Joe then sought to instill this in his son as well. Over time, they both learned to harness their sometimes ferocious tempers and use them to their advantage in non-violent battles on picket lines and in boardrooms.

✳✳✳

"Whether my father was a Mob boss or a real estate broker, there was no denying his knowledge of and passion for the Italian American people. He would become incensed about the social injustices he read about in the papers. I'd hear him exclaiming, 'Would you look at this?' when he'd come upon some financial scam or political scandal. He responded with particular rage to a story about millions missing from a school budget; not only because it wasn't being investigated by the feds, but because it was only a tiny article hidden way in the back of the paper. I remember the first summer when I met Nelson Rockefeller, I was very excited. He was, after all, an extremely powerful person. When he offered to take photos with us my father refused to participate. Soon after, during a League meeting, he spoke about the importance of organizing against corporate giants. He reminded those in attendance about the brutalization and exploitation of hard- working immigrants, which could invariably be traced to some wealthy industry man indifferent to human suffering. He told us about Rockefeller's father and the Ludlow Massacre. This was a story about a group of underpaid, overworked immigrant miners that organized for more humane working conditions. Their appeals were ignored, and as punishment for their insubordination, they were evicted from their homes, along with their wives and children. They were forced to live in a makeshift camp while they struggled to make a deal and return to work. Before long, National Guardsmen arrived at the camp in an armored car with a mounted machine gun. The guardsmen surrounded the camp with weapons drawn. Then, without provocation, they opened fire, indiscriminately killing men, women and children. My father emphasized that this was only one of many atrocities committed with impunity by industry superpowers. It was this kind of suffering and subjugation that impelled workers to organize and ultimately form unions.

Although he was most informed about injustices towards Italians, my father also recognized the similar experiences of other disenfranchised immigrant groups. He sympathized with everyone alike, and took great pride in his knowledge of history. One day, as we walked through Greenwich Village, he pointed up to a building and said, 'You know what happened in this building?' I shrugged, 'No, Dad.' 'This was the Triangle Shirtwaist Factory. In 1911, over a hundred workers died right here. Most of them were young women, no older than your wife. They were garment workers, just like at Catania, but back then there were no unions, no fire codes, and no fire escapes. Before unions, factory workers had no rights. Young women were subjected to the worst conditions. Their bosses locked these workers on their floor, so they couldn't steal clothes or leave work early. One day, a fire broke out. The foreman escaped with no injuries and took with him the key to the door that could have saved all those people. Two Italian men who operated the elevators saved as many women as they could, but they stopped because the elevator ended up busting. Young women were in flames, throwing themselves out the windows.' My father spoke with great sadness about this event; almost as if he'd known the women personally. He felt profoundly connected to all working-class people and their hardships."

***

The League was undeniably an agent of social justice. If someone had a problem too big to fight alone, the League would not hesitate to offer support. Financial aid reached a wide variety of distressed citizens. Member support ranged from distributing gifts to the underprivileged during the holidays, to physically laying down in the street to prevent vehicles from disrupting protests. The IACRL established over thirty-two chapters with over fifty thousand members in less than nine months.

In the summer of 1970, a young Italian lawyer arrived at a meeting with a group of homeowners from Corona, Queens to discuss an urgent matter. The City Planning Commission planned to bulldoze a few blocks of homes in order to build a new high school and athletic field. The lawyer had been battling the City Planning Commission for a few years, defending the group of Italian-American residents who had lived in the neighborhood for three generations. They were known as "the Corona fighting 69." Around eighty young men from that neighborhood had been soldiers in World War II, half of whom never returned home. Their families had used the insurance money to pay the mortgages on their homes. These citizens were deeply committed to their peaceful and productive community; they cleaned their own streets, repaired the sidewalks, and had achieved status in Queens as a "low crime" area.[xcv] The residents had proposed a number of alternatives to the bulldozing, all of which were summarily rejected by city officials. The city simply cited eminent domain laws, but residents were being offered a mere $10,000 for homes valued at closer to $60,000. Joe was very moved by the plight of these residents, and assured them that the League would provide whatever assistance it could. When the meeting concluded, he and Anthony introduced themselves to the young lawyer who had described the community's plight so eloquently. His name was Mario Cuomo. He would eventually become the 52nd governor of New York State.

In the months that followed, the campaign to save the 69 Corona homes gained momentum. Among its supporters was Vito Battista, a State assemblyman who demanded a full-scale inquiry from the State Investigation Commission. When the homeowners received a visit by state officials, they showed them eleven alternate sites that the city had disregarded.[xcvi] The State Commission maintained that its choice was already "approved by the city site selection board as the best of the many alternatives after a public hearing more than three years ago... Delaying it now to resurrect alternatives that were thoroughly, publicly, and conclusively considered would deal a serious blow to the students that need the school."[xcvii] Battista would not relent. Along with Anthony Colombo and other League members, protesters picketed City Hall day and night. Although the Mayor received dozens of letters from League officials, state senators and assemblymen, he didn't lift a finger to help. Battista, Colombo, Marcone and a few state legislators waited for weeks to plead their case in person to the Commission. In late September, a new group of protesters arrived at City Hall with a different agenda. The small group from the Bronx was nowhere near the size of Battista's, and had only been there a few hours before they were ushered right in to speak with the Mayor. Battista was insulted and became enraged. He climbed on top of a large truck. "Charge the barricades!" he yelled, urging the entire group of Italian-American protesters to shove past the barriers into City Hall. The mounted police began to crowd their horses together and the foot patrolmen began physically fighting with the protesters. "Go in there! Go in there!" shouted

Battista.[xcviii] Police inspector Dennis Noonan screamed at officers to put cuffs on Mr. Battista for inciting the chaos. Battista avoided police and kept his distance from the inspector until the storm was quelled. As order was restored, Deputy Mayor Richard R. Aurelio agreed to meet with Anthony Colombo. He listened to Anthony's account and promised to "look into the equities of the situation" in Corona.[xcix] After months of peaceful but futile protests, it appeared that more radical measures were proving effective.

***

Dennis Dillon entered the Cantalupo Realty offices rather imperiously, accompanied by Ray Tallia, who scratched dandruff from the wisps of his greasy hair. The two men received some disapproving stares from the salesmen at their desks. Unlike Bernie Welsh, neither Tallia nor Dillon had the personality to win respect from any of the men in Colombo's circle. Before Dillon could even ask for Joe, Anthony Colombo, wielding a silver spy camera walked right up to Dillon and snapped a photo of him. Before Dillon could even process what just happened, Anthony slid apart both ends of the tiny camera and snapped it again. Dillon was outraged and yelled, "Who is this guy? What is he doing here? He can't take pictures of me! Arrest him!" Tallia asked, "Arrest him for what? Taking pictures? It's not a crime." Dillon yelled, "I want to know who this person is!" Anthony offered his business card and informed him, "I'm the Vice President of the Italian-American Civil Rights League." Tallia explained to Dillon, "This is Joe Colombo's oldest son." Joe Colombo stepped out of his office to see what the commotion was. Dillon, overwrought, turned to Joe, "What kind of respect is that? What do you teach your children? I am a United States Attorney." Joe replied calmly, "He's not doing anything to disrespect you. My son is the Vice President of the Italian-American Civil Rights League and taking pictures is part of his job." Dillon asked incredulously, "That's his job? Taking pictures?" "He is supposed to document any suspected case of harassment against Italian-Americans, so, yeah, that is his job." Dillon was clearly unable to compose himself, so Tallia grabbed him by the suit coat and guided him to the exit. "Come on Dennis. Let's Go." Dillon shook off Tallia and stormed out of the realty offices, seething with rage and embarrassment. As he exited, he cast a final glare at Anthony assuring him that this event would not be forgotten.

Colombo: The Unsolved Murder

Brooklyn Homicide dusting for fingerprints at the Shore Road crime scene after two bodies were found in the rear seat of the vehicle. *(Getty Images)*

14-year-old Joe Colombo with his Grandfather and sister, waiting outside the precinct to identify his father's body. *(Public Domain)*

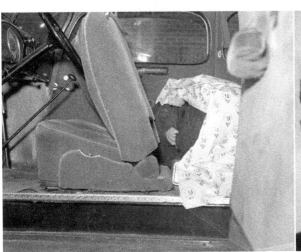

The hand of Anthony Colombo as his dead body was found in the backseat of his Pontiac. *(Getty Images)*

Mug Shot of Anthony Colombo aka "Tony Durante" *(Public Domain)*

From the deck of the U.S.S. Falgout
(Author's archive)

Joe Colombo & Lucille "Jo-Jo" wedding photo –
Our Lady of Peace Church. Brooklyn, NY May 28, 1944
(Author's archive)

Colombo: The Unsolved Murder

Mugshsot line up Brooklyn, 1958.
L-R Joe Calabro, "Joey Notch", Joe Colombo, Patsy Greico, Frank Urdan, John Campanella
(Public Domain)

Jo-Jo with Joe Junior, Anthony and Vinny in their Blooming Grove home.
(Author's archive)

Joe checking the swing on his golf club in front of his Blooming Grove estate. *(Author's archive)*

Anthony Colombo in uniform at Valley Forge Military Academy in 1961. *(Author's archive)*

Joe sitting on his horse, "Joey's girl" in front of his Blooming Grove estate. *(Author's archive)*

Colombo: The Unsolved Murder

Anthony and Joe Jr. with their friends and girlfriends at the Copa Cabana in the mid-1960's.
(Author's archive)

The Colombo Family at Anthony and Carol's wedding. L-R Joe Larosa, Vincent Colombo, Joe, Jo-Jo, Carol, Anthony, Joe Jr., Vincent De Goia, Loretta Colombo-Larosa, Mary Faiello, Christopher, Catherine Colombo-De Goia.
(Author's archive)

Joe putting his hat on after answering questions to the grand jury, January, 15 1970.
(Getty Images)

The first public interview with Joe Colombo done by Daily News Reporter Bill Federici. Joe's lawyer, Barry Slotnick, sits in the middle.
(Getty Images)

Colombo: The Unsolved Murder

Anthony gives his first speech at the first Unity Day Rally in Columbus Circle.
(Getty Images)

Joe calms protesters in front of the FBI building after the 1st Unity Day Rally in 1970.
(Corbis Images)

The aftermath from the bombing at Barry Slotnick's law office on Park Row.
(Getty Images)

Colombo: The Unsolved Murder

March 6, 1971, Joe in handcuffs being escorted by agents for falsely reporting his criminal history on his real estate license application.
(Getty Images)

FBI picket line, winter 1971.
(Author's archive)

210 The famous photo of Nelson Rockefeller with the League's pin on his lapel. From L-R, Anthony Colombo, Joseph DeCicco, Secretary of State John Lomenzo, Nelson Rockefeller, Nicky Bianco and tk. *(Author's archive)*

Colombo: The Unsolved Murder

Congressman Paul O'Dwyer, Democratic Leader Meade Esposito, Sammy Davis, Brooklyn Borough President Sam Leone and State Senator Basil Patterson.
(Author's archive)

Joe with Ed McMahon and Frank Sinatra's manager, Kenny Rogers, going over last minute details for the Felt Forum benefit in 1970.
(Author's archive)

Anthony and Franki Valli at the Felt Forum, November 1970. *(Author's archive)*

Joe with singer Connie Francis at the Felt Forum. *(Author's archive)*

Frank Sinatra performing at the Felt Forum Benefit, November 1970. *(Author's archive)*

During a Christmas toy drive at the League's downtown Brooklyn Chapter. From L-R, Nat Marcone, Hugh McIntosh, Chapter President, Joe Colombo, Carmine Persico and Anthony Colombo. *(Author's archive)*

Joe with his mother, Catherine Colombo-De Goia. *(Author's archive)*

A happy Joe Jr., Jo-Jo and Joe Colombo after receiving an innocent verdict in the coin melting case, February 26, 1971. *(Getty Images)*

Italian American Civil Rights League picket lines on 3rd ave in Manhattan, 1971. *(Bob DAlessandro)*

Colombo: The Unsolved Murder

Joe Colombo, Anthony Colombo and Steve Aeillo guests on the Dick Cavett show.
(Getty Images)

Joe with Meir Kahane (JDL founder) in front of the Brooklyn Federal Courthouse.
(Getty Images)

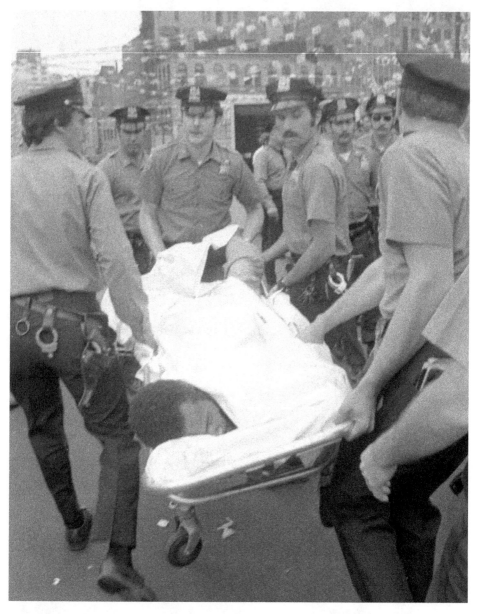

NYPD officers escort a still living Jerome Johnson out of the Unity Day Rally. The officer at Johnson's feet is Giuliani "Tony" Schiozzi, who first apprehended Johnson and disarmed him.
(Getty Images)

Chapter 8.

"I've Got the World on a String"

(Fall 1970)

Barry Slotnick had just received a visit from his wife Donna and their son Stuart. He kissed them both goodbye and they made their way towards the elevators of his thirteenth-floor law offices. As they left, they passed and received a small nod from Caesar Vitale and Fat Philly, who were arriving for an appointment with Barry. Caesar and Philly both looked exhausted, and they sank heavily into the chairs at Barry's conference table. The hot August sun had both of them toweling the perspiration off their doughy olive-skinned faces. Barry leaned on his desk, looked the two big boys over and said, "I hope you two already ate lunch."

Donna and Stuart waited for the elevator at the end of the long corridor. She bounced the baby in her arms until the bell chimed and the doors opened. A young black man with short hair stepped out, looking momentarily surprised, but then offering Donna a quick smile. Donna stepped inside the doors and quickly turned to face him. She tapped the lobby button and watched the man walk hesitantly down the hallway, pretending to be lost. She noticed a bag which he seemed to hold protectively. She kept her eyes on him until the steel doors joined together and her view was gone.

Back in the office Philly and Caesar sat comfortably at the conference table while Barry's partner, Ray Narral, shuffled through a large box of paperwork. Caesar watched as Fat Philly peeled open a Hostess cake. He seemed much more interested in the snack than in what Barry was saying. The phone rang and Barry rose to grab it from his desk. A sudden, thunderous explosion ripped through the room. Bewildered and frightened, all the men ducked for cover. The walls shook as paperwork flew and pictures clattered down. Cesar shouted, "What the hell?" Philly took an educated guess; "That must have been a bomb." Barry looked down at the obese genius and said, "What gave you the first clue?" The men were all unharmed. They looked around the room and at each other. He stepped to the large wooden door and cautiously opened it into the next room. The waiting room looked like a demolition zone. The metal ceiling grid was in pieces with the tiles broken and the ground littered with rubble. Light fixtures dangled uselessly like broken limbs. Barry exhaled as the men all stood in the doorway examining the damage. Philly looked at the ceiling and said, "Somebody doesn't like you, Barry."

***

On August 24, 1970, police stood outside Barry Slotnick's office, examining the remains of the pipe bomb explosion. Although both the police and the bomb squad had arrived within minutes of the bombing, they were never able to find any leads on the case. Joe wondered whether this bombing was connected to the infamous Bonanno bombings in Tucson, Arizona. Exactly one month before the attack at Barry's office, Joe read an article in the New York Post covering the Tucson trial that directly linked the FBI to the crimes. Special Agent David Hale was identified in open court as the mastermind behind the 20 bombings that took place in Tucson in 1968. Paul Stevens, an ex-marine and demolition expert was the first man apprehended in the case. William J. Dunbar was his accomplice. During their interrogations, both men gave statements that an FBI agent named David Hale had recruited them to do the bombings. Dunbar shared with the judge in court that he was "told by Hale that [his] felony [record] would be expunged and that there was nothing illegal in what he was doing. Furthermore, if there were any repercussions, Hale assured [him] that he was working under the auspices and protection of the FBI and would not be prosecuted." Judge William Frey shook his finger at FBI special agent Hale, telling him, "You have led two young men down a primrose path."[c] When Hale was forced to take the stand, he pled the fifth to avoid answering any questions. The judge recommended a Grand Jury investigation into Hale's involvement.

Hale resigned from the FBI on August 12, 1969, the same day of Stevens' and Dunbar's arraignment. Dunbar and Stevens provided further testimony about Hale's orders, one of which was to kill Bonanno's bodyguard Peter Notaro. Attorney General John Mitchell informed Judge Frey that Special Agent Hale would be free to testify in court, as long as it did "not directly [involve] FBI matters."[ci] The Justice Department's official stance was "it has no cause for action against Hale."[cii] The only official statement made by the FBI concerning the allegations was, "The special agent alleged to have been involved is no longer employed by the FBI."[ciii] The judge was appalled, commenting with contempt, "Fantastic... I think it's a disgrace that the nation's top law enforcement body should neglect the prosecution for this case."[civ]

***

"The expansion of the League was necessary in order to raise sufficient funds for larger-scale projects. My father didn't just think big when it came to rallies and protests. He had plans to establish a youth outreach program, a nursing home, a rehabilitation center, and a hospital. He appointed a team of professionals to look for property and draw up a budget. These projects were all extremely ambitious and seemed out of reach. Even with the League's rapidly growing membership, we wouldn't even be able to generate enough money for a down payment. That's when my father dreamed up the benefit concert. He called me into the office one day and told me, 'Ant, I want you to go over to the West Side and sit down with Frank Sinatra. He's interested in this concert, but he wants to get a feel for the League and what we are doing here. So I want you to go explain to him everything we have done and what we intend to do.' Of course, I agreed to this. I felt thrilled and privileged to meet Frank Sinatra. I was a big fan of all his music and movies. I also admired him as a man's man, because he didn't take any shit from people. If he was criticized he never hesitated to defend himself, even physically if necessary.

I was brought to Frank's office by his associate Ken Roberts. Frank's workplace was located in an apartment a little north of Hell's Kitchen. When I arrived, he was sitting behind his desk looking sharp in a beautifully tailored suit and fancy cufflinks. He rose to greet me, but could not shake my hand. Both of his hands were bandaged from a recent operation he'd had to repair damaged tendons or ligaments. We both sat down and began to talk. He had the secretary bring me lunch and we had coffee and biscotti. We spoke for about five hours that day and covered every imaginable topic about Italian-Americans. We spoke about political affairs from JFK to Nixon and about discrimination, to which he was no stranger. He told me about his early experiences in music and in Hollywood and how disparagingly people had spoken about him. When it came to facts about Italian-Americans, he was as sharp as my father. When I asked him if he knew that an Italian-American had signed the Declaration of Independence he answered quickly, 'William Paca.' After we had discussed both the accomplishments and the hardships of Italians in this country, we talked about Mob stereotypes. He told me how he had been warned at every point in his life not to talk to certain people, and that he'd always responded the same way. His friends were his friends and he wasn't going to stop talking to anyone simply because of their personal or professional associations. He asked a lot of questions about the League and I told him all about the things we wanted to do. He loved all of the ideas and immediately agreed to help us raise the money. The only thing he wanted was to make sure it went specifically to the intended cause. He knew that a lot of organizations raised money and spent it over time on expense accounts, conventions, and awards dinners. We told him our books were open at any time to anyone who wanted to see them. Then we got into discussing the upcoming league benefit concert at the Felt Forum. Frank wanted to take care of the whole event. He was immediately very passionate about it. He would bring his orchestra, in addition to the best musicians in the area, from the Four Seasons to Connie Francis. He said he would also arrange for Ed McMahon to be the master of ceremonies. We talked for a while longer and when it came time to leave I looked at his hands, smiled and asked, 'You going to be ready to do the show?' He answered, Absolutely Anthony.'

That Friday night at the Felt Forum I attended a show I will never forget. My whole family went together. My mother, my wife, and all the other women made getting ready a whole day affair. They got their hair done, makeup, nails and everything. We took limousines to the garden and "walked a carpet" inside like celebrities. Frank made it a VIP affair for all the League officers and distinguished guests, and he had a receiving line set up so everyone could meet him. While we were on the receiving line that night, I remember as my wife reached Frank something happened in a moment that might have affected the entire event. My wife is a very beautiful woman, and she was especially stunning that night, so naturally Frank noticed her. He probably didn't know who she was, but that didn't matter to me. I was a jealous bastard back then. And Frank was well known as a lady-killer. He had looked at my wife in a way that made me rage. It might very well have been all inside my head. My wife didn't even know what was going on, but most of the time women don't notice that sort of thing anyway. I immediately turned back toward him, intending to put my hand on him. Now, here I was, the same person who'd just recently met with him to ask him for help. I was in such awe of who he was and yet the way he looked at my wife; I was ready to fight with him in a heartbeat. Before Frank got a chance to see me, my father grabbed my hand and whispered in my ear, 'What, are you crazy?' He was watching me closely. I woke up from the rage quickly. He slid me from the line and put his arm around me and walked me over to a table. When we sat down I told him about the look. In his typically cool tone he said to me, 'So what? Your wife is a very attractive woman; men are going to look at her. Learn to deal with it.' I protested, 'Dad, but did you see the way he looked at her?' He said, 'Anthony it doesn't matter. Take it as a compliment.' Still not convinced, I said, 'All right Dad, if he looked at mom like that what would you do?' Very matter of fact, he replied, 'I would have beat the crap out of him.' So we both started laughing about it. He was often good at making a joke in order to lighten up a serious situation.

    The concert was extraordinary. I know it was the talk of the town for a long time after it ended. A number of people had helped to organize the show but could not afford the hundred-dollar ticket price, and I remember my father pulling out of pocket to make sure they got to see the show. The line-up was amazing. It began with an overture conducted by Don Costa, and then Ed McMahon took the microphone as master of ceremonies. He announced the first act and the room erupted with cheers as Frankie Valli and the Four Seasons took the stage. I remember looking over at my father who smiled as we sat together and watched the show. Godfrey Cambridge and Ross Martin both spoke about social activism and performed parts of their comedy routines. Then we watched Connie Francis, Guy Marx, and Vic Damone. After Vic Damone was an intermission, we mingled with the guests; League members from all over the tri-state area were in attendance. We saw Sy Kravitz and a bunch of producers and staff from NBC. The second part of the show began with The Pee Jays, followed by Morty Storm, Trinny Lopez, and Pat Henry, who was another comedian. The grand finale was Sammy Davis, Jr., followed by Sinatra. It was just spectacular. After the final encore, we handed out some honorary awards to League members and a few people made short speeches. Dick Cappazola, a League officer, had made three special League pins out of solid gold. He presented them to Frank Sinatra, Sammy Davis and my father. My father really liked Cappazola; he wasn't a jeweler or anything of the sort, but was so passionate about the League that he'd do anything to contribute. We then announced that the concert had been a success; enough funds had been raised that night to allow us to build Camp Unity, a summer retreat for underprivileged kids. We were ecstatic; everyone felt amazing about being a League member. We had the sense that we could accomplish anything. After the show, a large group of us went to the Copacabana with some of the entertainers and special guests. It was pretty big to be rolling around with the likes of Sammy Davis Jr., Connie Francis, Gina Lollobrigida, and Godfrey Cambridge. We raised half a million dollars that night at the Felt Forum. Four thousand people had attended the event. Raising money had seemed to be a significant obstacle to the League's endeavors, but we had again witnessed my father's ability to make any obstacle disappear."

***

Agents Boland and Welsh eyed the back of the gold station wagon on the corner of Mott and Worth. The station wagon hooked a hard right and disappeared from their view. They followed the lead and watched as the car pulled over to the left and parked behind the court building. The station wagon sat idling, and so did Boland and Welsh in their car nearby.

Joe Colombo sat in the passenger seat of the '69 Buick next to Rocky Miraglia. They'd only been there for moments when a metal ring tapped on the glass of Rocky's window. Joe and Rocky looked outside to see the two agents standing outside in the cold. Rocky rolled down the window. "Rocky, we have a warrant for your arrest." Joe asked, "For what?" Bernie pulled out a piece of paper. "It's a perjury indictment." Joe, upset, protested, 'This guy's got nine kids Bernie, don't you people have anything better to do with your time?" Boland said, "Come on, Rocky, get out of the car." Rocky obeyed. Bernie glanced into the car again. "Let me see that bag on the seat." Rocky said, "It's not mine." "I don't care. I want to see the bag." Rocky stood there looking stone-faced at Welsh. "I want to see if you got a weapon, now gimme the bag." Rocky replied, "There's no weapon in there." Rocky grabbed the bag to hand it to Welsh. Joe yelled, "That's my bag!" Boland snatched up the bag. "Now it's mine." Joe hopped out from the passenger door in a fit of rage. "You can't take that bag. That's not his!" Boland retorted, "He had his hands on it, we are arresting him, anything in this car is his and we can take it in." "I'm telling you the bag is mine, it belongs to me and you can't take it." Welsh began to cuff Rocky, "The bag is coming with us, Joe." Joe responded, incensed, "You have no authority to touch that bag. It is property of the Italian-American Civil Rights League." A squad car crawled to a stop on the street. Two uniformed NYPD officers exited their vehicle to see what the commotion was. One of the cops asked Welsh, "Everything all right here, fellas?' Bernie flashed his credentials. "FBI, we are taking this gentlemen and this bag into custody." Joe continued to scream at Welsh over the bag. Finally, Boland spoke harshly. "Listen, Joe. We are taking Miraglia and the bag and that's final. You can either stay here, or you can come with us. In cuffs." Joe shouted, "This is an illegal seizure!" "If it is, then you can have the bag back." Joe was helpless, wild with frustration, boiling over. Smoke pumped from his nostrils into the cold December air.

***

Two days before Christmas, Joe Colombo was in court awaiting the verdict of his five-count perjury trial. Joe was accused of lying to the Division of Licensing Services of the New York Department of State. The State placed the small perjury trial at the highest level of priority. While typical procedure is for the Assistant District Attorney to take part in the trial phase, Alfred J. Scotti sat in personally to try the case. As a Chief Administrator it was rare for him to do more than supervise the one hundred plus prosecutors who worked below him.[cv] After a twelve-day trial the jury was ready to deliver its verdict. Joe's entire family and a large group of friends listened as the foreman read the verdict. "Not guilty" was read for the first three counts, but for the second two, Colombo was found guilty. Barry Slotnick immediately motioned for an appeal and Judge Harold Baer released Joe on bail. Sentencing was postponed until February 1971.

It was during that December trial when the FBI seized Joe's briefcase while he and Rocky Miraglia were speaking in a parked car in the lot behind the courthouse. The FBI bragged to the press about a number of large donations cited on the documents found and about the "many well known names" that were on it.[cvi] The FBI made photocopies, returned the originals to Colombo and then brought the paperwork to US Attorney Dennis Dillon. The list was a record of League contributions and had no properties that could be traced to illegal activities. In his FBI report Dennis Dillon advised the FBI:

> THIS LIST WOULD FORM AN EXCELLENT BASIS FOR A FEDERAL GRAND JURY INVESTIGATION UNDER TITLE 18, SECTION 1962, UNITED STATES CODE, WHICH MAKES ILLEGAL THE INVESTMENT OF FUNDS DERIVED FROM RACKETEERING ACTIVITIES IN ANY ENTERPRISE AFFECTING INTERSTATE COMMERCE.[cvii]

The memorandum went to William Sullivan, the head of domestic intelligence and second in command to J. Edgar Hoover. The Grand Jury would take place in February and Dillon would call every suspected organized crime member that attended the concert.

The FBI became well aware of the financing and operations of the League as they opened an IRS investigation into all of the League assets as well.

Joe's professional and emotional investment in the League grew tremendously over the first year, as did the FBI's man-hours and tax dollars into investigating the League. What was formerly an inchoate organization, whose priorities mostly centered on combating defamation, had now become a formidable opponent of drug addiction, poverty, government corruption and police harassment. Almost any person or group could expect to receive assistance from the League if needed. Joe was an ideal leader for the League's altruistic campaigns; he had an innate ability to connect with people. He could listen to a person's problems and evince complete understanding of his situation. He was also a keen political strategist, which had even been demonstrated in his purported involvement in organized crime. As aforementioned, he was widely believed to be the man who effected the peace agreement in the longstanding and bloody Gallo-Profaci conflict. He was a mediator who naturally commanded respect, but also made people feel comfortable and significant. A longtime friend and associate described Joe by saying, "He was the type of guy that could take an Italian, a black, a Puerto Rican, and a Jew that were all at each other's throats for something, sit them down in a room for ten minutes, and afterwards, they'd all walk out laughing with each other like they were the best of friends." Colombo understood the mechanics of a good relationship. He celebrated people's individuality and adapted his own language to suit the situation. He was remarkably able to listen to someone's problem and immediately envision a way of helping. He found that the majority of the people who sought his help had an antagonist in their lives that they felt was too overwhelming to fight. Sometimes he helped people who needed money, most of the time he helped battle injustice. He repeatedly offered his help in situations where someone was being exploited, disenfranchised, or bullied. Above all, Joe Colombo despised bullies.

By 1971 the League was in full blossom. Despite continued arrests and police harassment of Colombo, membership and support for the IACRL grew exponentially. Twenty-five chapters throughout the five boroughs now represented it. That winter, while most of the city was suffering financially, League members handed out 25,000 toys and tons of ice cream and treats to needy children in New York. Joe himself made the rounds, and frequently visited children's hospitals and orphanages. He was often accompanied by heartier-sized League members who donned Santa Claus suits, giving the children a reassuring feeling that Santa was there for them regardless of their financial or family situations.

When disaster struck in Pakistan in the form of an earthquake, a benefit dinner was held at the Chez Royal in Brooklyn to raise money for the surviving families. Joe personally handed the $8,000 check to Pakistani Minister Consul General, M.N.I. Chaudury. Chaudury humbly thanked Joe, telling him, "Your generous assistance to my people has touched me very profoundly, and hundreds of my people will live because of it."[cviii] As the League flourished, Joe increasingly focused his efforts on civil rights activism and philanthropy.

The League's numerous humanitarian campaigns still escaped the attention of the press, however. Anthony addressed this at a meeting of League captains in February. "It is apparent that some people ignore the good that the Italian-American Civil Rights League has done and continues to do," he spoke emphatically to the packed room, "Our anti narcotics program is already showing results although it was only recently started, our members made thousands of children happier last Christmas when they distributed toys to those who were hospitalized and institutionalized throughout the city, but not one word of that was mentioned in the newspapers. We are now over 40,000 strong and growing everyday and the FBI is still trying to destroy us. But the Italian-American Civil Rights League will have a membership of over 250,000 before this year is over, and no one will ever take us apart."[cix]

    Anthony's passion for the League was largely inspired by his father. Not many children have the opportunity to work alongside their fathers, and Anthony's work with the League enabled him to feel that he was guarding his father and protecting his interests. If he had any lingering uncertainty about those illicit activities his father was being accused of daily, he had no doubts about the League and all of the good it was doing. The League's accomplishments under Joe's leadership served to reinforce what Anthony wanted to believe of his dad, that he was the real estate broker with many dear friends in the underworld. His father was a very convincing person and when he told Anthony that the stories about him were nonsense, Anthony believed him; enough to never ask again. He felt too embarrassed to question his own father about his possible involvement in organized crime. His father was loved and respected by everyone in his family and community. Any revelations about his criminal activity would have devastated him. It was much easier for Anthony to move forward, refusing to believe anything the FBI or newspapers said about his father. The more he participated in the League, the closer they became, and the more he could focus on the undeniably admirable aspects of his father's life.

To the FBI, Joe Colombo was an elusive trophy; a prize to be captured by the most skilled hunter. No matter what the IACRL accomplished, the only Joe Colombo law enforcement wanted to know was the man who operated one of New York's biggest crime families. In fact, as Joe's reputation grew as a social activist and humanitarian, the FBI increased its efforts to destroy him. Agents worked at putting Joe on the front pages of the papers with bold headlines about his criminal lifestyle. To achieve this in 1971, they would have to dig back into their case files from years prior. Previous indictments were based on flimsy evidence, and Colombo's lawyer knew well that most of the charges were weak and unlikely to result in a conviction. Colombo had consistently challenged the validity of his arrests and exposed the harassment of law enforcement right to the media cameras

Less then one month after his perjury conviction, Joe Colombo was named "Man of the Year" by the Tri-Boro Post. The weekly newspaper, which was regarded as the official voice of the Italian-American community, announced a ceremonial dinner to honor the man who had done so much to help his people, and beleaguered people of all minorities."[cx] In January 1971, New York Magazine writer Dick Shaap published his list of the Ten Most Powerful Men in New York, placing Joe among city leaders and business giants like David and Nelson Rockefeller, Harry Van Arsdale, John Lindsay and Abe Rosenthal.[cxi]

Joe's health began to deteriorate as a consequence of stress and long hours of work. During the FBI pickets in the winter of 1971, he suffered a relapse of the Bells Palsy that had afflicted him years prior. Against his doctors' wishes, he still made it to the picket lines every night, pulling his hood tightly over his head to conceal his condition. Joe never displayed any signs of weakness to his family or friends; but the relentless pursuit by the FBI, and the demands of his various careers were wearing on Colombo, and his worries were betrayed by the sagging of his face.

In 1970 the Federal Government assumed jurisdiction over gambling cases. Local gambling operations and underground social clubs became prey for the FBI. There were many in local law enforcement that did not bother with these such gambling institutions. They refrained from raids and making arrests based on special relationships or moral beliefs. With the new FBI involvement, those men would face more serious corruption charges and federal prison time. In addition, U.S. Attorney General John Mitchell overturned a former ban on wiretapping at the federal level. It was rumored that Colombo issued orders to his men not to make mention of his name in any transmissions.[cxii] Led by U.S. Attorney Dillon, the Organized Crime Strike Force began a wiretap campaign to dismantle some of Joe's suspected gambling operations in Brooklyn and Long Island. At the same time, Dillon was at the close of an eight-day trial against Joe Junior for the silver coin melting conspiracy.

***

"We were all gathered in the Federal Courthouse awaiting the jury's verdict for my brother's case. It seemed entirely evident to us that my brother was innocent but the decision lay in the hands of the jury, so naturally we were terribly anxious. My entire family was sitting in the first two rows of the courtroom. The judge called a break for lunch while we were awaiting the jury's verdict. The tension in the courtroom was very high during these hours. Sitting across from us were James O. Druker, the Special Attorney for the Department of Justice, Special Agent Ray Tallia, and a few other government men. When we got up to exit, Dillon leaned over to Tallia and said audibly, 'You better get the exterminator and fumigate these pews!' Immediately, my father grabbed me, knowing intuitively that I was inclined to react with rage to this comment. He held me with his gaze and settled me down pretty quickly. He simply allowed them to pass by us without paying them any mind. When they'd left he said, 'Go grab Barry, walk down to their offices as a representative of the Italian-American Civil Rights League, and register a complaint with them for their conduct.' Although reluctant, I always wanted to respect my father's decisions, so I went downstairs with Barry and a few others to Dennis Dillon's office. When we knocked on the door, Dennis Dillon answered. Barry told him we were there to file a complaint. As Barry was talking, I looked past Dillon into the office and noticed a picture of my father on the wall with darts sticking in it. It was a pretty funny thing to see. When Barry finished speaking, Dennis Dillon looked at us and asked flatly, 'Are you finished?' Then he just slammed the door in our faces.

We stood there regrouping for a few minutes and then we walked over to the elevator. The door opened up and over came Drucker, Tallia, and Dillon to get on the elevator with us. They were so pissed off when they saw us that I felt Dillon and his team had the jury room bugged. If he did, he would have heard by then that they were going to clear my brother against all charges. We all crammed into the elevator together. I was with Vinnie Vingo, Fat Philly, and Barry Slotnick. Vinnie Vingo was an ex-fighter, Fat Philly was twice my size, and Barry was one of the tallest guys I'd ever seen, so we were a pretty good crew if a fight were to break out. Tallia had his gun, which was a very big revolver holstered right into his vest, no jacket, visible for all to see. He was standing right in my face, eyeing me boldly, and right in front of my lawyer he said to me, 'Anthony, I'm going to get you.' I didn't flinch and I said to him, 'You're going to get me? You take your best shot, Ray! Any way you want it, guns, fists or knives!' Then, Tallia made a little move, and because we were so cramped, Vinnie Vingo thought he was trying to clock me, so he stepped up to throw a punch at Tallia. Barry, who towered above everyone in the elevator, blocked the punch with the back of his shoulder. Then the elevator erupted into a pushing and shoving match. Words were exchanged and there was a good amount of time before the elevator and the fighting stopped. Barry's shoulder hurt pretty badly from the punch, but he had helped Vinnie avoid assaulting a Federal Officer.

The moment the elevator door opened, Dillon ran into the courtroom, waving his arms and screaming to Judge Judd, 'Your Honor, Anthony Colombo and his men just came downstairs and threatened us. They threatened my life and asked how I wanted it, with a knife or with a fist?' Dillon was beside himself; he had hated me ever since I snapped his photo back at Cantalupo Realty. I immediately cut in, 'Your Honor, that man is a liar. I never threatened him.' My father saw what was going on and he started yelling, too! The whole courtroom exploded. The Judge pounded his gavel, shouting, 'Order in the court! Please, please, everyone settle down. I know this has been an emotional day, but the jury has reached a verdict, so please, everyone, settle down.' The judge looked over at our group and added, 'I don't have to remind anyone about threats to Federal Officers.'[cxiii] All I could think was how it was okay for a Federal Officer to threaten me, though. When everyone had settled down a bit, the jury came out and announced its verdict, 'Not guilty.' Joey was free. My father was very emotional. This case was vindicating for him, not just because it established my brother's innocence, but because it was proof of the false and contrived nature of the accusations against our family."

***

The case against Joe Junior was weak from the beginning. The information regarding the case came to them in bits and pieces from Greg Scarpa. The more information Scarpa gave the government the more he asked for lump sum payments. He felt, especially with the coin melting case, that his information was leading to arrests and more money was justifiable. Around the same time, Scarpa had furnished the FBI with information in two truck heists. During the trial, the New York Offices again strongly recommended more cash from Washington for Scarpa.[cxiv] The cash was easy to obtain for the feds, and they were confident the case on Colombo Junior would stick. A conspiracy charge is not difficult to achieve at the Federal level, as no concrete evidence is required.

A conviction can be obtained solely from the testimony of a witness. The case against Joe Junior hinged entirely on the testimony of Richard Salamone. While on the stand, however, he recanted his initial sworn testimony against Joe Junior, and stated instead that the FBI had coaxed him into making false statements by offering to help save his home and business from financial collapse. His change of heart came when he realized that the FBI could not, or would not honor its promises to him. He testified that Special Agent Ray Tallia offered to recover the fifty thousand dollars Salamone had lost in a business deal. In addition, Attorney Dennis Dillon was to phone the IRS on his behalf and put a hold on fines he owed for back taxes. Dillon had also supposedly called Bankers Trust, and stopped them from foreclosing on Salamone's home. Finally, agents had promised they would help him to find employment and reissue his pistol permit.[cxv] These were all instances of bribery at the Federal level. Once Salamone had recanted his statements and testified against the FBI, the government wasted no time in locking him up.

Shortly after the verdict was announced, Richard Salamone was indicted for perjury and taken into custody that evening. Salamone had embarrassed the entire prosecution team during the trial. What Salamone reported to the court especially angered Agent Ray Tallia. He provided a detailed account of the many instances in which Tallia gave him money, including a card for the birth of his daughter. The card read, 'Here's a little something to start an account for the baby girl, signed Ray and the boys.' Further proof of the specious charges was introduced by the defense in a recorded conversation between the codefendant, David Lennard, and an FBI agent. Lennard, who was the man accused of actually melting the coins, had taped a phone conversation in which the agent told him they were not interested in convicting him; they were after bigger names.

Outside the courthouse, Colombo smiled as he walked with his arm around his wife. Reporters rushed over to him for a statement. "I don't care if they indict me and I'm found guilty. I'll go to jail for the maximum, the maximum. But when they frame my boy, I don't go for that. They framed my son and now the truth is out. Let's see if anyone investigates the government for the crimes they have committed." Like the David Hale case, this was yet another instance of the FBI engendering and committing crimes without any legal repercussions.

Chapter 9.

"Stormy Weather"

(Winter 1971)

Trucks roar out of the Staten Island Advance parking lot like a small military convoy. One of the drivers, Joseph, anxiously checks the rearview mirror as he cruises down Hyland Boulevard. He pulls into a small plaza to make a delivery. His assistant Michael grabs a bundle of papers from the back and walks up to one of the storefronts. Joseph notices a suspiciously slow car on Hyland Boulevard making a stop in the right lane. He doesn't like the looks of this. "Michael, let's go! Leave them on the curb and get in the truck." Michael asks, "Leave them here?" "Get back in the truck. We're being followed." Michael looks behind them and can't see anything. He hops back over to the truck and Joseph floors the beast out of the mall lot and back onto the Boulevard. Michael asks, "What is it?" "That black Buick. I think they're following us." Michael turns around and tries to get a look behind them. Joseph says, "Trust me." Michael watches the car from the side rearview mirror, "I think you're right. They are speeding up. They're coming up on your side." The Buick flashes its lights. The passenger waves his hand out of the window, signaling for the truck to pull over. "He is waving me over." Michael asks fearfully, "What are you going to do?" Joseph refuses to surrender. "I am not pulling over. Fuck him." The engine of the late model Buick roars as the car almost hops forward, nosing past the truck and pulling up directly beside them. The passenger, shrouded in a black ski mask, hangs out of the window yelling, "Pull over." Joseph speeds up, but the Buick is too quick and runs right up to the front of the truck. The passenger screams, "I said pull over!" Joseph shoots back, "Fuck you! I am not pulling over." The truck yanks a hard right turn down a side street off Hyland. Laying chase, the Buick fishtails, spins its tires and tries to catch up. The Buick quickly gets back alongside the big truck and, passing the nose, he cuts the truck off, forcing him to either stop or crash into their car. Mike braces himself in the high truck seat as they screech to a halt. "Fuck, Joe! What now?" Four masked men quickly exit the Buick. Mike locks his slider door as Joseph exits the truck. "Don't leave!" Mike is begging. He watches as the ominous men surround Joseph and begin to rough him up. "Fuck," he says softly, and jumps out of the vehicle. A husky man is shoving Joseph as another with a deep gravelly voice screams, "You guys think this is a fucking game? Why don't you get the fuck out of here and start walking back to the plant before you have some real problems?" "Get the fuck off him!" Joseph yells, and a fight ensues. One of the masked men hops into the truck as another man by the Buick picks up a tire iron from the trunk and walks over to the scuffle. As the men wrestle, Joseph shouts, "Guinea motherfuckers!" Joseph gets belted over the back with the tire iron and falls hard to the ground. Michael gets thrown against the side of the truck as the husky man delivers a few good kicks into his ribs. Three men from the Buick step back from the wounded. "Now you can fucking limp back!" Inside the truck, the fourth masked man with ice-blue eyes squirts lighter fluid on the stacks of newspapers. He removes a Zippo from his pocket. He tears off a page of newspaper, rolls it up into a cone, and sets it alight. The edges of the cone quickly curl and he touches the smoldering torch to the pile of papers. Flames snake out in every direction as thick black smoke begins to fill the truck. He jumps out. "Let's move," he yells to his crew. They run over to the Buick, slam the trunk shut, and get inside. The Buick tears off into the distance. Injured and disoriented, Joseph and Michael drag themselves away from the burning truck. They watch helplessly as flames consume the thousands of newspapers inside. The heat and smoke issuing from the fire make the sky above appear wavy.

✱✱✱

Across the Verrazano Narrows that day, a large group of the League's supporters were picketing the headquarters of the Staten Island Advance newspaper. The paper had recently run a story about a Grand Jury investigation of the League's activities. When the League called to ask the newspaper's director John Malone about the article, he denied knowledge of any such investigation. Anthony and his father, along with 4,000 supporters, rallied to protest in front of the Advance's offices, demanding that editor Everett Harvey be fired and that the paper publish an apology.[cxvi]

Dennis Dillon called for Grand Jury investigation into two of the incidents that occurred during the week of February 22, 1971. The first was the skirmish in the courthouse elevator. Dillon made certain that Joe Colombo was brought in for questioning, despite his knowledge that Colombo hadn't been in the elevator at all. Nor had Joe been present during the attack on the Staten Island Advance newspaper trucks, the second incident for which Dillon sought an investigation. Even the court questioned what federal laws were being violated in the picketing of a newspaper. While he could not specify any violations, Dillon continued his pursuit of the League.[cxvii] When Joe left the Grand Jury room, reporters rushed to him. He told them, "They were still very interested in the list they took from me in December. This was the topic for the day, not the Staten Island Advance.' When a reporter asked what was on the list, Joe removed the list with confidence and showed it to him, offering the same story he'd told during the Grand Jury investigation months prior. The names and figures were all from the benefit concert at the Felt Forum. Colombo added, "I did not take the Fifth Amendment in this Grand Jury. I didn't invoke any rights and I answered every question." "What about the Staten Island Advance protest, did they question you at all about that? " "No," Joe replied. "And what about the trucks that were burned? The men that were beaten up?" Joe insisted, "That had nothing to do with the League. If you want to learn something about the League then I can tell you, but that's not the League. We have close to 60,000 members. We raised 487,000 dollars at the concert the police were so interested in. We put the money towards a 3.5 million dollar property on Cropsey Avenue near the Belt Parkway. We purchased ten and a half acres to build a complex which will include a rehabilitation center, a senior citizens' home and a youth center." With a mix of pride and humor he told the reporters, "You should print that in your paper!"[cxviii]

***

On behalf of the IACRL, Anthony Colombo and Nat Marcone requested an investigation into the FBI's Organized Crime Strike Force in New York City. The testimony of Richard Salamone was sufficient to obtain an indictment. In any court of law if a person made such offers, he would be charged with bribing a federal witness. The statutory maximum for federal bribery is ten years, and twenty for witness tampering. Tallia and Dillon both avoided indictments. It took almost twenty years for the law to catch up to Agent Ray Tallia. On November 7, 1990, Tallia was indicted on sixteen counts of providing false statements and one count of conversion of government funds.[cxix] He retired from the FBI in June of 1990 during the investigation. On March 15, 1991, Tallia pled guilty to three of the felony counts against him and was sentenced to three years probation and a $4000 dollar fine.[cxx]

Back in the 1970's the League, in addition to other civil rights organizations, began a letter writing campaign to Senator Ervin of North Carolina, chairman of the subcommittee on constitutional rights. This subcommittee was the most likely to influence FBI policy, especially concerning the grey area of harassment where legality is not clearly defined. It was only a few more months before Congress, led by Senator Ervin, was forced to acknowledge the abuse of power and often illegal tactics being used by federal law enforcement.

***

"The FBI was constantly harassing my wife. They had been to the house numerous times with subpoenas from the IRS. They wanted her to testify against my father about his earnings for his income tax evasion case. The first time they subpoenaed her she was pregnant with our son, Joey, and then pregnant with our daughter, Lucille the second time. Barry Slotnick had the subpoenas lifted both times and Dennis Dillon commented to him in court, 'Is your client perpetually pregnant?' She despised Dillon and Tallia for constantly badgering her about my father's finances, so when Ray Tallia rang the bell after the incident with Boland and Welsh, she just cracked the door, took the subpoena from him and slammed the door in his face. With all she had experienced, she was through being civil with them. Then they would stand outside the house and shout through the window. 'Tell your husband we have a deal for him. You take it and you're both going to be okay; you don't, and your husband is going to go to jail for a very long time.' She knew they would go down the street and do the same things to Joe Junior's wife. Sometimes they would just shout, 'Stay away from your father-in-law! Tell your husband to stay away from his father.' My wife was proud of what I was doing with the League, and she knew well that I was a law-abiding citizen. Her only fear was that they would try to frame me like they did my brother Joey. She was also afraid that they would try and hurt me if given the chance. I had been on the news talking about the FBI to reporters, and had even spoken out against them on radio and talk shows. I knew the FBI was watching. I wasn't afraid, I figured the worst they could do was put me in jail, and then my stock as a civil rights activist would go up, so I was almost waiting for that day to come.

One day when I was leaving my house, headed to the League offices in Manhattan I saw agent Welsh parked behind my car in my driveway. I just looked at him and said, Bernie, I don't have time for this, I have to go.' Welsh got out of the car and smiled as he approached me. Boland stood back, leaning against the hood sneering at me. 'We have to talk to you, Anthony.' I said, 'Bernie please, I have nothing to say to you people, there's nothing to talk to you about. I'm not going to stay away from my father; can't you just leave me alone?' He says, 'It's not that, we really have to talk to you. This is for your benefit.' I said, 'What could you possibly have to say to me that would be for my benefit?' He leans in and starts talking softly. 'What we want from you is simple. We don't want you to rat, we don't need you to tell us about crimes, we just want you to tell us everywhere your father is going, and who he is meeting with. If you don't know where he is going maybe you can give us a little heads up when he's leaving so we can follow him; stuff like that. We're going to give you two thousand dollars a week and no one will ever know. You'll never have to enter a police station, FBI office or a courtroom, no witness stand, nothing. It will be our little secret.' So I look up at him with an interested face and said, Bernie, you're going to give me two thousand dollars a week?' He gets excited and says, 'Yeah, two thousand.' I said, 'Bernie, tell me again what I have to do to get this money?' He says, 'Just a little surveillance on him, that's it. You would never have to testify against him, never spend a day in court, and we can give you two thousand a week.' And he stresses the money again, 'Two thousand a week!' I'm nodding my head okay. And then I ask, 'You sure you're going to give me that two thousand every week?' He said, 'I guarantee it.' I said, 'Okay, Bernie, but I have one condition.' He's so satisfied, thinking he just turned Joe Colombo's son, and with great enthusiasm he says, 'Name it, name it!' I think even Boland was smiling a little at this point, and that man never smiled. 'Bernie, for two thousand I can do it, but I need you to give me the money in a check.' He is still excited, thinking I'm actually going along with this and he says, 'No, no, we are going to give it to you in cash.' As serious as I could be I replied, 'No Bernie, I need a check.' He's arguing, 'No we will give it to you in cash. Why would you want a check? You don't want a check.' Now I've got the big fish on the hook. He is looking down at me a little anxiously and I say, 'Because, Bernie, I have to claim this money on my income tax.' Right when I said that he knew I was yanking his chain. His demeanor changed so fast, he looked like I'd just shot his dog. He yells at me, 'You little cocksucker!' I yelled back, 'Leave me the fuck alone, Bernie! When are you going to stop with this shit? I have nothing to talk to you about, ever.' I got into my car and started it and they just stood there staring furiously at me for a few moments before they got into their car. They looked at me as fiercely as they could. I just sat there and got a little laugh out in the car and then they pulled off and that was it."

***

"PAPA COLOMBO GOES TO JAIL" was the bold headline of the March 6, 1971 edition of the Daily News.[cxxi] The charges stemmed from a $750,000 jewel heist which was executed in 1968. The robbery was an inside job and, according to the DA, masterminded by Robert Aaron, former manager of the Long Island Diamond and Jewelry Exchange. Another former employee aided him and three other men were indicted as co-conspirators. The jewels were fenced for $160,000 and Colombo was accused of being a mediator between the thieves who were arguing over their cut. Colombo was charged with first-degree grand larceny and second-degree conspiracy, and was ordered to be held without bail. Barry Slotnick knew immediately these were trumped up charges, but was out of town at the time and unable to be present for Joe's arraignment. Attorney Frank A. Gulotta Jr., serving as Colombo's counsel, filed a writ of Habeas Corpus, but State Supreme Court Justice Paul Widlitz denied the motion.[cxxii] Joe was remanded to the county jail.

Joe knew that this was retaliation for his public campaign against the FBI. District Attorney Cahn was rumored to have ties to FBI leader J. Edgar Hoover. Cahn was honored with an award at the National Convention of District Attorneys in 1968. Hoover was in attendance, and it was remarked that the two got along well. While Colombo sat in jail, members and supporters of the IACRL, many of whom were women, flocked to the Nassau County Courthouse to protest his imprisonment. A number of picketers carried signs claiming D.A. Cahn was a tool of the FBI and a bigot. The protesters were fervent enough that Cahn requested and received 24-hour police protection.[cxxiii] Cahn himself faced various criminal charges years later. First, he was jailed for gambling violations.[cxxiv] Then in 1974, he was involved in a corruption scandal in which hundreds of thousands of dollars were looted in a "party loyalty" scam.[cxxv] Unlike Colombo's legal exploits, the crimes of Cahn and other public officials did not appear on the front pages of the newspapers. Cahn was convicted, but only served one year in jail and was then welcomed home to a plush job as executive director of the World Association of Detectives.[cxxvi]

Anthony addressed his frustrations over his father's imprisonment to the press, "This is a vendetta against the Colombo family. This is a blatant attempt on the part of the U.S. Justice Department and the District Attorney to frame and stigmatize Italian-American people. My father has five children and three grandchildren and he loves his family dearly." He described a number of recent social projects he'd begun with the League. Supporters of Colombo could do little to affect the press, however. A photo of Joe Colombo in handcuffs appeared in every publication in the five boroughs. That image was a powerful weapon in the media campaign against Joe. Readers were simply more fascinated by Colombo the Mob magnate who ran rackets from Rhode Island to Miami. Law enforcement viewed this sinister depiction of Colombo as a victory, and did everything possible to capitalize on it.

Barry Slotnick returned to New York and immediately held a press conference at the League's offices to discuss Colombo's unconstitutional and unprecedented detainment. He told reporters that there was no legal reason for Joe to be denied bail.[cxxvii] He claimed the denial of bail was a violation of Joe's constitutional rights. Bail was intended to be set according to the defendant's likelihood to return to court. Joe had never missed a court appearance. Slotnick argued, "I have clients accused of first-degree murder who are walking the streets, but I'm afraid Mr. Colombo has become very political. I have never heard of bail being denied in a grand larceny case." Barry then accused law enforcement of monitoring a conversation he'd had with Joe at the Nassau County jail. This would have been a direct violation of the attorney-client confidentiality privilege. When the reporters asked if Joe was innocent, Slotnick answered them, "Joe told me, 'I'm innocent of all charges against me. I swear I had nothing to do with those charges. I swear on my children this is another frame.'"

As a result of a report written by the County Probation Department, Joe was released on Monday March 6th from the Nassau county jail on $25,000 bail. After dinner that evening he was on 3rd Avenue and 69th Street picketing the FBI. He was wearing his fedora and grey parka, and was joined by his sons and a crowd of supporters, which grew into the hundreds as the evening wore on. Reporters snapped photos of Joe and printed more articles describing him as the alleged head of one of New York City's Mafia families. [cxxviii] Joe spoke with passion through the bullhorn to the crowd. His resilience and tireless efforts were inspiring to those who knew him. Even Anthony questioned his father's source of strength. It was as if he never slept. He had no choice but to adopt his father's schedule. At nights they would come home from League functions, frequently very late, and after a quick snack and a nap they were up at the crack of dawn for another day of battling for the League. Joe demanded that tasks be completed quickly and exactly. He disliked enlisting the help of others for important work. To insure the job was going to get done right, he invariably preferred to do it himself. It often seemed that Joe's absorption in the League was a way for him to escape the ceaseless war being waged on him by the FBI. Two days following his release on bail, he received the sentencing for December's perjury conviction. The prosecution was demanding the maximum of five years for each count and Slotnick had already warned Joe that he might be facing some hard time. On March 11th he entered the Brooklyn courthouse to hear the verdict.

***

The courtroom is silent. Joe sits composed, awaiting the pronouncement of Judge Baer. Joe's family and friends are all packed into the room, patiently awaiting the same message. Directly behind Colombo, Jo-Jo sits beside her sister Rachel. She clutches Rachel's hand and wears a veil of hope across her face. Anthony is expressionless; stony. Baer speaks. "With this conviction, I will not agree to the maximum penalty of five years requested by the prosecution. I will however, enclose half that time, sentencing you, Joe Colombo, to two and a half years for each charge. The sentences will run concurrently." Joe evinces only a hint of defeat as he briefly closes his eyes and inhales deliberately. Barry Slotnick has been prepared for this. "Your honor, the defense would ask a continuance of bail until March 23rd. We are pending an appeal for this case and will be asking for a writ of reasonable doubt in hopes of remaining on bail during the appellate process." Judge Baer considers Slotnick's request, knowing this is not much to ask for. Personally, he would like to remand Colombo immediately, but instead says, "Bail will be continued until March 23rd." Joe's family is elated. He looks back at Jo-Jo with his customary confident demeanor and gives her a little wink. She looks at once relieved and discouraged. Joe assures her warmly, "Everything's gonna be okay."

Outside the courtroom, reporters swarm around Joe, pressing their cameras and microphones to his face. Joe says to them, "This unfortunate incident occurred because I checked the wrong boxes. They have one set of rules for the average man and a special set for Joe Colombo. I hope to God they let me out on bail while this case is appealed and leave me alone to do all the good things I want to do." Joe captivates the reporters as they vie for his attention. They are supposed to inquire about the hearing, but the truth is they wish to get answers about the one topic he avoids. They want to know the truth about his involvement in the Brooklyn underworld. They want to know if he is "The Don."

Chapter 10.

"There Will Never be Another You"

(The Godfather)

Although Mario Puzo wrote many stories about mobsters, he did his best to avoid them in his personal life. Puzo grew up in the 1930's on the West Side of Manhattan in a Neapolitan ghetto known as Hell's Kitchen. As a child he was a bit of an outcast, an unpopular kid who didn't have much success with sports or girls. Lacking companions, he spent much of his time observing others and inventing stories about them. His angst and isolation as a child, coupled with disdain for the older generation of immigrants and blue collar workers in his neighborhood shaped his perspective and infused his dramas with a sense of dark realism.[cxxix] On March 10, 1969, Mario Puzo released a book that would radically change both his life, and the face of Italian organized crime in the United States.

The fictional novel *The Godfather* (originally titled *Mafia*) became an instant success and swept the nation, selling over 700,000 hard cover copies and a few million more in paperback in its first few years. The story Puzo wrote was a 'Greek tragedy' about a father who watches as his son, whom he hoped would become a politician, is inadvertently drawn into a life of crime. It was not intended to be a novel about organized crime; it was a family epic with the criminal lifestyle as its backdrop. While so many Italian gangsters from the sixties claimed this epic film was based on their lives, Puzo maintained that the character of Don Corleone was based on the late crime boss Vito Genovese. While Marlon Brando was developing the character of Don Corleone, producer Al Ruddy furnished him with some tapes the FBI had of gangster Frank Costello, so Brando could mimic the raspy, commanding voice of the then prime minister of the Mob underworld. The film and book were so replete with real New York crime legends that it gave readers and viewers a sense of authenticity rarely achieved in fiction.

In the opening scene of the film, funeral parlor owner Amerigo Bonasera goes to Don Corleone and asks for help after two men beat his daughter. In an interesting parallel, Anthony recalled that among the many people who went to his own father seeking help was the proprietor of a Brooklyn funeral parlor.

***

"In Brooklyn, a funeral parlor owner's son was having problems. He was fooling around with hard drugs, running around in the streets and doing things that; unfortunately a lot of Italian kids were doing in Brooklyn at that time. The parlor owner came to my father and asked him if he would speak to his son. He told him he had tried everything to straighten him out and his son just wouldn't listen. He feared for his son's life and safety. People in the neighborhood had always known my father to be a peacemaker of sorts, so naturally he accepted the challenge, and sent for the man's son.

Before he met with my father, the boy's clothing was disheveled and his hair unkempt. But right after the first time he came to see my father, there was a noticeable change. He cut off his long hair, shaved his face and started dressing like a gentleman; even his demeanor seemed immediately improved. After that initial visit, he kept coming in to see my father at his office a few days every week, and my father always made time to talk to him. I never asked my father what he was saying to him, but the funeral parlor owner came to my father several times to thank him for helping with his son. He would tell stories to people in the neighborhood about how happy he was with his son's transformation, how he was so energetic again and back to being a supportive member of his family."

***

Don Corleone was simultaneously a crime boss and a peacemaker with zero tolerance for drugs. This position was mirrored in a real order issued by the Commission in 1958, which was essentially, if you used, you died. Three of the five bosses didn't adhere strictly to this dictate and would allow men to get involved in the lucrative business of drug trafficking. But the remaining two, Vito Genovese and Joe Colombo, were rigidly opposed to profiting from drugs. During this time, it was typical for wise guys, as opposed to police, to enforce social regulations and maintain order in the neighborhoods.

Many of the story elements in *The Godfather* corresponded directly to events in the "Profaci/Colombo" crime organization. During the death scene of character Luca Brasi, the line "He sleeps with the fishes," was borrowed from the disappearance of the most feared Gallo enforcer, Joe "Joe Jelly" Gioielli. Lenny Montana, the actor who played Luca Brasi was an intimidating man, standing over six feet four inches and weighing close to three hundred pounds. Joe Jelly, although only a few inches over five feet, was probably just as wide and heavy as Montana. Rumors of his death circulated after a bundle containing Gioielli's clothing wrapped in newspapers and lined with seaweed was dropped off at a Gallo hangout. Informants knew Gioielli frequently spent time fishing with Sally D. and Junior Perisco on Sheepshead Bay. The Gallos decoded the message of the seaweed- wrapped clothing. Joe Gioielli would never come back from his fishing trip. Gioielli had been missing for several weeks when detective Ralph Salerno questioned Joey Gallo, "Where's Joe Jelly, Joey?" Joey looked at him. "Don't waste your time, go catch a bookmaker, and maybe they'll make you police Commissioner. But don't waste your time looking for Joe Jelly, you'll never find him."[cxxx]

Another story appropriated by Puzo, which was mentioned earlier in this book, was the attempted murder of Larry Gallo at the Sahara Lounge in Brooklyn, 1961. In just the way Frank Pentageli unsuspectingly went to meet the Rosato brothers in *The Godfather Part II*, Larry Gallo went to meet John Scimone to discuss a truce during the Gallo/Profaci war. Although Scimone was a Profaci associate, Gallo believed him to be an ally, and was thrown off when he was handed a mysterious hundred-dollar bill. The gentlemen went in the empty bar to sit down and talk. As Scimone went to use the bathroom, the barman Charley Clemenza made small talk with Gallo. Then from the shadows a sash cord was looped around Gallo's neck. He fought until he lost consciousness, but he did not die, and police believe he was given a message during the near-fatal struggle. At that moment, exactly as in the book and film, a patrolman entered the dark lounge, questioning the manager. Clemenza assured him everything was okay, but while the officer scanned the dim room, he noticed a pair of legs on the bar floor; Scimone and the two gangsters escaped through the front door, passing Officer Malvin Blei. One of the hoods, presumed to be Sally D., fired at Blei, hitting him in the face with a slug. Larry Gallo and the officer survived that day. The police believed Larry was kept alive so his attackers could discover the whereabouts of his crew. A more popular belief was that Persico and Sally D. wanted to relay a message to him about what they'd done to his good friend Joe Jelly.

Additional stories from Puzo's book can also be linked to other real crimes that occurred in New York during the 1960's. The fictional assassination of Sonny Corleone could have been an adaptation of the attempt made on Bill Bonnano's life during the shooting on Troutman Street where, unlike Sonny Corleone, young Bonanno survived.

***

The interesting facts about this film don't just lie in the similarities between the Colombo organization and Corleone family. Most people do not know that Joe Colombo was directly involved with producers of the film before shooting even began. In 1971, during their anti-defamation campaign, the Italian-American Civil Rights League became pivotal in the film's history, first by protesting production, and later by aiding the producers and contributing to the film's authenticity. At first the announcement that the book would be turned into a film scandalized Italian-Americans, as they were concerned about their stereotypical and unfavorable depiction. Both the local Italian-American community, and also associations such as the Order of the Sons of Italy (OSIA) and A.I.D. viewed the book and the film as harshly and unfairly stigmatizing Americans of Italian descent. While the letters and protests directed at Paramount Films had little impact on the film, the influence of the IACRL under the leadership of Joe Colombo would prove to be formidable.

Many stories about Joe's involvement in *The Godfather* paint a picture similar to old Hollywood gangster flicks with clichéd one-liners and strong-arming from thugs and hoods. Bob Evans, an executive at Paramount, claimed Joe Colombo personally called him and threatened him if he moved forward with the picture. Evans copped out quickly, arguing that he wasn't making the film, Al Ruddy was. According to Evans, Joe responded, "When we kill a snake, we chop its fucking head off."

Anthony doesn't confirm or deny that his father spoke to Bob Evans, but he does insist that his father would never make a statement like that; he would never call someone on the phone and threaten him. It was simply not in his father's character to do so. Further, since his phone lines were all tapped during those years by the FBI, if he'd made a call threatening Bob Evans, wouldn't agents have done anything in their power to arrest him? Anthony says, "The truth was we didn't need to make threats to stop the picture, if we didn't want it made in New York it wouldn't have been made, period. At the time the League had over 40,000 members and the majority of them were blue-collar workers who believed in the power of protest. The entire Italian-American community was waiting to hear our next move with the picture. My father stressed the importance of non-violence because he knew that strength lay in the hearts of the people, not in their fists."

The purpose of the League was to combat defamation and stereotyping, especially in motion pictures and television. To that end, the League planned to organize a union strike, which would deprive the film crew of drivers and deliveries. League captains instructed members to stop all communication with the film's producers, who had intended to use many of their Long Island and Little Italy homes and businesses as shooting locations. There were Italian-American actors and entertainers who also dropped out of the picture because of their loyalty to the League. Frank Sinatra, who was a leader of the Americans of Italian Descent, was vociferously opposed to the film being made, calling Puzo a thief of news stories who sold out his own people to pay off his gambling debts.

***

Francis Ford Coppola strolls down Broome Street in Little Italy, with his cinematographer Gordon Willis. They meet up with a duo of production assistants who have just finished parking the giant, sparkling clean Cinemobile. The group gazes admiringly at the truck, which is a truly impressive vehicle. An assistant asks Coppola, "Should we take out the boxes, get the camera set up right here?" "No," he replies, "let's walk around first and get an idea of what we want to shoot. We can grab lunch and take in the neighborhood while we eat." As the group strolls down Mulberry, Coppola inspects every inch of the street. This neighborhood is his set; the backdrop for his picture, and he pores over its details like a shopper looking for the perfect fruit. He combs his burly black beard with his fingers and squints behind his tinted glasses. Gordon rather nervously adjusts the pinky ring on his right hand.

They reach Hester St. and take a table inside Umberto's. They are greeted warmly by the wait staff and are served a generous meal of pasta and seafood. Excited to begin production, the men make their way back to their van after they eat. Francis keeps them laughing while he tells them about Bob Evans' ridiculous suggestion for the role of Michael Corleone. He hates Evans, not because he is his superior, but because he knows nothing about the art of film. As the group turns the corner onto Broome, they fall silent upon seeing the empty parking space where the Cinemobile was supposed to be. An assistant asks, "Is this the street?" Francis is confident, "Yeah, it is." The men all look at each other. Their prized vehicle and all of their camera equipment have vanished. Apparently no one in the neighborhood has seen a thing, and the crew realizes how presumptuous they have been. They are not welcome here; the residents of Little Italy have not given them permission to film, and Paramount will need to revise its strategy if The Godfather is going to be realized.

***

Bob Evans could either work with the IACRL or shoot the film on a back lot in Hollywood, without its star director. Evans' decision to collaborate with the League proved more than profitable. Ruddy recalls, "Bob Evans called me and said you have to go see this guy Joe Colombo; they don't want this movie to be made. So I planned on going to the Park Sheraton and speaking with these men about the picture."

On March 10, 1971, just one day before Joe was to be sentenced for his perjury conviction, Al Ruddy arrived at a League meeting to discuss the film. Ruddy was up against an army of around six hundred League supporters at the Park Sheraton that evening, and one wrong statement could have proved ruinous. A full time schoolteacher and league officer, Dick Cappazola remembers that night; "I was very opposed to the picture being made at all, and I think in hindsight I was right. But Joe thought the picture and the alignment with Hollywood could help the League. Well, when I spoke that evening the room was filled to capacity. I wasn't for it being made, and I was never a yes man in my life, and Joe knew I was coming to the mic' with some harsh words. Before I got a chance to speak Joe says, 'I want everyone to know who this fellow is that's coming up to the microphone. This is Dickey, and he is my button man.[2]' I said to myself, 'Holy shit'. I had the place looking at me sideways for a minute until Joe explained to everyone that I had designed the League's logos and buttons, and was in charge of producing them. It was good for a laugh, even Joe smiled."

During the meeting, concerned Italian-Americans harshly criticized the book, while others asked questions about Ruddy's intentions. Al was given a fair chance to explain the film and how it was not meant to defame Italian-Americans. His firm demeanor, raspy voice and guileless answers were the elixir Paramount needed that night to assuage the League's fears. He explained that other ethnicities in the film were similarly portrayed in a negative light. He also argued that despite their occupations, the members of the Corleone family were the heroes of the story. Joe Colombo didn't do much talking; he allowed Nat Marcone and the other League officials to work with Ruddy. Joe just listened and watched, carefully monitoring the emotions in the room and carefully studying Ruddy. Al recalls:

"I knew very little about the League before I went to the meeting. I really didn't know much about Joe either. I had heard he was a very levelheaded and fair guy. At the time there were a lot of people in the community that didn't want to see this movie being made, and I understood that. When you keep talking about the 'Mob,' people automatically assume you're talking about Italians, when really there's organized crime in every ethnicity, from Russians, Irish to the Jews. But Hollywood was in love with the Italians. Joe hated the term 'Mafia,' because it gave people the

---

[2] Hit-man

impression that the Italians were the only ones committing crimes. I had no trouble understanding what Joe was talking about at the meeting. At the time, I didn't just agree to take the words out, but I understood the man. After the League meeting, I invited Joe to come down to my office and have a more personal meeting and maybe look at the script. Joe showed up to my office that next day with Caesar Vitale, and Butter, Colombo's driver, and I showed them the 150-page script. The meeting only lasted five or ten minutes so there was no way anyone was going to read it. Joe told me his concerns about the story and how he wanted certain words removed from the screenplay and I told him I would have no problem with that, and we made a deal. We had a very short meeting and Joe got what he wanted and so did I. After we'd agreed to work together, Joe felt it was a good idea to get the word out to the community about the alliance. He asked me to come down to the League offices and do a press conference. I thought there would be a few cameras from some local Italian news stations; I had no idea the entire media would be there."

As Al Ruddy strolled into the League offices on March 19th, he was a bit surprised to see the mass of news reporters waiting. Ruddy did his best to answer questions and explain the simplicity of the deal that was made, but reporters disbelieved the collaboration could have been so legitimate. During the press conference, Ruddy agreed to allow the League to make a few changes to the script by removing the words "Mafia and "La Cosa Nostra," and he also offered to donate the premier's proceeds to the League's hospital benefit fund. With that announcement, Ruddy had obtained the key to the Italian-American community; the full support of Colombo and the IACRL.

Anthony reflects about Al Ruddy and the deal:

"He deserves a lot of respect, in my eyes Al Ruddy was the hero of *The Godfather*. Even though Bob Evans spent a lot of his life taking credit for that movie, I heard he was afraid to come to New York during production. Al was the perfect man to come and negotiate with my father. If Hollywood had sent a man like Bob Evans to New York to negotiate, things would have ended differently. Al was very straightforward; he was a native New Yorker so he could speak the language. Hollywood guys can get a little ahead of themselves, and that kind of pretentiousness would have turned my father off immediately. Al was a likeable guy, and you could feel his strong sense of commitment. That type of passion and confidence demanded respect, and he got it from my father.

He knew Hollywood made millions exploiting certain groups and promoting violence. Producers walked into any neighborhood in the nation and people were usually impressed by their presence, so they were used to getting whatever they wanted. I think Paramount was in shock more than anything when they got wind of how much control we had in the city. My father explained to me the importance of the alignment with Paramount. I remember riding in the car and discussing the deal with him and he told me, 'This is bigger than a few words in a script. This display of non-violent protest and its results will again prove to the people in our communities that we are results driven. The press, the politicians, Hollywood, they can hate us now, but in time they will all follow the people. So we make this win for the people.'"

***

Media coverage of the press conference was extraordinarily inconsistent. Some praised the League for its accomplishments, saying the League "showed its strength and unity."[cxxxi] But only a few papers ran the story the way it happened; many attempted to depict the alignment as a backdoor deal Ruddy made with mobsters. Articles insinuated bribes and coercion, and even implied that Paramount was working side by side with the 'Mafia.' One article claimed that Puzo believed Italian-Americans controlled organized crime in America.[cxxxii] As calls poured into the Gulf and Western offices, cantankerous CEO Charlie Bludhorn demanded in a fit of rage that Ruddy be fired immediately for getting involved with Colombo, a reputed mobster. The irony of this tirade would be revealed years later, when Bludhorn himself was almost jailed for having ties to Mob-connected bankers in Europe.[cxxxiii]

While Bludhorn controlled the future of Paramount Pictures' financing, he lacked the vision that Al Ruddy possessed. Even as Bludhorn was chastising him, Ruddy responded calmly, "If you think I'm going to apologize for what I did, you're mistaken." Bludhorn shouted, "You've wrecked my company! I've tried to go legit all of these years and look what you've done! I'm firing you and disavowing everything you've done!" Al said, "No hard feelings. I got my deal, my money, it's your company, see you around." He left the meeting, returned to his hotel room and packed his bags, planning to head back to Los Angeles.

After the meeting, Ruddy recalls, "Bob Evans was out of town at the time and he called me. And told me the reason I got fired was for not apologizing for what I did. I said I wasn't going to apologize, so what can I tell you, I'm out. Bludhorn called Francis [Ford Coppola] up and said 'Al Ruddy is a fucking nut. He's just wrecked my company and he was fired.' Francis told him, 'You better not let Al Ruddy leave New York or the movie will stop.' Needless to say I got a quick call telling me to go back and see Charlie Bludhorn. I went back up to Columbus Circle to the Gulf and Western offices and he said, 'If you ever talk to anyone in the press I will kill you with my own hands!' I said, 'Calm down, Charlie.' And I was back on the movie again. The only reason Bludhorn fired me was the way they wrote the story in the media, saying we had made a deal with the 'Mafia,' and that was his prerogative, but it was my prerogative to make a good movie and I did what I had to do. And I was never going to cop out, and I didn't apologize for what I did and that's why they fired me."

***

A number of editorials criticized the League's alignment with Paramount Pictures. Some claimed the caricatures of Italian-Americans on TV and in films were innocuous, that the League was out of touch with the "real world" and that broken English was a "charming manner of speech."[cxxxiv] Senator Marchi strenuously objected, calling such depictions a "monstrous insult" to millions of "loyal Americans of Italian Extraction."[cxxxv]

Pete Hamil, an editor for the New York Post lampooned Joe and the IACRL. He ridiculed the League's efforts to ban words like "Mafia" and "La Cosa Nostra," and suggested that these were the only "injustices" the League was combating. He described the typical League members as ostentatious, clad in suits and diamond pinkie rings, while the guy who works for an honest living is demeaned. The Mob guys take their glossy blonds to the title fights, drink the best whiskey, and have the wife at home.[cxxxvi] There could be no greater mischaracterization of Joe than that he was living this plush life while the workingman was supporting the League. Joe believed the League belonged to the people and it would be impossible to find a person in the organization that put in more hours or took on more responsibility. Joe received plenty of support from his wife Jo-Jo and his sons, Anthony in particular. Joe encouraged Anthony and guided him politically, hoping that he would one day cross over from community activist to public official. While the leaders of other Italian organizations tried to claim credit for many of the League's accomplishments, Joe knew it was Anthony and the other League officers that were battling in the trenches and surmounting overwhelming obstacles.

✸✸✸

The Godfather encountered obstacles at every turn, even before the presence of the IACRL. Although they had a number-one best seller in their possession, the executives at Paramount did not believe America would be interested in *The Godfather*. Actors were backing out, and the ones that Ruddy and Coppola wanted, the studio and parent company (Gulf & Western) didn't want. The Hollywood elite is like the political elite, always claiming they know what the people want, when the truth is they are so far removed that they usually achieve just the opposite. Stanley Jeffe was so vehemently opposed to having Marlon Brando in the film he screamed there would be no way Brando would play the Don as long as he was president of Paramount. Bob Evans would consistently get infuriated with Coppola and his casting choices. He referred to Al Pacino as "Little Dwarf," and made suggestions for actors that, had they been adopted, would have likely ruined the cinematic masterpiece. But both Ruddy and Coppola were stubborn and fought tooth and nail for their visions of the film. Eventually the cast they had hand-picked were all signed onto the groundbreaking picture.

When production finally began on the movie, many roles were given to members of the League as a result of its new relationship with Al Ruddy and Paramount. It only made sense that if they wanted to portray authentic New York Italians, they would cast some actual New York Italians. The wedding photographer in the opening scene was the IACRL photographer Joe Labella. Actor Gianni Russo credits Joe Colombo for his entire career in entertainment, which began with his role as Carlo Rizzi in *The Godfather*. He remembers meeting with the producers of the film at the Gulf and Western offices, along with Joe, Anthony, Caesar and League Attorney Barry Slotnick. According to Russo, "I wanted to be in the film and I know Joe's influence gave me the role of Carlo. If not, I would have probably been some guy in the crowd somewhere. In hindsight I don't know what I'd be doing today if I never got in that film."

After its film debut, *The Godfather* went on to win three of its eleven Academy Award nominations, five of its seven Golden Globe nominations, and it currently sits in the number two slot in the American Film Academy's top one hundred films of all time. But it is the making of this film, which was fraught with conflict and mystery that has become the topic for numerous books and documentaries.

"Everyone that was on that movie was born to be there," Ruddy recalls. "I know that beyond a shadow of a doubt. Gordon Willis, Francis, Me, Marlon. When something like that happens, it is unexplainable in this business, it's the perfect storm. There were all kinds of problems, no one wanted Marlon [Brando], no one wanted Al [Pacino]. They called him a midget and didn't want to see him in it even after we began shooting. We had to fight for everything, especially the money. Paramount had just made 'Brotherhood' and it didn't make any money, so even with a best-selling book they didn't want to risk a penny. After we made the deal with the League, we were in the New York Times and the Wall Street Journal. The movie was escalated right up into the headlines. Then you had the shootings in New York that were right around the time the movie was being filmed. Things started feeding off each other and it became a real event. It was a constellation of the gang wars, Hollywood turmoil, the League, and the newspapers. But something magical happened with this film." Ruddy reflects, "All the right people showed up at the right time."

During the shooting of *The Godfather,* Al didn't get to see much of Joe Colombo. Joe was contravening frivolous indictments by the FBI, protesting alongside League members, and spending time with his family. Ruddy remembers that, "Joe didn't look like the type of guy to care about a Hollywood movie set. I met Joe again in Staten Island; he had helped me secure the location for the house used in the opening wedding scene. I have to say, Joe was very helpful. He offered things that we couldn't get and they were delivered to us at no cost, no questions asked. It was all out of respect. He was a businessman and you got that from the way he carried himself. Now that I think back, I never really got to know Joe Colombo. I should have tried to spend more time with him, I'm sure he was quite an amazing guy. I remember an FBI agent I knew, many years later saying to me, 'You know what, Ruddy? You lived in the salad days of crime in New York with the Colombo gang.' I said, 'What do you mean?' He said, 'Al, these were businessmen, they were family men that lived by a code, they're not like these half-wit wannabes that are out there now, shooting and killing people for no reason. Joe Colombo, he was from a different class of organized crime. You saw the best when you met those guys, and now those days are over.' I mean just to think back, when I made the deal with Joe, we shook hands and that was the end of it, and that doesn't happen in Hollywood, ever! Without our making the deal with Joe and the League, I don't think that movie would have ever been made, and even if it had, it wouldn't be the movie we call *The Godfather* today."

Chapter 11.

"Why Try to Change Me Now"

(March & April 1971)

Nearly two hundred people are packed into the Huntington Town House catering hall in Long Island to honor Joe Colombo as "Man of the Year." The impeccably attired guests feast on baked salmon in champagne sauce, followed by chateaubriand and honeyed Belgian carrots.[cxxxvii] *Nat Marcone stands at the podium at the edge of the dance floor. He looks out at the room full of guests and says with pride, "It is my privilege to introduce to you the father of our entire organization; the man we are honoring on this beautiful night, Mr. Joseph Colombo Senior." As the band strikes up an entrance tune, the guests filling the dining room stand, raise their drinks, and applaud. Joe Colombo walks slowly across the floor with a humble smile as he buttons the top button of his suit. The guests chant in unison, "One! One! One! One" Nat Marcone holds up the 14-karat gold plaque for Joe, shakes his hand and says, "On behalf of the officials and all of the members of the Italian-American Civil Rights League, I present this gold plaque to Mr. Colombo, Man of the Year." Joe allows a few moments for the applause to die down and begins his acceptance speech. "Thank you very much. I have said before that we are building a stairway to heaven, and on this night we take one more step on our way to*

God." He holds his finger up like a warning from a parent. "I want you to remember one thing." Joe steps off the podium with the microphone in his hand. "We've got a lot of work to do and we can't get discouraged. Don't ever let them say to you it's Joe Colombo's League." He shakes his head emphatically. "It's not. It doesn't belong to me, and it never did. I am proud to say that you blessed me as its father, but I would die brokenhearted if this League would ever let the people down. This is our struggle, and together we will triumph." He picks up a rose from a vase on a table. "This rose symbolizes the plight of the Italian-American people in this country. From the thorns a thing of beauty has grown. Do you pledge your continued support tonight? Will we continue to work together to demonstrate our strength, our commitment, our solidarity? Now I want to hear your applause." The audience roars. Colombo replaces the microphone and moves away from the podium. He turns and smiles and catches his daughter in his arms as she runs over to him. Everyone in the room chants, "One! One! One! One!"

Everyone in the room knows a different Joe Colombo. Many are acquainted with him only recently through his work with the League. Some are old cohorts from the neighborhood who have watched him become a community leader over the years. There are numerous family members who know Joe on a more intimate level, having shared holidays, vacations and personal memories with him and there are a handful of men suspected to know him in a more clandestine capacity. Regardless of how these people came to meet Joe or how much they actually know of him, they all acknowledge Joe's impressive character. At one time or another they have observed his great generosity, his integrity, his composure under pressure. Whether they have witnessed him

Colombo: The Unsolved Murder

attack or defend, love or educate, their image of Colombo cannot be assailed by any newspaper reporter or FBI agent.

***

Reporters loved Joe Colombo. Never in the history of organized crime had there been a suspect so willing to talk. Following his speech at the awards ceremony, Joe was surrounded by cameras and microphones, and immediately, he was asked, "Mr. Colombo, are you a boss of the Mafia?" Unruffled, Joe answered politely, but directly, "No, I am definitely not a crime boss. They [the police] have been following me around for years. I am kept under such surveillance, I couldn't possibly do anything wrong if I wanted to."[cxxxviii] The reporter continued, "Is there a Mafia?" Joe replied firmly, "No, there is not!" The reporter was unconvinced. Few people doubted the existence of the Mafia. The FBI had a team of street informants all reporting that Colombo was not only a member of, but the leader of one of the five "families" of Italian organized crime in New York City. Joe steadfastly and publically denied that such an organization even existed. This may have been due in part to the fact that many men in organized crime did not adopt the labels "Mafia" or "La Cosa Nostra." Nonetheless, it certainly appeared paradoxical that one of the IACRL's principal goals was the removal of such terms from the public's vocabulary. Colombo's insistence that the Mafia didn't exist seemed foolish and duplicitous to most people. For those who were unacquainted with Joe's work with the League, he was perceived as a dishonest man trying to dupe people by creating a civil rights league. The media employed every opportunity to exploit this flaw in Joe's image, and tried to blanket the entire Italian-American Civil Rights League with this sense of illegitimacy and dishonesty.

Aldo Tambellini, an Italian artist and activist living in the Lower East Side of Manhattan, knew nothing of Joe Colombo before he first witnessed him at a Park Sheraton League meeting. After hearing about the League's courageous efforts against the FBI, but then noticing its unfavorable depiction in the press, he wanted to discover the truth. "I entered the filled to capacity ballroom at the Park Sheraton Hotel. We saw several men sitting on a stage and one of them was at the microphone addressing the audience. I learned later that the speaker was Nat Marcone, the president, a former union leader. He was delivering a report on the League's recent activities. Anthony Colombo, the vice president, spoke and then Joe Colombo addressed the audience. Here was a short, energetic, very charismatic man in his mid-forties who in a reasonable time had the audience's total attention. As he spoke, he became larger than life-size."[cxxxix]

Tambellini described the League meeting as "highly informative, heightening my awareness and providing supportive data of the realities of the time." At a later date, Tambellini contacted Joe, and with his permission began documenting the activities of the League. Tambellini soon recognized evidence of a conspiracy many of the League officers were complaining about. "Despite all of these positive activities and a swelling of membership drawn from blue-collar workers and family people, the New York media had unleashed a defamatory attack on the League to discourage participation and membership."[cxl]

While friends and family admired Joe for his valiant efforts with the League, his role as a social reformer was highly objectionable to his associates in the underworld. Carl Gambino, Joe's most trusted friend, gradually withdrew his support for the League. It was suspected that Carl was displeased with Joe for his frequent public appearances and his willingness to talk to the media. Colombo was inviting unwanted attention, and despite his insistence that the Mafia didn't exist, other leaders of organized crime didn't want it to be the subject of discussion. Carl did not attend the benefit dinner at the Town House and had not been to a League event since the Felt Forum concert in November. Criticism from his clandestine counterparts did nothing to dissuade Joe from advancing the League's agenda. In fact, as a man who was only motivated by opposition, he grew more stubborn and emboldened. Joe must certainly have known that in distancing himself from these once powerful allies, he was likely creating equally formidable enemies.

On March 23rd, Joe was intended to begin his prison sentence for his perjury conviction. The appeal however, was still pending and Slotnick succeeded in getting the sentencing postponed for a few more weeks. Outside the courtroom a reporter asked Joe, "What is your reaction to Judge Baer's decision today?" Joe answered, "I believe that the law of our land and the judges are fair. I should be treated the same as anyone else." The reporter then remarked, "But you feel you're being railroaded?" Joe replied, "I definitely feel I'm being railroaded." Regardless of Joe's feelings for the FBI, he still maintained faith in the judicial system. His protests were not directed at the entire government. He believed there were a select few responsible for the harassment of his family and Italian-Americans in general; specifically, FBI director J. Edgar Hoover and Attorney General John Mitchell. Joe did not believe that the suspension of civil liberties was intended to protect national security, particularly since these new laws were targeting neighborhood gambling operations.

Indeed, other government officials echoed his beliefs. Emanuel Celler, Chairman of the House Judiciary Committee, said of Mitchell's wiretapping laws, "If there are no brakes placed upon the right of the Attorney General to tap wires, we're certainly tending toward a police state."[cxli] NBC correspondent Sherman Jackson reported, "Last year, the League's protest against the FBI culminated with a march on City Hall, This year they promise to march on Washington. They are protesting what they describe as harassment tactics by the Organized Crime Strike Force under Attorney General Mitchell." Anthony Colombo told Jackson during an interview outside the FBI offices, "We are asking the FBI for justice. Ultimately, we will achieve it, but I would say there are two ways this could go. Either in a month and a half we will end it (the picketing of the FBI offices), and have a mass march on Washington. Or we will let it run right into Unity Day, which will be June 28th in Columbus Circle."[cxlii]

***

"During our fight against the Organized Crime Strike Task Force and the FBI I learned things about people that changed my perception of the world. My father had always told me to respect every man I met, from the President of the United States to the bum on the street corner. This changed when they framed my brother. It was the first time I ever witnessed the deception of which our own government was capable. Our tax dollars were actually being used to investigate innocent people. I still shudder to think of the amount of money and time that was wasted following my family and friends. They had carte blanche to investigate whomever they wanted. In early April of '71, I received phone call from a reporter named Judith Michaelson at the New York Post. She told me she was running a piece highlighting the public officials who were sympathetic to our cause. She asked us to send her a list of all of the officials who were both honorary and actual members.

The next day she phoned me at the offices and asked, 'Anthony, are you sure this information is accurate?' I said, 'Of course it is.' She warned me, 'You can't lie to the press.' I told her flatly, 'I'm not lying.' She said, 'Well I called Governor Rockefeller's office and they said he is not associated with the League; he's not an honorary member and he never was.' I said, 'That's not true.' She said, 'If we find out that you are lying to us, Anthony, we will never print a piece for you again, and we will never believe you when you speak on behalf of your organization.' By this point I was frustrated and probably a little belligerent. I said, 'The governor's lying.' She said, 'How can you say that? You're telling me that the governor is lying and not you?' 'That's exactly what I'm telling you.' 'Well, that doesn't make any sense, Anthony.' I suggested to her, 'Come down to our offices and I will give you absolute proof that he was an honorary member of the League. Then you can determine for yourself who's lying. If you find that I'm lying to you, you can print that in your paper. But if the governor is lying, I want you to do the same thing to him.' She came down to the offices and I produced the photos we had of Governor Rockefeller at a League event wearing his honorary League pin. She was rather stunned and said, 'I guess the governor was lying.' The next day, on the second page of the New York Post next to our article was a photo of the Governor wearing the League pin on his lapel.

***

The piece on the Italian-American Civil Rights League was titled *The Colombo League's VIP's*[cxliii] The article listed all of the politicians and assorted leaders who had been associated with the League, and did not fail to mention the denial of honorary membership by a spokesperson at the Governor's office. Michaelson didn't explicitly call him a liar, but she printed the photo of Joseph DiCicco affixing the League pin to Governor Rockefeller's lapel. Michaelson interviewed Deputy Mayor Richard Aurelio, who said there would be no reason to refuse honorary membership status "unless an organization is proved to be doing something contrary to the law."[cxliv] Aurelio continued, "The League has shown tremendous initiative, fantastic, the very fact that they would get all the leading people to become honorary members...The record should show that the League has worked with the city in a constructive way ... This project for a hospital in Brooklyn is not an insignificant project. It's one of the most interesting things they've done. They were helpful to me personally in getting the community in Corona to accept the compromise [on the houses], at a time when the [Vito] Battista people were claiming it was a fraud. They supported the plan, and played a very constructive role there."[cxlv]

Deputy Mayor Aurelio and Mayor Lindsay had been proponents of the IACRL and in fact, Mayor Lindsay beat two Italian candidates in the fall election of 1970; Mario Procaccino and State Senator John Marchi. Marchi, who was strongly opposed to anything the League was doing, alienated himself from the Italian voters who were sympathetic to the organization. Marchi was one of the only politicians who spoke out against the League. He was vehemently opposed to its activities because of Joe Colombo's involvement. Marchi found it impossible to separate Joe's alleged Mob ties from his work with the League. He believed that no man with Joe's reputation could do anything good for society. Until the formation of the League, the Italians hadn't been considered a voting bloc and they were largely ignored during political campaigns. The League did not endorse a political party or support any one candidate, but Lindsay astutely recognized that the community had been estranged from politics for years, so he made efforts to address the concerns of this constituency. After this election, all New York politicians recognized the Italians as a solid voting bloc, and endorsements or not, they needed to be on the good side of the League.

***

On April 2nd, the FBI indicted Joe on two counts of gambling and conspiracy. He and 30 other men were accused of operating a 10 million dollar a year gambling ring. Joe was alleged to be the mastermind of the entire operation. According to the indictment he, "supervised, managed, and directed the financial and record-keeping phase of the illegal gambling activities, as well as controlling the operation."[cxlvi] Leading the investigation was the head attorney for the Organized Crime Strike Force, Denis Dillon. During the arraignment, one of Colombo's lawyers, Jacob Lefkowitz, told Dillon they had already known about the indictment, which is why they'd offered to surrender Colombo to the FBI before they arrested him. Lefkowitz claimed they had a wiretap on the Justice Department's downtown Brooklyn offices. Dennis Dillon admitted he received the call from Colombo's lawyers well before a warrant was issued; he told the judge, "Apparently there's been a leak." Lefkowitz boasted, "That's right, there was a leak. There was a tap on your line."[cxlvii] Dillon became incensed, demanding that Lefkowitz explain the taps on the government lines. Lefkowitz didn't reveal much beyond raised eyebrows and a smirk, which only infuriated Dillon further. Joe viewed Dillon's loss of composure as evidence of his insecurity. Joe himself was always perfectly poised in court; impeccably attired in his custom tailored brown pin-striped suit, he was stoic, never betraying anxiety or frustration. The Magistrate called for order and demanded to get on with the bail proceedings. Despite knowing that the maximum sentence for the charge was five years and a $10,000 fine, Dillon pushed for $100,000 bail for Colombo. Lefkowitz cited Colombo's flawless court appearance record and he was granted bail for $25,000. A tiny smile of satisfaction flickered across his face while Dillon's jaw clenched from stress.

Joe Colombo continually eluded the FBI. The more difficult he was to snare, the more alluring a target he became. He only used a telephone on rare occasions and when he did it was for personal use. He was extraordinarily well-insulated and avoided contact with any neighborhood bookies or loan sharks. He had a few suspected associates who managed all of his business dealings; Nicholas Mainello, Peter Candarini, and childhood friend, Joseph "Joey Notch" Iannaci.[cxlviii] The FBI tailed these men to suspected stash houses in Brooklyn on Cropsey and Bath Avenues. Mainello was photographed picking up and dropping off suspicious brown bags, which Dennis Dillon argued in court contained money and policy slips. Dillon was armed with 95 days of recorded conversations in which suspected Colombo racketeers complained about "sloppy records," along with other incriminating statements.[cxlix] At Petey's Leather shop on Cropsey Avenue, agents confiscated an adding machine and a few stacks of policy slips.[cl] Dillon did not have much to tell the judge about Colombo's direct involvement other than an eyewitness account of Joe entering the shop on February 15, 1971. The FBI knew their source could not be used as a witness in court. Greg Scarpa had been feeding them information about Colombo's suspected rackets for close to ten years and they could not risk outing him for a simple gambling bust. He claimed pay offs to the local Police were up to 5 grand a month and the weekly grosses were sometimes totaling 100 grand. He was also expanding on intelligence from the normal truck heists he told them about to newer rackets in stolen securities. In the eyes of the FBI, Scarpa was considered a "close confidant of Joe Colombo." They would continue to approve cash payments and gather intelligence.[cli]

One day before Joe's gambling indictment, he was granted another twelve-day stay by Judge Harold Baer for his pending perjury sentence. Outside the Brooklyn courthouse, Joe bumped into defense attorney William Kunstler, a civil rights attorney and activist, who had been described in the New York Times as "without a doubt the country's most controversial and perhaps its best-known lawyer, period"[clii] After the two men embraced, reporters flocked to Kunstler and asked him for a few words about Joe. Kunstler replied, "He's a fighter for civil rights."[cliii] When they turned to interview Joe, he announced he would hold a press conference about the ruling at the League offices. At the press conference, he discussed the FBI's intrusive tactics and argued that the nation was on its way to becoming a police state. "They're everywhere we are. They've even bugged our bedrooms. And I say, our bedrooms today, yours tomorrow."[cliv] The reporters listened attentively to Joe, but they did not honestly believe him. He came across as an affable man with intelligence and a knack for evading prison, but they viewed this rhetoric about the FBI as nonsense. They generally accepted the stories fed to them by the police and FBI that all of the League supporters had either been duped or coerced into being members. Joe enumerated the League's goals and accomplishments as much as he could, but again, the reporters were really only interested in his criminal ties.

***

Four men from the IACRL sit at either side of the massive podium in the Park Sheraton Hotel's Grand Hall. Chandeliers drench the room with a warm white light through thousands of dangling crystals. Hazy spirals of cigarette smoke hang in the air. From the rear of the room, a wheelchair slowly rolls along the carpet, as dozens of men and women stand aside to allow its passage. The young boy seated in the chair can be no more than ten years old. He is escorted by Father Louis Gigante. At the dais, Steve Aeillo, a distinguished looking young Italian man, passes the microphone to Father Gigante. He adjusts his glasses and gazes for a moment at his attentive audience. "Ladies and gentlemen, I have with me tonight a very special guest who has traveled all the way across the Atlantic Ocean to be here. Now, just a few short months ago, some of you may remember we received a letter from a family in Italy asking for our help in transporting their son to the United States to have surgery. He suffered from a rare heart condition which could not be treated in his small village. As a result of your contributions, Antonio is here tonight only a few weeks after a very successful surgery. He wanted to say a few words to you all." Tears are already streaming down the faces of the women, and many of the men in the room. Gigante continues, "He cannot speak English so I am going to translate what he has to say." The priest leans down and listens as the boy whispers a few sentences into his ear. "He wanted to come here and thank everyone that answered his prayers. He could not have received this medical attention back in Italy. He has also come to meet the man who helped save his life, Joe Colombo. Without his help, he does not think he would be alive right now." Everyone turns to look at Joe, who takes a slow breath and rises from his seat to walk over to the young boy. Joe reaches the young boy and very tenderly and respectfully shakes his hand. He looks into the child's eyes with an affection that is palpable to everyone in the room. In his best English the boy says, "Thank you Joe Colombo. It is an honor to finally meet you." Joe kneels down next to him and replies, "It is my honor to meet you. You are a brave young boy, and I know from looking at you today that you are going to be fine. God is with you." The boy smiles broadly, sincerely convinced by the words Colombo spoke to him; as if they are the only inspiration he needs in moving forward in his life.

✳✳✳

On March 11, 1971, Joey "The Blonde" Gallo was picked up from Sing Sing after serving a ten-year sentence for his extortion case back in 1961. During his 10-year sentence he bounced from facility to facility, encountering problems everywhere he went, beginning in "the Tombs" of Manhattan where the first attempts were made on his life. While Profaci was still alive and in power he'd wanted to have Joey assassinated in prison. He felt Joey was the main antagonist in the territory disputes and wanted him removed from the picture for his disloyalty. It was rumored that Profaci tried to have Joey poisoned while he was staying in the Tombs. Not knowing which plate would go directly to Gallo, the plan to poison Gallo would have involve killing every other prisoner on the block who would eat that evening. Profaci wanted to avoid arousing Gallo's suspicions. Instead of killing Gallo and the rest of the inmates dining that evening at Gallo's table, the cook gave word to the chaplain and Joey was sent upstate to begin serving time in a prison.[clv]

Gallo was transferred to Attica prison only to be shunned by the Italian inmates for his rebellion against Profaci. Gallo's bodyguard and driver Pete the Greek recalled stories of Joey's early days in prison, "In the slams the Profacis had tried to nail Joey. They put ground glass in his chow, sent big guys to work him. Joey almost bit one guy's tit, and another time bit off a guy's ear."[clvi] An inmate who served time with Gallo recalled the message being sent out that "Gallo was taboo."[clvii] Gallo spoke to his wife Jeffie and convinced her that he would be killed in Attica soon.[clviii] Jeffie then enlisted the help of her psychiatrist and wrote the Department of Corrections, requesting that Joey be moved to a new facility. Her request was granted, and Joey was transferred to Clinton Correctional in Dannemora, New York. At Clinton, however, Joey encountered the same animosity, perhaps even worse. Clinton's prison population included a large amount of Profaci supporters from New York City. Seeking whatever allies he could, he fought his way into earning respect from the black and Puerto Rican inmates. Gallo was a small man, only about 5'6", but he was a vicious and tenacious opponent. Pete recalled, "Since Gallo wasn't accepted by anyone he started hanging around with Puerto Rican and black guys. It happens with all white inmates who are in prison who are stool pigeons or who aren't accepted. The black guys will sort of give him a sort of protection."[clix]

In 1967 he was transferred again, this time to Greenhaven Prison. There, he survived a number of attacks on his life that included a near stabbing in the chow hall. It was also rumored that he was doused with gasoline in his cell.[clx] Gallo was then shipped to Auburn, where he ran into some odd luck. During a riot, Gallo rescued a white prison guard from a group of black insurgents. Although Gallo had numerous assault tickets and convictions, the clerks at Auburn rewarded his good deed by granting him an early release in the spring of 1971.

The day of his release, Gallo was greeted at the prison gates by a crew of his closest friends, Pete "the Greek" Diapoulos, Tony Bernardo, Louie "the Syrian" Hubela, Bobby Boriello, his nephew Steve Gallo, and his younger brother Albert. After taking a short nap on the way back down the Taconic Parkway, he woke up agitated. He began interrogating his brother about their business affairs and especially wanted to know about the current situation with Joe Colombo. Albert discussed some business, avoiding the topic of Colombo. Joey pressed him, "But what about Colombo? This car got no wire. We can talk."[clxi] He was insistent, and his younger brother finally relented, knowing it was futile to refuse him. Joey Gallo had a temper that none of his companions wanted to ignite. His behavior was often erratic and his outbursts unmanageable. Albert knew his brother's time in prison had been difficult, but he couldn't deny that while Joey was away things around President Street had quieted down. Everyone in the vehicle agreed that Joey was not thinking straight. Joey had failed to earn respect with Profaci before his prison term, and now demanding it from Colombo would place the crew back into peril. With Larry Gallo and Joe Gioielli gone, no one had the guts to stand up to him.

Regardless of the mutual respect between Larry Gallo and Joe Colombo, Joey Gallo resented Colombo and wanted to confront him. Gallo was preoccupied with what he felt he'd been deprived of at the close of the Gallo-Profaci war; a piece of Brooklyn's gambling rackets. He was intensely envious of men like Anthony "Tony Shots" Abbatemarco, son of the late Frankie Shots, who'd inherited his father's territory after he was murdered. Gallo felt entitled to such a portion as compensation for the time he'd spent in prison. Joe Colombo, as Profaci's successor, now held all the cards, making him in Gallo's estimation, an obstacle and enemy.

After his release from prison, rumors began to circulate that Joey was building an army of black gangsters, although the men in his crew denied this. Pete the Greek knew Joey had helped a few of them from the neighborhood find work, but he didn't appear to have much of a relationship with them beyond that. Joey had certainly not sided with them in Auburn during the riots. In fact, he'd remarked that if they'd had pistols at the time "they would have shot some white dude who never did anything to them…shoot a guy for something somebody did to them twenty years ago, or something some rednecks in the KKK did to their uncle or old man."[clxii]

Upon his release, Gallo fell right back into local rackets on President Street. Driven by seething resentment and a sense of entitlement, he sought to exploit anyone he disliked or viewed as an easy target. He began with Dolly the bookkeeper. In 1967, it was rumored that a few ledger books went missing from the Gallo crew. Their bookkeeper Dolly claimed she couldn't find them. Dolly was suspected by the group to have had a crush on a Colombo soldier named Nick Bianco. The Gallo crew wasn't fond of Bianco. He was purportedly made a member of the Colombo organization during the Gallo Profaci conflict, and instead of staying with the Gallos in Redhook went directly under Colombo's wing. Although he had no evidence, Joey was convinced that Dolly had stolen the money and hidden the ledger books. Joey figured Nick Bianco was also in on it, and by virtue of association, Joe Colombo. Joey spotted the short Italian mother of three walking across the street to a café. He sent one of his men to drag her over to him, and then he ripped her bag from her arms. She was a tough woman and struggled for the purse, but when she finally laid eyes on Joey, she shuddered. Joey yelled at her, "Hey cunt, get off the fucking block. Leave everything you got." Convinced of the earnestness of Gallo's threats, Dolly returned to the apartment where she lived with her father and daughters, and the family quickly fled from the neighborhood. Joey intended to send a message out to the underworld; any perceived enemy would be confronted. He continued to torment various local storeowners and residents, until finally Joe sent a few men down to talk to him and find out what his grievances were.

✱✱✱

Inside the small Roy Roy's Café on President Street, Joey and Albert Gallo sat across the table from Rocky Miraglia and Nicky Bianco. The tough, shiny skin on Joey's face was stretched into a rather menacing grin. Joey looked across the table at Miraglia, whose mere resemblance to Joe Colombo was enough to make Joey hate him. Joey glanced to his left and watched as Pete the Greek counted a few crisp hundred-dollar bills from an envelope. The Greek put the money on the table and said, "It's one thousand." Joey was not happy. "Nine and a half years I did in the fucking slams, and he gives me a thousand. Who the fuck needs this money?"[clxiii] *Albert interrupted the exchange and tried to muzzle Joey before things got any worse. "Excuse me, Nicky, Rocky, I want to speak to my brother a minute. All right?" Albert rose and walked with Joey over to the front counter. The Greek stood like a sentinel while the Gallo's argued in whispers. Bianco sat tall and confident in his small metal chair. He looked up and gave the Greek a faint, cryptic smile. Rocky Miraglia kept his fedora on his knee while he watched the heated exchange between the Gallo brothers.*

Joey and Albert returned to the table after a few more minutes and sat back down. "Listen, Nick," Joey said, pulling his chair in closer, "there's nobody who knows better than you what was said and what was supposed to be done in our peace agreement with Profaci. You remember the promise of Mr. Colombo, Mr. Joe Colombo."[clxiv] Nick cut in, "Joey, excuse me. I'm in no position to discuss this now." Joey snapped back, "There's nobody in a better position than you." Gallo knew it was Bianco who had sat in during the peace talks with his older brother and Colombo back in '63. Miraglia turned away, tuning him out, while Bianco remained expressionless. Both men now recognized the futility of this meeting. "There's nothing else I have to discuss with you. Just tell him like I told you."[clxv] Joey threw the envelope at the men. "Take this back to your boss," he sneered, "and tell Mister Colombo I told him to shove it."[clxvi]

Across the street from the café, Colombo's two emissaries sat inside Miraglia's Buick station wagon for a few minutes before pulling away. Bianco finally raised his voice, "Can you believe the sense of entitlement of this guy? I think he forgot he just robbed a box of cash. He's out of his mind." Rocky started the car. Bianco continued, "We come down here to talk about straightening his mess out and he's still living in 1963. He really is ubatz!"* Miraglia echoed his disgust. "Fuck him. We got better things to do

---

* Sicilian word for "crazy" (slang)

than sit on this god forsaken block. Thanks to his mouth, we ain't ever coming back here." As the Buick pulled off down President Street, Albert Gallo watched from behind the glass of the café; he knew this wasn't good.

Chapter 12.

"My Way"

(May & June -1971)

In the large lobby of the Brooklyn Federal Courthouse, Barry Slotnick looked around at the mixed crowd of law enforcement, lawyers, staff and defendants. He pulled Joe Colombo aside and spoke to him confidentially. "Joe, I have another client who's in court today. You know of him, his name is Meir Kahane. He is a fighter like you and I think the both of you would get along; maybe form a coalition together." Joe told Barry, "Sure, I'd like to meet him." Barry continued, "There's a catch, Joe. He's here for an arraignment and he's not going to make bail." Joe asked, "How much is his bail?" "Twenty-five thousand." Without hesitation, Joe responded, "Call Al Newman and tell him to set up the bail for Mr. Kahane. And tell Mr. Kahane I'll be waiting for him when he gets released. I'd like to get to work with him as soon as possible."

Barry entered the courtroom and walked past a few bailiffs and lawyers up to the bench where Meir was seated with his co-defendants. Meir seemed relaxed and very comfortable; his legs were crossed with both hands resting on his lap. He was dressed in a muted grey sport jacket and tie, and his short black hair was topped faithfully by a satin Yarmulke. Barry leaned in to speak to him. "I just spoke to Joe Colombo. He is in the hallway outside.

You know who he is, don't you?" Meir replied, *"Of course I do." "He's waiting to meet with you outside in the lobby. He is offering to help you with your bail."* Meir pondered the offer. He turned his head and looked down at his men beside him and responded carefully. *"Well that is very good news, and I'm honored that he would want to do that for me. As much as I would like to walk out of this courtroom right now to meet with him I cannot accept the offer."* Barry was a bit shocked. *"Why is that? You don't need to be in here right now. If this is some kind of statement, I assure you the better move is getting out of here as soon as possible. There are plenty of press people outside waiting to see if you make bail." "I agree with you on all points, Barry. But I am sure that Mr. Colombo would understand that I couldn't walk out of here today and leave my men behind. What kind of message would I be sending to my community with a move like that? Tell Mr. Colombo I regretfully decline, unless of course he would want to spring all eight of us."* Meir looked at Barry, who did not immediately discard this idea.

✸✸✸

On the morning of May 13, 1971, Meir Kahane was released on $25,000 bail from the Brooklyn Federal Courthouse. Kahane was in court that day for conspiring to purchase firearms. The indictment had resulted from a yearlong investigation that had implicated Kahane in the sale of over thirty pistols and rifles. The prosecution claimed the weapons were transported from Warrenton, Virginia to New York, increasing the charge to interstate trafficking of weapons; a federal violation. That morning Joe Colombo covered his bail and also took care of his seven associates at a cost of ten thousand dollars each. As soon as Slotnick spoke to Joe about Kahane's refusal to leave his associates behind, Joe's respect for the rabbi deepened, and he agreed immediately to help his entire group.

The lobby of the courthouse was filled with Jewish Defense League supporters. Joe Colombo observed that the JDL supporters were mostly middle-aged men and women, some with their children in tow. They reminded Joe of the many loyal League supporters who came out to show support during all of his court proceedings. As they emerged from the building, the two leaders posed for the press with a handshake and warm smiles. When Joe was questioned about his relationship to Kahane he told reporters, "Rabbi Kahane is a man of God, and his cause is just. He is fighting for his people in Russia and we're fighting for our people here."[clxvii] Colombo and Kahane told the press that the alliance was made in order to support one another's social agendas. Kahane told reporters that if he were asked by Joe to picket the FBI offices with the League, the JDL would gladly be there. Joe echoed his sentiments, "If they need our support, we will give it."[clxviii] One reporter asked Kahane, "What is your philosophy behind this alliance?" Kahane replied, "I'm not a philosopher this morning, I'm a defendant."[clxix] However, he explained, "It's not about Italians or blacks; it's the right to dissent in a manner that is not popular. We have a right to do outrageous things if they are legal. And the right to do these things without having to bear the tremendous pressure of the government."[clxx]

Barry Slotnick made the perfect match by joining Kahane and Colombo. The two men came from different ethnic backgrounds but were equally devoted to the expansion and protection of civil liberties and the celebration of their respective heritages. Both had been similarly disappointed in seeking the support of established civil rights groups. In the Italian-American community, Joe had been rebuffed by groups like C.I.A.O., the Order of the Sons of Italy, and A.I.D. Kahane had been turned down by B'nai Birth, the New York Board of Rabbis and the American Jewish Congress.

***

"When my father first made the alignment with the JDL I was a little apprehensive. As far as the different things my father was accused of and arrested for, I believed he was truly innocent. Most of the charges they had on him weren't that serious. He had been arrested for things like tax evasion, perjury, and gambling, never anything involving guns or violence. But some of the things that were being written in the paper about Meir Kahane and the JDL were pretty heavy to me. Meir was accused of making bombs; in the paper they made him out to be some kind of radical terrorist. In the neighborhoods all you would hear is about how the JDL had more guns than the army. One evening on the picket lines I pulled my father aside, unsure if he had done the right thing by starting a coalition with them and I questioned him. 'Dad, are you sure this is a good idea?' 'What's that?' he asked me. 'These guys, some of the things they say about them in the newspaper are pretty serious. Maybe we shouldn't get involved with the JDL.' My father stopped and looked at me and said, 'Anthony, you're guilty of doing the exact same thing to the JDL that we are fighting against being done to us. You have to find out who people are on your own. You don't let some newspaper or TV reporter tell you if a person is good or bad. This is not an honest way to judge people. Never go by what another man tells you unless you trust him already. You certainly can't trust the press.' My father was right. I was so wrapped up in what was being said about them I had momentarily forgotten everything we were about and everything that had been done to us.

As we drew closer to the second Unity Day, League membership across the US had grown to over fifty thousand. But with more members came more problems, and my father wasn't the type to leave anyone out in the cold. If something was brought up at a meeting he wanted it handled right then and there. We were concluding a few big projects that spring. One was the Brooklyn Hospital and Rehabilitation Center headed up by Dr. Sam Leoni, a very dear friend of my father's and a loyal League supporter. Besides the hospital work we also did a major blood drive in New York City. This was something of a regular occurrence and a service we wanted to offer at the medical center once we got it up and running. Within about a week we donated 190 pints of blood to the Leukemia Society and the Greater Red Bank of New York, a local affiliate of the Red Cross. My father was thrilled by the success of the drive, until he heard some disturbing news. At the next League meeting, John James, the son of the woman who had coordinated the blood drive, told my father that his mother had lost her job with the Leukemia Society. She was so distraught that she had admitted herself into a hospital for depression. James explained that when the treasurer for the Leukemia Society found out the blood was donated by the League, he'd demanded, "I want to know who is responsible for bringing in this blood!' When he was informed that it was Mrs. James he had her fired, announcing, "We don't want any more of that gangster blood in our bank. It won't be accepted!'

We were really aghast when we heard this story. It was difficult to believe that someone could be this bigoted, and even more astonishing that he would express it so openly. We found out that the treasurer's name was Mr. Bateum, and he worked full time as the vice president of Chemical Bank on Broadway in Brooklyn. My father announced the plan of attack, "Many of you must deal with this bank. Many must put your money in this bank. And now, many of you people have to go into the bank and take your money out and tell the president why." Dozens of our members had accounts with this bank; they began withdrawing their money. I drew up letters with Steve Aiello and sent them to the Bank and the Leukemia Society. The biggest blow came when my father spoke to Carl and found out Brooklyn Unions had holdings in that back. Within one week, 22 million dollars in union funds were withdrawn from the bank. Soon after, we received a phone call from a representative of the Red Cross. He said they would gladly take all the blood that was refused by the Leukemia Society, in addition to any more we had to give. We felt somewhat vindicated by this, albeit still disturbed by the prejudice we'd encountered.

We also had to overcome some obstacles to accomplish our other major project, Camp Unity. There was a beautiful piece of property in Tom's River, New Jersey, which we thought was a perfect location. We sent our lawyers down in the springtime and got all of the contracts and financing together. Approval seemed imminent, until the buyers and the community leaders found out it was going to be a camp for underprivileged Italian kids. They expressed intense disapproval and word got back to the League that they didn't want us in their neighborhood. Our first reaction was to fight, but their refusal ended up being a blessing in disguise, since we soon found property in upstate New York ten times the size of the Tom's River land and half the price. The camp became my father's primary focus. He pulled out all the stops and enlisted the help of everyone he knew in order to realize this project. I knew more than anyone why the camp meant so much to him. He wanted to give inner-city kids a chance to get away. The same chance he was given as a child."

During the spring of 1971 a few newspapers ran stories about the League's success and rapid growth. Many even printed their pieces without including the obligatory back-story of Joe's alleged Mob ties. New York Times editor Fred Ferretti wrote a thorough piece called "Italian-American League Power Spreads."[clxxi] The Brooklyn Graphic headline read "Italian-American League Active On All Fronts."[clxxii] Time Magazine featured Colombo in *The Nation* section in a piece titled, "A Night For Colombo,"[clxxiii] and New York Magazine contributor Nicholas Pileggi wrote an elaborate eleven-page story called, "Risorgimento: The Red, White, and Greening of New York." Risorgimento is Italian for "rise again." In his story, Pileggi remarked that the League's accomplishments over the past few years were a sharp contrast to the previous seventy-five, in which the community experienced virtually no forward movement or social growth. The League's current efforts to eliminate ethnic slurs and boycott discriminatory corporations were elements of its principle goal; to threaten the status quo by empowering the lower and middle class residents of New York City. The IACRL accomplished more during its first year than all its ancestors and contemporaries combined. Even Joe's unfavorable portrayal by the media couldn't diminish his efficacy as a leader and activist. By May 1971, Joe Colombo was being interviewed by Walter Kronkite, holding court with city officials, and engaging in debate with congressmen. However impressive his achievements, Joe never rested or felt satisfied. He was always focused on his next battle, knowing his enemies were doing the same. Joe clearly knew he was pressed for time and at some point the contradictions between his private and public personas would collide.

***

According to a number of articles in the New York Times, Colombo was the head of a criminal organization with over 200 men at his beck and call. Law enforcement asserted that this organization represented "a new generation in the Mafia."[clxxiv] A federal agent stated, "Most of its members are American born, freewheeling men not so bound to tradition and eager to find new ways to exploit the system."[clxxv] New York Organized Crime Strike Force Director Holman claimed that Joe Colombo was pioneering avenues of fraud and theft within Wall Street and the mortgage and loan industry. As a result of all the press about Colombo, the State of New York appropriated funds to run a complete investigation, with detectives assigned to build a complete profile on him to report back to the State Senate. The investigative team was lead by William B. Gallinaro, a man who had known Joe since childhood. For over a decade Gallinaro had pursued Colombo, and he "found it pure pleasure to be working with a Senate Committee which had the jurisdiction and the will to put together the full story of Joe Colombo, without being hemmed in by an indictment that was confined to only one aspect of the Colombo operation."[clxxvi]

Other suspected members of the Colombo crew were followed as well. One agent reported, "Like Colombo, the family's capos are well spoken, polished and innovative."[clxxvii] The FBI believed Joe had successfully evolved a once ruthless class of ruffians into a more refined organization of business-minded men. Agents and lawyers were alarmed by this transformation and outraged that Colombo could have been profiting from over twenty legitimate businesses. Joe's suspected interests ranged from the Glen Oaks Nursing Home in Long Island, to Catania Clothes on 5th Avenue in Manhattan. All of his businesses were investigated by the FBI but no illicit activity was uncovered. Joe was listed in most of the books as a partner. Law enforcement claimed to have discovered through wiretaps that Joe was the leader of his own crime organization, which was distinctly structured and profiting from numerous rackets primarily in Brooklyn and Long Island. Rackets included sports betting, hi-jacking, fencing, and loan sharking. Agents told the press unconfirmed details about Joe's suspected operations as if he were already clearly convicted. "Our informants tell us that Colombo's family has at least $3 million in the street."clxxviii Colombo's operation was still considerably smaller than the Gambinos, which had three times the suspected members and whose financial activity purportedly reached all the way from Boston to central Pennsylvania.

At the 1971 McClellan Subcommittee hearings, which were aimed at furnishing intelligence about organized crime to Congress, The FBI claimed one of "their most sensational witnesses was Robert F. Cudak, a confessed thief," and an associate of two suspected Colombo crew members named "Cangiano and Peraino."clxxix These prolific and accomplished hijackers had operated for years at JFK, amassing millions of dollars worth of stolen goods. Attorney General John Mitchell personally stepped in to arrange immunity for Cudak, who agreed to provide more details about Colombo's operations.clxxx

The FBI expanded its efforts to leak information to the press about Colombo's criminal connections. This propaganda campaign against Colombo was a form of psychological warfare. COINTELPRO operatives sought to tarnish his reputation by writing unfavorable articles for or furnishing damaging information to 'friendly' media sources who could be relied upon not to reveal the Bureau's activities. Field offices also had "confidential sources" (unpaid Bureau informants) in the media, and were able to ensure their cooperation. The objective was to 'expose' and discredit target groups.clxxxi

Particularly popular were quotes from Sam "The Plumber" DeCavalcante, who was recorded on illegal wiretaps lambasting Colombo and the other members of the Commission. The feds erroneously called DeCavalcante a "colleague",[clxxxii] of Joe's. Such incendiary measures were intended to debase him and the League in the public eye, and potentially aggravate him enough to retaliate against DeCavalcante. According to a congressional report:

> Approximately 28% of the Bureau's COINTELPRO efforts were designed to weaken groups by setting members against each other, or to separate groups which might otherwise be allies, and convert them into mutual enemies. The techniques used included anonymous mailings [reprints, Bureau-authored articles and letters] to group members criticizing a leader or an allied group; using informants to raise controversial issues; forming a "notional" -- a Bureau run splinter group -- to draw away membership from the target organization; encouraging hostility up to and including gang warfare between rival groups; and the "snitch jacket.[clxxxiii]

A "snitch jacket" was a manipulative tactic in which law enforcement started and spread rumors that an individual was an informant. This was an attempt to promote discord and mistrust in suspected criminal organizations; but which could certainly have resulted in a death sentence for the falsely accused.

Agents also plied media sources with stories of Crazy Joey Gallo's return from prison, and encouraged the idea he was ready to cause trouble in Brooklyn again. One article read, "Colombo is a little more than uneasy at having him back in circulation."[clxxxiv]

Another article claimed Colombo and his loyal friend Carmine Persico were at odds. Persico was a zealous follower of Profaci and the article erroneously suggested that Colombo had failed to support the late boss in the war against the Gallos."[clxxxv] In addition it claimed that Persico, "has always felt that Colombo did not deserve to be given the leadership of the family over more experienced capos."[clxxxvi] While Joey Gallo had always been favored to rebel against leadership, the Bureau's reports about the rest of the Colombo organization told a different story. One report stated, "Informant concluded with an evaluation of Colombo by stating that there was no one within the family who at present was a challenge to Colombo's leadership and that presently [men] prefer Colombo as boss rather than any of the logical successors."[clxxxvii] In addition, Colombo and Persico's relationship had actually grown stronger over the ten years prior. The rumors agents circulated contradicted their own reports.

Agents continued to pursue Colombo and his associates, but they remained unable to issue a serious indictment. Their IRS case was inconsequential; Joe was accused of evading $19,169 in a five-year period. It was a scant amount for a prosecution and even if convicted, he would only be fined. His implication in the Long Island jewelry theft was flimsy at best; their claim that he'd acted as a negotiator for the accused would be very difficult to prove in court. A gambling indictment had resulted from over 95 days of legal wiretapping, but none of the voices heard on the tapes were positively identified as Colombo's. While the wiretaps offered some evidence that was usable in court, agents had also learned that Colombo's associates were aware of many of the taps. They would have conversations to deliberately incriminate the agents themselves. One recording ran, "Hey, Joey, You better clear out

now. I'm expecting Bernie Welsh to come by for his payoff."[clxxxviii]
On May 5th, the FBI encountered another defeat when Joe's close friend, Rocky Miraglia was acquitted of the perjury charges he'd been slapped with in December, when Federal agents arrested him and confiscated Joe's mysterious League briefcase and list. The jury reached its verdict after only three hours of deliberation.[clxxxix] Colombo and his lawyers predicted this outcome. They knew the charge was simply another instance of police harassment and a pretext for the confiscation of his briefcase.

In May, Camp Unity was established in Rosendale, New York. The land purchased was over 150 acres around two large spring-fed lakes. The area was very familiar to Joe; it was about thirty-five miles away from his home in Blooming Grove. He knew many of the young kids growing up in Brooklyn had never seen the beauty of upstate New York's mountains and countryside, and he recognized how formative these experiences had been for him as a child. Joe was personally involved in virtually every aspect of this project. Within two weeks of purchasing the land, he and his team of League officers had built roads and refurbished the thirty cabins on the property with new beds and bathrooms. Joe also ensured that every inch of the camp was handicap accessible. He was almost fanatically devoted to the completion of this camp and he was equally anxious that an enemy, most likely the FBI, would find some way of derailing him. One afternoon while walking up a mountainside with League officer Dick Capozzola, he pointed down to the two big lakes on the campgrounds and said, "Dickie, I need someone to survey these lakes." Dick looked a bit confused and Joe continued, "I don't want any trouble from the government. I don't want any bodies showing up here later." Joe was convinced that such a measure as planting corpses in his lakes was well within the FBI's capacity. Dick assured him, "Okay, Joe. I will take care of it."

Building Camp Unity was the perfect escape for Joe from the city and the news media frenzy that followed him daily. However, he was working almost to the point of exhaustion. Some days he would arrive at Cantalupo Realty by 8 a.m., leave at lunchtime to pitch in at the camp and then leave the camp at dark for a meal with Jo-Jo at their upstate home. Joe never felt he had sufficient time to accomplish what he intended to. He sacrificed all of his leisure time, as well as hours of sleep each night, in order to attend to his endless obligations.

***

One of the League's principle goals was to protect merchants, their customers, and residents from harassment by the FBI or law enforcement. Since its inception, the League instructed its members about civil liberties and provided round the clock support for anyone suffering from police intrusions or bullying. In late May, 1971, Anthony and other League officials began receiving numerous calls from citizens in the Red Hook neighborhood of

Brooklyn. Apparently, Gallo was threatening shop owners and forcing them to take down posters promoting the upcoming rally for Unity Day. He was telling shopkeepers, "Colombo's just using the dues from poor Italians to pay for his lousy fight with the FBI."[cxc] League officials told the shopkeepers to ignore Gallo and return the signs to their windows. Informants told agents that Gallo was "determined to get Joe Colombo to disassociate himself from the Italian-American Civil rights League and is doing everything possible to disrupt all League plans as long as Colombo is its leader."[cxci] In early June, Gallo even tried to arrange for an appearance on the local news in order to antagonize and discredit Colombo. The pretext would be a discussion of his upcoming film project, *The Gang That Couldn't Shoot Straight*, a movie loosely based on his crew. Once the interview was underway, Gallo would "shift the conversation over to the Italian-American Civil Rights League" and begin thrashing Colombo and his League.[cxcii] After discussing it with his cohorts, however, the plan was dismissed as a bad move and hypocritical, since he would be doing exactly what he was criticizing Colombo for; speaking openly to the public.

The rumors of Gallo aligning with the blacks continued. But mainly within law enforcement and media. It was known that Gallo got close with some blacks in prison, but only to obtain a measure of protection from Profaci's men who wanted to kill him.[cxciii] To show gratitude for this protection, Gallo sent word to his brothers back home, asking if they'd help a few of them out once they were released. "Blast (Albert Gallo) said he'd try to get them jobs, but he never really tried."[cxciv] When Gallo returned home, a few blacks would call for him on President Street, but his associates would simply tell the ex-cons they were afraid Gallo would violate parole for being near any of them. Although Gallo had lent a few of them money and helped others, he'd fallen out of favor with them after an incident in Auburn, and he told his crew that they could never truly be trusted.[cxcv] Just before he was released from prison at Auburn, some black inmates incited a riot during which he and another inmate saved the life of a white prison guard. Gallo was thereafter viewed as an enemy and became a target of the blacks. When the riots were over Gallo was "threatened by Negro inmates."[cxcvi] Without allies among either the black or the white inmates, Gallo was again forced to transfer prisons. As a measure of gratitude for saving the guard, he was granted an early release by the Bureau and spent his remaining few months in Sing Sing. On May 26, the FBI received a report that Gallo was shot at near one of his haunts. According to the report, "Gallo saw his assailants and it was definitely Negros."[cxcvii] Gallo believed the shooting was a reprisal for his role in the Auburn riot.

There were rumors that Gallo wanted to take a shot at Colombo, but they never made it into official FBI reports. In any event, an attempt to depose Joe Colombo would have been an extraordinarily difficult maneuver for Gallo. Michael Franzese, an associate of Colombo who later became an informant noted, "In truth, few imagined that Crazy Joe had aspirations to take over the family. A prison term had weakened his power, and his soldiers had never been loyal - a factor attributed to his tightrope walk with sanity."[cxcviii] But Gallo could have been thinking like he had during his crew's war with the Profaci's ten years prior; remove the boss and assume control of the rackets in Red Hook. Gallo also knew his unconcealed contempt for Colombo could likely result in retaliation, thus making this in Gallo's mind a kill or be killed scenario.

In late May the Gallo crew devised a plan to hit Joe from the roof of Kaplan Buick as he exited the luncheonette across from his office at Cantalupo Realty.[cxcix] However, this plan was quickly abandoned for fear of missing the shot. The next plan was to hide a shooter in the trunk of a parked car in hopes of catching Joe on the street. This also seemed unreliable, though, so they scrapped the single shooter idea and decided it was better to have two shooters to ensure he was killed. Gallo's close friend and trusted bodyguard, Pete the Greek suggested having two shooters sitting inside of a custom-built box truck. They would cut small holes in the side of the truck, just large enough for gun barrels to pass through. Then they would line the thin steel truck walls with mattresses to "muffle the shots."[cc] The Greek and Bobby Darrow first parked their truck outside of Prospero's funeral home on 86th Street. After failing to see Joe there for a number of hours, they moved the truck to 83rd Street in Dyker Beach where Joe lived, but Colombo's block was so heavily patrolled by squad cars that the two decided to abort the mission entirely. The crew discussed other options, even bringing up the idea of hitting Joe at Unity Day, but they decided that it was too risky; the Greek thought, "The rally wasn't any good. It just wasn't feasible."[cci] There would be too many police and federal agents present, so they would execute the hit afterward. While the FBI received reports that he had planned "something," all the informants could tell them was "whatever it is the Gallo's are planning will demonstrate that Colombo does not have unified backing in his leadership of the League."[ccii]

***

Harassment of storeowners by suspected gangsters was already a sensitive issue for the League due to complaints from the previous year's rally. They'd had to respond to "unconfirmed but stubborn reports that some muscle had been used to encourage storekeepers to close prior to the Unity Day event."[cciii] Anthony spoke to the press, assuring them that the League would offer support to any shopkeepers who were in need. "Guys might try to hurt our image by pressuring people. So we have promised to provide protection for anyone who reports being threatened."[cciv] The press seized upon the opportunity to print stories of League intimidation, so reporters began their investigation in Joe's neighborhood, Bensonhurst. A Board of Trade official who was interviewed noted, "Many of the businesses owned by Italians in the area are barbershops, beauty parlors and restaurants, and most of them are closed on Mondays anyway."[ccv] When questioned by the media, the State Commissioner of Human Rights told reporters that he had received no complaints thus far about merchants being pressured to close, however at a news conference called by the Commissioner to discuss various allegations of bias made by Italian-American groups, one participant told of such a threat.[ccvi]

On June 25th, just four days before Unity Day, twenty Italian-American groups met with State Commissioner of Human Rights Jack M. Sable to discuss complaints of discrimination. Leaders from a few groups made it clear to the Commissioner that they were not affiliated with the Italian-American Civil Rights League and informed him that they had planned the meeting without the League's knowledge. Virtually every other Italian political, civic, labor, and church group was represented at this meeting.[ccvii]

The exclusion was a terrible insult and betrayal to Joe and the Italian-American Civil Rights League. During a press conference after the meeting, Commissioner Sable and the other groups were asked if they were discriminating against the newly formed IACRL. Sable told reporters, "There is no particular reason they're not here. I do not believe they were invited."[ccviii] The topics discussed at the meeting were eerily similar to the issues that were dearest to the IACRL, such as improved care for the elderly, better health facilities and drug rehabilitation. The League's absence was especially odd, given that it had accomplished more towards these goals in a little over a year than all the other organizations included in the meeting. When reporters asked if the IACRL had been successful in its goal of eliminating defaming labels and racial epithets in the media, Alfred Santagelo, president of Italians of American Descent, claimed the League had nothing to do with it. He stated, "You people are giving credit where credit is not due."[ccix] When Santangelo and a few of the other leaders were asked if they would attend the upcoming Unity Day Rally in Columbus circle they refused to comment.[ccx] This exclusion of the League from an important political gathering was likely a COINTELRPO tactic. The "covert action" to undermine the League involved not only the propagation of misinformation and false media stories, but also the establishment of pseudo organizations and the planting of agents into existing groups in order to manipulate leaderships and divide activists and supporters.[ccxi] Indeed, after some investigation into these organizations, which had ostracized his League, Colombo discovered that many of them had recently aligned themselves with, and received sizeable grants from various government agencies. Colombo suspected the FBI had planted undercover agents in these organizations, and even expressed concerns about infiltration within the League. As the

307

rally approached, Joe grew increasingly agitated and suspicious. At one of the last League meetings before Unity Day, an angry Joe Colombo gripped the podium for one of his final speeches at the Park Sheraton Hotel. "What if I tell you that the President of the United States is so worried about you that he is offering money to other Italian-American organizations? To make them stronger. To divide and conquer. To kill your League. They are now funding organizations that have done nothing but drink the blood of our people. You know what Italian organizations they are! They will only better themselves. Rob the money!"

***

On June 11th, just two weeks before the rally, Eugene Gold, District Attorney of Kings County issued warrants for 46 suspected mobsters in New York City. The men were all charged with contempt of court from a 1968 Grand Jury investigation.[ccxii] Given the length of time between the trial and the arrests, many of those arrested believed this was just another tactic to aggravate mobsters before the upcoming rally. Attorney Gold, at a press conference, simply stated, "We are going to pursue the lawless conduct of organized crime relentlessly."[ccxiii] The men were mostly from the Gambino, Colombo, and Bonanno organizations. The FBI had been receiving reports of an imminent gang war in New York, and believed it would affect all five organizations. A decision was made by Dennis Dillon and the Organized Crime Strike Force to place Carl Gambino, Joe Colombo, Joe Bonanno, Tommy Ryan

Colombo: The Unsolved Murder

and Carmine Tramunti, the five leaders of the New York organizations, on twenty-four hour surveillance.

A few days after the surveillance was initiated, Michael B. Pollack, an attorney who worked for the Organized Crime Strike Force under Dillon, returned from vacation and was called into Dillon's office. "We are going to pull surveillance off of Joe Colombo," Dillon told him. When he asked about the other bosses he was told they were only pulling away from Colombo. Puzzled, he asked if there had been any new developments that would account for this change in plan. Dillon replied, "No, we're just not protecting Joe Colombo at this time." The government justified the 24-hour surveillance as "protection" for the bosses during these heightened times. Pollack, subordinate to Dillon, left confused by his decision.

***

"Months before the second Unity Day, the newspapers were running articles about my father, Joe Gallo and Carl Gambino. A number of the stories were about Joe Gallo taking League placards out of stores in downtown Brooklyn. I remember even reading something about Gallo saying in effect, 'Fuck, Joe Colombo.' One evening I was driving with my father upstate. This nighttime ride had become part of our routine during the League years. We'd had a long day of driving around to all the different chapters and making sure everything was going smoothly for Unity Day. We were both tired and eager to get home, but I was feeling troubled

309

and couldn't help expressing it to him. I started to tell him about some of the things I was reading in the paper about him and Uncle Carl being big Mob bosses, and of course the stories about Joey Gallo coming home from prison. I'd also heard rumors about Gallo being angry with my father. He was doing his best to ignore the topic, but I could tell he was a bit agitated that I'd even brought it up. He told me not to believe any of the nonsense written in the paper. For years I never questioned him about what the newspapers where saying about him, but I kept pressing.

We had just crossed through a toll plaza, and I said to my father, 'Dad, maybe you shouldn't go to Unity Day." That was probably the worst thing I could have said; it was like I'd hit him in the head with a hammer. He blew his top and started yelling at me. For the first time in my life, I raised my voice back. It wasn't out of disrespect, it was out of concern. So now we were both arguing, yelling back and forth at each other. He was screaming at me, 'You and your mother are both doing the same thing to me!' He yelled, 'pull over the car!' So I pulled the car over a little ways up on the side of the thruway and asked, 'what now?' He was enraged, yelling, 'Get out! Get out of the car!' I said, 'what do you mean get out?' he said, 'I want you to get out of the car!' 'What do you want me to do then?' 'Get out of the car!' he yelled, "I'm leaving you here. I don't want to hear from you anymore. Now get out of the car!' He was dead serious. 'Get out of the car! Now, Anthony!' I said, 'I'm not getting out of the car. What am I supposed to do, walk?' He snapped back, 'I don't care what you do. Just get out, now!' It was pitch black outside and there wasn't a soul on the thruway, there was no way I was getting out of that car. I said, 'Dad what do you want? I'm afraid something may happen.' He said, 'How many times do I gotta tell you to stop believing the newspapers?' 'I said, 'Dad, I don't, but it looks like someone might really try to hurt you. I just don't think it's worth it for you to go. Stay home and I'll take care of it for you. I can handle the speeches and everything.' He was beside himself with anger. In the brief silence that followed, I added in a calmer voice, 'Dad, we can always have another League, but I only have one father.'

We were about thirty miles from the house. The rest of the car ride was dead silence. When we finally reached the house he just got out of the car and went inside. Normally, when we returned home, I'd make a sandwich, offer to make him one, and he would say he wasn't hungry. Then when I had finished making mine, he would eat half of it with his winning grin and we would both laugh and have some little conversation before bed. There was no conversation that night. I know my father felt betrayed because I'd challenged him. No one ever challenged him. I walked past him in the kitchen and said, 'goodnight, dad.' He gave me a mumble and a head nod and I went off to bed. I was truly nervous. I knew he was mad at me, but I wasn't going to back down this time. It was the first and only time I'd raised my voice to my father.

The next day when I woke up for breakfast he sat down with me in the kitchen. He and my mother must have had a long talk after I fell asleep. He said, 'Anthony, I understand you're concerned. I really do. But what you're reading in the paper is not true. I have nothing to do with Joe Gallo. All that stuff is not a concern. And Carl is still my close friend, no matter what they say in the news. Don't worry about anything because nothing is going to happen to me.' I said, 'Okay, Dad.' And that was the end of it.'

***

As resilient and strong as Joe Colombo appeared to be to his friends and followers, his wife noticed he was beginning to fatigue. Psychological stresses were compounded by intense physical exhaustion from his frenetic work schedule with the League. As the League expanded, he felt increasingly persecuted by law enforcement and increasingly estranged from professional associates. His colleague, Joe Cantalupo noticed Colombo had begun carrying a pistol, which he had never done before.[ccxiv] His wife Jo-Jo had been asking him to slow down for months, hoping he would consider taking a brief vacation, but Joe told her there was no chance given all the work he needed to do to open the camp. Even if he could put aside all the demands from the League, his bail conditions would require him to obtain special permission from the courts in order to travel.

He did, however, take one final trip with his wife near their beloved Blooming Grove Estate. A few weeks before the second Unity Day, just after celebrating their 27th wedding anniversary, he and Jo-Jo took their horses out to Tomahawk Lake for a ride across the Orange County plains and creeks. Since they'd met as teenagers at the Franklyn Factory in Greenpoint, the couple had survived a world war, gang wars, arrests, and trials; all while building a strong, loving family. Jo-Jo had watched her husband grow from a young tough kid from the streets of South Brooklyn into a loving father and a respected community leader. She trusted him blindly, but recently she feared for him. She knew better than anyone how stubborn Joe could be, and her protests over the upcoming Unity Day Rally fell on deaf ears. Joe understood his family's concerns, however, and did not want them to worry. He assured Jo-Jo and Anthony that his relationship with Carl was intact, despite the fact that they had been spending less and less time with him. Joe cited Carl's failing health as a reason, as well as his own cramped schedule, but Jo-Jo remained anxious. After their long ride through the countryside, Joe told his wife that he would go and speak to Carl in Brooklyn.

***

Carl spoke softly. "You can no longer be around this League." Joe protested with excitement, "Then everything we worked for, everything you helped me do, it would all die in vain." "That is not your problem anymore. If it cannot work without you than it does not deserve to." Joe tried to explain, "If I walk away now then I have backed down from my own fight." "This is a fight you can no longer win, Joseph. Why can't you see that? Can't you see how angry they are with you? All of these arrests. This thing you say you care so much about. These people. You are infecting them." Joe took a breath and absorbed the harshness of the words. "What would you have me do then?" Carl said simply, "Let the rally happen without you." "Carl, I cannot do that. They need to see me there." "Who needs to see you there?" With a hint of sarcasm Carl asked, "The FBI. The media?" Carl looks at him sharply and continues. "They want to lock you up in prison for the rest of your life. Is that what you want? Then what happens to your League? What happens to your family? You're not making any sense, Joseph." Joe pleaded, "I have been preaching to everyone in that organization for two years not to be afraid and not to back down. If I back down, what kind of message would I be sending them?" "You should have never given them that hope. You have commitments that are much more important." Joe exhaled his frustrations and began, "Listen, Barry says I'm going to have to spend some time in jail for the perjury case. It is the perfect way for me to step aside without letting people down. While I am away, Nat and Anthony will take over and the people will continue to support them. I will go to the rally, but only to show my face. I will not speak. I will only be there as a spectator." Carl's eyes catechized Joe. He then said, "I told Scotto, Brooklyn's waterfront will work on Monday. I cannot go back on my word. They are trying to prosecute him and this would give them more incentive." Joe listened patiently as Carl continued, " There are many men that are afraid to show their faces that will not be there on Unity Day. You should be one of them." But Carl, I cannot go back on my word. It would not look good for me to change my position." "I understand, Joseph, and I would never ask you to go back on your word with anyone, but now more then ever, you need to worry about yourself. They are trying to take you away from your family, and your family should be your number one concern. At this rate, with what you've done, they will keep coming after you, until they are rid of you."

Chapter 13.

"Five Minutes More"

(Unity Day 1971)

The guest list for Unity Day in 1971 was substantial. Speeches would be made by over twenty distinguished state and city officials, including Manhattan Borough President Percy Sutton, Congressman Mario Biaggi, the League's education czar Steve Aiello, and City Comptroller Abe Beam. For the crowd's entertainment the League booked over forty acts, including Sammy Davis Jr., Frankie Valli and the Four Seasons, Tom Jones, Tony Darrow, BB King, and The Pee Jay's. Vendors prepared food for over half a million people. Expecting temperatures close to 100 degrees, hawkers would be walking through the crowds with coolers and carts filled with frozen treats and cold drinks.

The FBI was also preparing for the event. They would send every field agent from their New York offices to the rally. Agents took photos and videos at various locations. The New York City Police Department called in 1,500 uniformed patrolmen and a few hundred higher-ranking officers to monitor the crowd.[ccxv] In addition, Chief of Detectives Albert Seedman enlisted some of his own lawmen to attend. These men were different from the patrolmen. They were Seedman's handpicked elite investigators whose background was in organized crime. Seedman claimed,

"Most of the men assigned to Columbus Circle that day were specialists in Mob politics, any one of whom could identify hundreds of Mafia figures by the backs of their necks."[ccxvi]

Anyone associated with Joey Gallo was ordered not to attend the rally. Activist and League supporter Ti-Grace Atkinson received an anxious phone call from an acquaintance, David McMullin, a filmmaker who had been in contact with a relative of Gallo's. McMullin said he heard the Gallo's were threatening those who planned to attend, but Ti-Grace was a loyal friend of Joe's and disregarded the advice. Many of the underworld supporters who loved the League and wanted to support Joe feared the event might become an ambush from the FBI filled with frivolous indictments and arrests. Paul Vario, upon whom the character "Paul Cicero" was based in the movie *Goodfellas*, was a League organizer who a few weeks before the rally retired from the League, citing health issues. Vario had been under heavy scrutiny by the FBI at the time, and shortly after the rally he was indicted, convicted of perjury and sentenced to three years in Federal prison. Warnings about the rally even reached Hollywood producer Al Ruddy. He recalled that while working on the set of *The Godfather,* "I had an FBI agent approach me who gave me his information and told me to call him if I had any trouble with the League or Joe. He was just doing his job, offering protection in case someone tried to muscle me or anything. I never called him, but he would call me from time to time to check in. The night before the rally he called me and said, 'Under no circumstances are you to be in Columbus Circle tomorrow!' The way he said it, it was like an order. I didn't know what it was about, he didn't explain it. He just hung up the phone."

Colombo: The Unsolved Murder

***

Buses unloaded herds of supporters onto Broadway and 63rd Street. On a stage adorned with green, white and red flowers, a group of well-dressed men looked rather anxiously out at the crowd as they waited for the band to strike up at noon, signaling the beginning of the event. Towering behind them, the 70-foot statue of Cristoforo Colombo was festooned with streamers of green, white and red flags that fluttered in the sky above. Columbus Circle was filled with thousands of Italian-Americans looking around with excitement, dancing and singing Italian folk music. As more people poured into the streets, vendors rushed to set up their booths in the long rows of red, white and green decorated huts. Pretty Blondes and brunettes smiled as men pinned buttons to their shirts that read, "Kiss me I'm Italian" and "Italian is Beautiful." Little boys and girls waved pennants and flags and tugged at their mothers for Italian ices and gelato.

Joe Colombo wove through the press area with his usual decorum, accompanied by his towering lawyer, Barry Slotnick. A few people said, "Hiya Joe," and offered him a wave and a smile. He took photos with politicians and greeted everyone warmly. Despite all the rumors about Joe Colombo's second life as a crime lord, in person he made it very hard for people to dislike him. His smile was genuine and his sad dark eyes were inviting.

Officer Tony Schiozzi stood only a few feet away at his post on the barricades. He couldn't help but take notice of a black couple in the press area near Joe. The man was holding a film camera and the short woman beside him was following him closely with a camera around her neck. Their presence was puzzling to Schiozzi, since The IACRL was hardly a newsworthy event for the local black media.

Anthony's father in law, Tim O'Brien, approached Joe with a couple of League officers, one of them holding a brown satchel. Tim O'Brien said, "Joe I have a lot of money here, what do you want me to do with the bag?" Joe replied, "Hold on to it for a few minutes. Once we collect from everyone we can lock it up in the trailer." Joe turned and was met by Assistant Chief of Police, Arthur Morgan.[ccxvii] "Joe, we had a little bit of a problem." Joe asked, "What's the matter?" Morgan continued, "It seems a group of Greek men were selling ice in the rally and some of your guys chased them through the park. They came to us crying because they said they're selling ice on public property. What do you want to do with them?" Joe gave it some thought. "Our guys put a lot of hard work into making this happen and for some of them the only payoff is their vending. Tell the Greeks, they'll have their turn another time."

Joe strolled a bit further and saw his daughter-in-law Carol through a break in the crowd. She waved to him and smiled and he winked back at her, lowered his arm, and walked slowly to the podium.

While dozens of cameramen were nudging each other aside to get a good photo of Colombo, the slim black man disguised as a press reporter stepped behind Joe, lifted a small black pistol from his pocket and pointed it at the back of Joe's head. From a few feet away, he crouched slightly, pulled the trigger and rapidly emptied three bullets into the back of Joe's head. Witnesses recalled a haunting moment of silence just before the chaos broke.

Officer Schiozzi heard the first clap and turned right to the source. The shooter, Jerome Addison Johnson, had a small Lugar pistol poised behind Joe's head. Johnson then turned away like he was going to run, and Schiozzi ran right for him, tackled him to the pavement and smashed Johnson's right hand, hoping to free the gun. A fourth bullet fired off, miraculously missing Officer Robert Krisch, burning his pant leg, and flying past thousands of people.[ccxviii]

Joe lurched and staggered forward from the shots quickly losing blood and strength. He leaned forward to steady himself against the barricades in front of him, but it was too far to grab. He collapsed heavily onto the pavement as the crowd around him watched in shock and horror. The men nearest to Joe folded a cardboard box and rested his head on it. Barry Slotnick was knocked to the ground as a phalanx of cops rushed into the press area.

Not far from Colombo, officers Schiozzi and James Scott and Deputy Chief Inspector Thomas Reed had Johnson pinned to the ground. One officer had his knee in Johnson's back while Johnson screamed they stretched his arms behind him to be cuffed. Schiozzi freed the small pistol and immediately secured it by emptying the remaining rounds. By this time, a group of patrolmen were covering Jerome Johnson and they began to cuff him. Through the mesh of policemen a small revolver pressed against the center of Jerome Johnson's back and two more gunshots popped off, further startling everyone around.

The gun used to shoot Johnson hit the pavement and was quickly retrieved by police, but the shooter inexplicably escaped through a thick crowd of FBI, detectives, and a few hundred policemen. Johnson's accomplice, a black female, also managed to escape from the press area. While trying to exit the barricades, she was stopped by a pair of police officers. She negotiated her release with them by stating, "Stay there and get my head blown off? No, sir!"[ccxix] And they let her flee the scene.

It all happened within three minutes. Shouts and echoes of "They got Colombo!" and "Somebody shot, Joe" fanned through the crowd like the wind through the green white and red streamers. Joe was now unconscious and bleeding heavily. His pulse was faint. Driver Eugene Carpentier had an ambulance parked right behind the barricades. While cameramen snapped photos, Joe's friends lifted Joe onto a gurney and into the back of the wagon. The NYPD feared Johnson would be ripped apart by people in the crowd and ordered him moved to the hospital as well. Most of the people at the rally still had no idea what had just happened. Police did their best to control the area but made grave errors in doing so. They failed to secure a crime scene of any kind. Evidence was removed from the scene without being tagged. The bodies were not chalked. All that was left for evidence were Joe's glasses, an empty Bolex camera case, three guns, two briefcases, and a comb.

Not far from the scene, Carol Colombo stood frozen with shock. A patrolman recognized her as Colombo's daughter-in-law and escorted her to a medical trailer. After about forty minutes, two lawmen, dressed in plainclothes, came into the trailer to ask her a few questions. These weren't any of the federal agents she knew, and they wasted no time with small talk. One of them asked her immediately, "Did you see who shot the black man on the ground?" She answered, "I can only assume it was a police officer, since there were so many of them on him." Unsure of what she saw he asked, "But did you actually see a police officer shoot him?" She answered honestly, "No, I didn't. But they all had their guns drawn wherever I looked." The men were not interested in anything else. They didn't ask her about the girl, they didn't ask her about the shooting of her father in-law. The men asked her the same question again and again, and once they heard the same answer, they left.

***

The moment he arrived at Roosevelt Hospital, all of Joe's clothes were removed, his wounds cleaned, and a sheet spread over his naked body. The chief neurosurgeon wanted X-rays immediately so he could begin extracting the bullets, two of which were lodged in his skull, and the third in his neck. Joe's hemorrhaging wasn't severe and he stabilized relatively quickly. The waiting area outside the operating room was crammed with detectives, agents, police officers, family, friends, city officials, and reporters. A physician shouted at a detective, "For God's sake, we're trying to run a hospital here." Doctors began begging police for some assistance in removing people from the building.[ccxx]

By noon radio broadcasts all over the city announced, "Joseph Colombo Sr. has just been shot three times in the head at Columbus Circle." At around 12:30 p.m. the Associated Press told police and media they received a phone call from a group claiming responsibility for the shooting. The caller had identified himself as a member of the "Black Revolutionary Attack Team",[ccxxi] Chief of Detectives Albert Seedman did not believe this was the work of a black militant, but told the press, "Unfortunately, we have not been able to rule out one sort of possibility or another.[ccxxii] Mr. Colombo is in serious condition and he's in the operating room right now. He was shot three times in the back of the head." A reported asked, "Do you have the weapon?" "Yes we do, we have the weapon used to shoot him." "What can you tell us about the circumstances surrounding the shooting, Chief?" "He was shot by an individual who appeared to be taking some photographs." "Was he wearing a New York City press pass?" "We haven't found a press card." The press pushes for answers, "Do you have the man?" Seedman replied flatly, "The man is dead." "Have you identified him?" "Well we have a tentative identification but before we confirm it, I won't give you his name." A female reporter asked, "Who shot the man who allegedly shot Mr. Colombo?" "We do not know." She pressed further, "Do you have any idea or any suspects at this point?" Seedman looked at the ground as he answered, "No we don't. We are trying to find out who shot him. We have several guns and are trying to match the guns against the spent bullets we have found." "Was he shot by a policeman?" Seedman ignored her and looked for another question. Another reporter asked, "Was Colombo's shooter a member of a militant organization? Was this a revenge kind of shooting?" "We don't have too much information about this individual. So far there is no apparent connection between this man and any known organization." The female reporter resumed her inquiry, "Was anyone shot by a policeman at the Italian Unity Rally today?" Seedman paused for a moment, "As far as I know, no." "So it was a shootout between people who were not members of the police department?" Seedman answered, "You said that."

Some eyewitnesses claimed to have seen Johnson standing by the press platform with a total of three other blacks. One recalled that Johnson was standing with "two other black men and a girl, all wearing press badges."[ccxxiii] One bereaved witness stated, "They [the bodyguards] weren't close enough [to Joe]. There should have been someone there watching him at all times." The reporter asked, "The cops, did they shoot the man who shot Joe right away?" The man nodded his head in sadness, "Right, They had to. The man had a piece on him." The report that a police officer shot Johnson came from several witnesses that day. Another who was interviewed told reporters that he'd observed a police officer pick up the gun that was wrested from the shooter, wipe it off, then place it into his pocket. One bystander was too distraught to respond to questions, and with his head down kept repeating, "Not Joe, please not Joe." Charlie Geraci, a League member from out of town said, disgusted, "I knew this would happen. They killed the president. They killed his brother and they killed [Martin Luther] King. How could they not kill Joe Colombo, these radicals? I swear I'm getting fed up with this country. What the hell is happening?"[ccxxiv]

The tens of thousands who'd assembled for Unity Day still lingered in the streets as news spread about Colombo's shooting. Father Gigante stepped up to the podium and told the crowd what news he had from the hospital. "My dear friends, today was a great day for us and a horrible event has occurred. But I can assure you that Joe Colombo, the man that has given his life to this League and the unification of all Italian-Americans, would say stay and enjoy this great day. I was just at the hospital and right now, his wife Jo-Jo and her sons are all together waiting and praying that God will see fit to save Joe. In the meantime, he is upstairs in the operating room with some of the city's best neurosurgeons. I give you this message because I believe if we believe, he can make it. Let's say another prayer for Joe Colombo." The crowd fell completely silent as Father Gigante recited the Lord's Prayer. Soon after, Rabbi Meir Kahane addressed the crowd after returning from the hospital. He tried his best to lift the spirits of the people by reminding them of their mission with Joe. "Let's go forward to build the kind of America that is meaningful."

Rabbi Kahane was shot and killed 19 years later on November 5, 1990 in a similar fashion after giving a speech at a small rally in New York. His assassin was an Egyptian Islamic militant who was found to have ties to the first World Trade Center bombers.[ccxxv]

***

Across the East River in Brooklyn, news of Colombo's shooting had reached Joey Gallo's closest associates. Pete The Greek and Albert Gallo were living in the same apartment building at the time and when The Greek heard about it, he ran down the hall to tell Albert.[ccxxvi] They were shocked, but knew it wouldn't be long before the police arrived. They had been under close watch by law enforcement since Joey's return from prison, and to make matters worse Joey had loudly broadcast his disdain for Joe, even to FBI and police officers.[ccxxvii] The group prepared for the police by first getting rid of all the weapons in their homes. Joey and Albert were brought to the precinct for questioning, and only a few hours after the newspapers began to run stories about Gallo as the main suspect. After Joey and Albert returned from the police station, the group assembled back at Armando's cafe, a Gallo hangout on Presidents Street. Joey walked in furiously, throwing his hat down and complaining, "What a bum rap they're laying on us over here. We clipped Colombo. Wish the fuck we did. But that J. Edgar Hoover must be creaming his fucking pants. He's going to have his own banchetto [banquet] tonight."[ccxxviii]

***

Down the packed second floor corridor of Roosevelt hospital, Anthony sees Dr. Hanson approaching. He and his family listen as the surgeon explains, "We just removed one of the bullets which was lodged in his head. There is still one more in his neck and a third in his cheek. He is stabilized now and his condition has improved slightly. We're going to monitor him for an hour and then go back in for the second bullet." Colombo's sons tighten their lips and hold back tears. Anthony says, "Thank you, Doctor."

A uniformed policeman pushes his way through the crowd of family members and friends, and heads right for Anthony. "Excuse me, Anthony, right?" Anthony doesn't recognize him and just stares back blankly. "You're Joe's son, right?" Overwhelmed and in shock, Anthony tries to process the simple question. He answers, "Yes." With a swift move the officer takes Anthony's hand and firmly places some items into it. With tears in his eyes the young officer tells Anthony, "These are your father's. I didn't want anything to happen to them." After a pause, he continues,

325

"Anthony, I'm real sorry about what happened. I was League member. Your father is a great man. I hope things here today get better real soon. I'll be praying for him." He then slips back into the crowd. Anthony opens his hand and looks down at the items: a small gold chain, a green scapular, his father's IACRL membership card, a handkerchief, a red ribbon with thirteen knots in it, and a roll of cash. As he picks up the gold chain the medallion of St. Jude dangles from the links. It is the chain his father wears every day around his neck. In this moment all the chaos surrounding Anthony subsides, and everything is still.

✻✻✻

Although law enforcement was still only speculating about why Jerome Johnson shot Colombo, the newspapers eagerly embraced accounts of the purported "feud" between Colombo and Gallo. The *Daily News* headline read, "Black is Slain at Rally After Hitting Mob Boss."[ccxxix] In the article, "the shooting of Brooklyn crime Czar Joseph Colombo"[ccxxx] was described as a "climax to months of a bitter struggle for power within his Brooklyn based family."[ccxxxi] This explanation for the shooting was both the most sensational and the easiest to understand. Reporters pointed out that Gallo had made friends with blacks in prison. And Jerome Johnson was black; it made perfect sense. According to the *Daily News*, Gallo had "organized a new gang consisting of black gunmen and racketeers operating in Harlem, Bedford-Stuyvesant and East New York and including some of his Auburn pen pals."[ccxxxii] Nicholas Pileggi, in a story for the *New Yorker*, claimed that Gallo "upon his release from prison" put "together an integrated gang. They [police] noticed that his two bodyguards were blacks."[ccxxxiii] These stories derived mostly from gossip, and were entirely repudiated by Gallo's associates. The Greek responded, 'What horseshit. I would have known if we'd sent Johnson in for the shot, even if Joey was working it on his own, because there wasn't a fucking thing we didn't talk about.'"[ccxxxiv]

The Gallo group, asserting its innocence in the Colombo shooting, speculated about other possible scenarios. They had access to more information than the NYPD about possible grudges within the organizations. They were aware of the rumors about Joey's association with the blacks, and they believed the use of a black shooter was an easy and obvious way to frame him. They discussed the possibility of Gambino having ordered the hit as punishment for Colombo's public persona, of which he disapproved, or of a coup within the Colombo group itself. Another theory related to the murder of Frankie "Shots" Abbatemarco. Frankie's son Tony blamed the Gallo group for the murder, and since a lot of his action was in Bedford Stuyvesant with blacks, he could have arranged the hit. This would result not only in the Colombos retaliating against the Gallos, but would also earn them the reproach of all of the New York groups for the dishonorable way in which the shooting was executed. When Joey himself was asked for his opinion on the various theories, he replied, "Who the fuck knows?"[ccxxxv]

Frank Illiano, one of Gallo's crew, was one of the first to espouse a theory, which extended well beyond Mob infighting. He argued that given Johnson's history with drugs and his desire to make some fast money he would have been easily manipulated by the FBI, especially if he was facing some heavy time. The Gallo crew initially argued with Illiano claiming the story was a bit far-fetched, but Illiano was insistent. "That piece of work on Colombo, that was a Mob hit? Think about it. Put your marbles together and *think*. This stunad,[stupid] this fucking Johnson, he's got the press pass, the professional camera, and he shoots. Where'd you ever hear of Mob guys doing some dumb shit like that with all the law around? Tell me. Where? In the fucking movies? But the CIA, that's how they do it. And who are they asshole buddies with? Hoover. And who does Hoover hate the most? Colombo. Hoover especially had everything to gain having Colombo clipped. Now here's a guy that's really going bananas with Colombo's people picketing the FBI. And how do we know this? The way he sent the feds down on everybody who picketed. Here's this stunad, scungil, [fool] Colombo, going against the biggest man in Washington next to the President, and in some ways he's bigger because he can do no wrong." Illiano described how the FBI could easily get to Johnson, convince him to kill Joe in front of thousands of people and the result would likely be a gang war. Afterward, "not only is he [Hoover] going to sit back and watch us kill each other, but there won't be any more stunad League. With Colombo taken off, is there a League? It's finito."[ccxxxvi]

***

"After my father was shot I was being followed everywhere I went. I couldn't turn any corner without someone lurking behind me or trailing me in my car. Most of the time it was the FBI but they operated very mysteriously so I couldn't always be so sure. Life for me changed drastically in a number of ways. I went from not having any fear at all to fearing almost every moment of my life. Fear that my father would die, fear that something might happened to my other family members, and at times fear that someone might try and take a shot at me. Naturally I began packing everywhere I went. When we were upstate at the house we would walk around the property with rifles and shotguns on us at all times. It was a very trying time for my family and me. I did not hide one bit; everyone knew where I was, which made me an easy target, especially entering and leaving Roosevelt Hospital.

I was with 'Chubby' (Phillip Rosello) walking in the hallway of the hospital a few days after my father was shot. When I opened the doors to one of the hallways, there were four men there waiting for me. These men were agents or detectives, dressed in the normal FBI costume, but I had never seen them before. They surrounded me. I told Chubby to go up ahead to check in on my mother. These men never provided any of their names, or said what agency they were with. I guess it was the leader of the group that said to me, 'Anthony, we need to speak to you.' I told them, 'I've got nothing to say to you people.' He said, 'No, we have to talk to you.' They made a wall in front of me so I couldn't walk around them. I said, 'Listen I told you I have nothing to say to you fucking people, so there is nothing to talk about.' Then this guy tried to suggest that they had something I needed to hear. 'No Anthony, we have some information for you.' I looked at him in disbelief and said, 'What information?' He said, 'We have serious word, from a credible source, that there is a plot to kill your mother and your sister.' It was pretty odd to me that the plot didn't include me or my brothers, just my mother and my sister. So I asked him, 'What's the plot?' He said, 'Well we can't tell you that but we can help you.' I asked, 'What do you mean you want to help me? Why don't you just arrest the people that are planning it?' Of course they had some official reason why they couldn't make an arrest yet. I said to him, bluntly, 'You have credible and good proof that someone is going to try and kill my mother and sister, but you can't do anything about it?' They wouldn't address my question and only talked about how they wanted to help by following me around. Confused, I asked, 'Follow me?' 'Yes, we can put guards on you wherever you go. This way we can protect you.' I said, 'I thought you just said they weren't after me, just my mother and sister. What do you want to protect me for?' Now he throws in, 'Well, they're going to kill you, too.' I paused for a minute and thought about what they were saying; then I spoke. 'So you're going to put guys on me and follow me everywhere I go to protect me?' 'Yes', he replied. 'So these men will be able to protect me if someone tries to shoot me or my family?' Again, he says, 'Yes.' I just stood there for a moment. I couldn't believe this preposterous bullshit he was trying to feed me. I was starting to get very angry about the whole thing. I said to him, "You had a guard on my father, right? Look what happened with that! I'll take care of protecting my family. Leave my mother and my sister alone.' I pushed my way past them as they all watched me, speechless.

Two weeks after the shooting I received a message from Carl that he wanted to see me. I drove to Brooklyn with my brother Joey to meet him at his son's home. By that time there were already a bunch of stories printed about him being tied to the shooting. The majority of them were written about my father and Joey Gallo, but I didn't believe anything that was being printed in the papers. When I arrived, Carl and his son Joseph, invited me and my brother Joey to sit down in the living room to talk. It was a very casual meeting. We drank black coffee and Carl asked me a bunch of questions. He said, 'Anthony, I am very sorry for what has happed. I can only imagine how your family must feel. I know what kind of man your father is in his family and I hope he recovers soon.' I thanked him and then he went on to ask about me and how I was handling all of it. He asked about my mother and brothers and of course offered to help in any way he could. When my father was mentioned again, Carl became sullen and his eyes welled up in tears. I don't think it is possible for people to understand the relationship my father had with Carl. I'm sure they had argued before and may have not seen eye to eye on everything, but my father loved Carl like a father and Carl treated him like his own son. It was reassuring for me to speak about my father. I didn't have to ask him any questions because I had no suspicions. You can tell when a person is truthful. He was emotional, concerned and obviously upset. We talked for a while more and after a light meal I went home.

Shortly after the meet with Carl, I was called to meet a man in New York who I will not mention by name. He wanted to see me to find out how my family was doing. He also wanted me to know that all of the men involved in the "lifestyle" were all supporters of the League when it began and many still were. If any man withdrew support later on when things got heated, it was unwritten law that no one was to touch the League. He assured me that many powerful men cared for it and felt it was needed. During our meeting he told me there was different kind of investigation happening on my father's shooting. This one by men within "the lifestyle." After months of gathering information they knew for certain it was not an underworld hit. Through the next several years this man would check in on me from time to time and make sure my family and I were doing okay. This man was someone the FBI and Media knew very little about. While the media and FBI were sure that Carl Gambino was the head of the so-called "commission" and the most powerful gangster in the nation, this man remained under their radar. The truth was, that during that era, he was a man even Carl wouldn't cross."

A few months after my first meeting with Carl the media continued to build awful stories about Carl and my father. They were also printing stories that claimed that Jerome Johnson had met Carl in a bar in Greenwich Village. Just because a man shows up at a bar the FBI thought was under Carl's control, that's a link? What if this guy frequented a precinct? Can we link him to the commissioner? Every time Seedman had a new theory on the case it was printed on the front page of the paper. An old judge once said the government could indict a ham sandwich if it wanted to, yet with all of Seedman's declarations they couldn't make one indictment. The scenario with Carl never made any sense to me. To know the intelligence and stature of Carl Gambino and to believe he would loose a man like Jerome Johnson into a crowd of 15,000 people with a gun, where he could have killed women or children, isn't rational. The margin for error in that situation is outrageous. But regardless of logic, and no matter how many times my father had told me not to trust the media, I couldn't stop reading the papers. I needed to see Carl again. I had to ask him to his face if any of it was true.

My brother Joey and I picked up Carl at his house on Ocean Parkway. He came out alone, and got into the car. I drove us up to Mary's restaurant on 86th Street, a place Carl used to frequent. We sat down and ordered dinner and while we ate I forced myself to ask the uncomfortable question, 'Carl, I've been reading all of these stories in the paper, and I may be out of line but with all due respect, for my own sanity and for my family's, is any of it true?' He looked at me and said, 'Absolutely not.'

The media did a good job of creating a believable story about my father's and Carl's relationship. There was truth in that Carl stopped supporting my father. It wasn't over League funding and Carl thinking my father was not giving him his fair cut. The truth was Carl knew how much money the League needed to survive because next to my father he was one of its biggest financial supporters. The divide that came between Carl and my father was caused by the League and my father's unwillingness to step down. Carl felt that the government would come after my father and try to put him away for life. He felt the League was aggravating them and they would stop at nothing to destroy it. Carl asked me what I was planning on doing with the League. He told me about how he had taken my father in as a child after my grandfather was murdered. He offered to help me find work and take me under his wing just like he did for my father. But he would do this under one condition. I would have to choose between working with him, or continuing my work with the League. I could not have both. He felt that any Colombo working with the League was going to be a thorn in the side of the government and he wanted no part of it.

In the back of my mind I thought about what leaving the League would mean. I could have money, power and respect, but I would turn my back on everything my father wanted for me. Carl asked me, 'You only worked for the League because you loved your father and you wanted to make him happy.' I told Carl that was true, but in time I grew to love the League on my own. I fell in love with the people, the fighting, and took pride in our accomplishments. I thought about the possibility of my father waking up. What could I tell him? I wouldn't be able to face him. I told Carl that I couldn't accept his offer. And with my refusal to back out, financially, I was on my own."

Chapter 14.

"No One Ever Tells You"

(Post-shooting)

Within two years, unable to survive without its founder, the League for which Joe had sacrificed so much disintegrated entirely. Colombo himself fared no better. On the morning of May 22, 1978, after lingering in a coma for seven years, Joe Colombo died from heart failure following brain surgery at St. Luke's Hospital in Newburgh, NY.

That week services were held for Joe at Saint Bernadette's in Bensonhurst. Father Louis Gigante held the mass services for his dear friend and urged people not to remember him for the things he was accused of in the papers, but for all of his great achievements. He closed by saying "shed no more tears for Joe Colombo, Joe Colombo is in the hands of God." Joe was buried in St. Johns Cemetery in Queens New York, beside his father and younger brother Lawrence, and along with many of the friends he had lost throughout the years. He would also rest near his mentor, Carl Gambino, who had died a year earlier from heart failure.

The assassination attempt on Joe Colombo was one of the most public and publicized shootings in the history of New York. If it was part of a larger conspiracy, and not solely the work of Jerome Johnson, it was executed flawlessly. After the shooting, law enforcement never produced a single indictment or arrest. The NYPD, led by Chief of Detectives Albert Seedman, investigated Joe Colombo's shooting based on three major theories. The first was that Johnson was a psychopath; a lone gunman who just wanted to kill Joe Colombo. The second was that Johnson was acting as a gunman for a black revolutionary group. The third was that Johnson had been hired by a member or members of organized crime to make the hit.[ccxxxvii] Seedman began by calling in over fifty detectives from all over the city.[ccxxxviii] He assigned three teams to look into each theory outlined. Immediately, an intensive investigation into Johnson's background was initiated.

The facts and evidence surrounding the shooting of Joe Colombo were plentiful, but there was not enough evidence to prove a conspiracy. There were numerous witness accounts identifying the black man, Jerome Addison Johnson, as the shooter. Johnson was then shot and killed by an unknown gunman, presumably either to silence him, or to avenge the shooting of Joe Colombo. Police knew Johnson was at the rally with an accomplice, a black female with a press pass and a camera. The NYPD recovered both the murder weapon that killed Johnson and the gun that shot Colombo at the scene of the crime. During press releases, police reported the weapons to be untraceable, but official reports leaned more towards a suspicious past for both of the weapons.

There was no shortage of people who were angry with Joe Colombo. Police and news writers eagerly jumped on stories that many members of the criminal underworld resented his work with the League and the unwanted attention it engendered. The public was well acquainted with Colombo's connection to organized crime, so the idea of a gangland shooting was easy to believe, even if the shooter was a black man unknown in criminal circles. Police knew if they couldn't solve the crime, they could still satisfy the public by imputing the crime to a complex plot laid out by the "Italian Mafia."

Seedman himself believed that the shooting had been ordered by one of two suspects. The first was Joey Gallo, whom police knew had had relationships with blacks while he was in prison. Gallo had a reputation as erratic and impulsive and was open in his hatred for Colombo. The theory that Gallo was behind the shooting was appealing for these reasons, regardless of the contradictory details and testimony that surfaced after the shooting.

The second suspect was Carl Gambino. Police believed Carl disapproved of the League and wanted to destroy it by eliminating Colombo. There were other rumors that Gambino felt entitled to and deprived of a portion of the League's treasure chest.[ccxxxix]

The investigation into Colombo's shooting was closed after less than a year. It was probably doomed from the beginning. All of the bias surrounding Colombo's life made it virtually impossible for the investigation to be run objectively. The following is what has been learned about the three aforementioned police theories, as well as a fourth theory never before introduced; the possibility of an FBI murder plot against Joe Colombo:

The Lone Gunman Theory

Jerome Addison Johnson, aka Jerry Johnson or Addison Rand, was a 24 year old drifter. The FBI knew him as "one JEROME A. JOHNSON, FBI Number 185 112 G, a Negro male, date of birth July 16, 1946."[ccxl] It is a troubling oddity that although Johnson had been issued an FBI number, the FBI denies entirely that it has any file on him. Johnson was raised in Waycross, Georgia by his maternal grandmother, until 1955 when he moved to New Brunswick, New Jersey to be reunited with his mother. After graduating high school he left for Hollywood to pursue a career in filmmaking.

The Hollywood shuffle proved arduous and Johnson ended up working odd jobs to make ends meet. In 1966, struggling to earn a living, Johnson turned to petty crimes and began having trouble with the law. He was arrested for burglaries and drug possession and eventually rape. Johnson spent a year and a half in jail in California and during his incarceration stabbed another inmate, leaving him with a 40-stitch scar.[ccxli] He was convicted of assault but was given three years probation for the violent felony.[ccxlii] During his first few months of probation, Johnson received special permission from his parole officer to travel back to the East Coast.[ccxliii] He moved back to New Jersey in the spring of 1970 and within a month, on May 9th, he was arrested for rape and assault in Greenwich Village, but again freed on bail. The case was still pending at the time of his death.[ccxliv] New Brunswick police disclosed records that he was involved in another attempted rape case.[ccxlv] The victim claimed she was tortured, raped and beaten by Johnson as he threatened her while wielding a machete.[ccxlvi] The case was never prosecuted and Johnson left for New York City where he began living with numerous white women, raping some, hustling others, always pitching them a line about who he was and what he was going to be. He was accused of rape again on May 10th, but the charges were later dropped. Although he had also been caught in possession of narcotics, police stated that since he'd been arrested on false charges they would not charge him with possession.[ccxlvii] A few days after he was released, Johnson inexplicably surfaced 2,200 miles away in Alberta, Canada. The trip was never investigated by law enforcement.

If Johnson had ties to the Mob, there was never any evidence of them. The truth was that he was a hustler; working at various times as a pimp, drug dealer, pornographer and filmmaker.[ccxlviii] He had enough intelligence to get him places and enough charisma to extract money or sex from those he encountered. He worked as a drug dealer, selling marijuana and cocaine, but almost everyone Johnson knew remembered him as always being broke. His friends and family never knew him to evince interest in politics or civil rights issues; he was more of a dreamer, a drifter, a pleasure seeker. The most interesting thing about Johnson was how he almost always managed to stay out of jail. While on probation Johnson kept adding new and serious charges to his rap sheet. Who was coming to the aid of Johnson to make these charges go away?

In the weeks leading up to Unity Day, Jerome Johnson was making preparations to actually record Joe Colombo on film. Johnson scrambled in the days leading up to the rally to try and hire extra camera operators for the rally. If Johnson were only planning on killing Colombo and being killed himself, it was suspicious behavior for him to be so concerned with having additional camera operators there the day of the rally. Johnson also showed his belief that he was going to leave that rally that day. Several of Johnson's friends told news reporters he was planning to take a trip to the Jamaican islands and had shown them a set of tickets.[ccxlix] If Johnson were truly prepared to commit murder and suicide, in a theory that profiled Johnson as a deranged lunatic, he would not have prepared for something like a "trip to the islands" after the shooting. These pieces of evidence even though they were small, cannot be disregarded, as they directly contradict the theory of a "lone gunman."

The B.R.A.T. Theory

The Associated Press ran the telephone call that came in at 12:30 p.m., purportedly from a group identified as the Black Revolutionary Attack Team. The transmission read as follows:

> We just assassinated Joe Colombo. This is only the beginning. One of our brothers was killed today. This is only the beginning. The racist society will pay for what they're doing to our black brothers.[ccl]

There were many black radical groups that emerged between 1954 and 1970, but no one had heard of the Black Revolutionary Attack Team. Ti-Grace Atkinson, a female activist, and friend of Joe's, was involved in the civil rights movement and well known among both white and black radicals at the time. Black radicals told Atkinson the group BRAT sounded like a "put up." This wouldn't have been a stretch for the FBI, as COINTELPRO was known to create fake organizations during the civil rights era. They reasoned that no political black person would have been involved in shooting Joe Colombo for two reasons: first, there was no way to get away with the crime, and second, no black radical would be willing to "die for whitey." Blacks told Atkinson the entire shooting felt like "pig" (FBI) influence. Both Gallo and Johnson seemed like the perfect fall guys for the operation.

Johnson possessed no attributes of a black radical, nor would the black radicals want to work or be associated with him. Further, a political group would have never approved the shooting in a public place, which put innocent people in danger. The radicals also felt that Colombo would be the last Mob boss a black group would want to hit because of his reputation for social activism and diplomacy. Colombo and the IACRL were well known for their ability to bring community leaders of different backgrounds together. The entire operation seemed like an attempt at creating racial bitterness between Italians and blacks. Like many of the COINTELPRO operations, the shooting may have been an attempt at inciting a war between FBI target groups; black radicals and Italian gangsters.

The Gallo Theory

On Friday July 2nd, four days after the shooting, Seedman called for a special conference with the city's Chief Inspector Codd and Deputy Police Commissioner Robert Daley. Seedman had just returned from a meeting with a source in Brooklyn and reported excitedly, "It was a Mob hit! According to my information the contract was let by Gambino himself. The price was $40,000. Furthermore, Colombo is supposed to be the first in a series of hits. Next on the list are Mrs. Colombo and the two oldest sons. It's to be a reign of terror, the object of which is to destroy both the League and the Colombo Mob completely."[ccli]

This informant's story claiming Mrs. Colombo would be murdered was completely inconsistent with Mob protocol and unprecedented. But Detective Seedman was so sure of this information he decided to call a press conference. Seedman wanted Deputy Police Commissioner Robert Daley to speak at the press conference so Daley could deny knowing the informant, and have deniability about other details the press would want to know.[cclii] This was a tactic often used by law enforcement when they did not have any tangible evidence in a case and made press releases in hopes of leading criminals to believe they had solid leads. The source of the story, which was complete hearsay, was an informant who "patronized" a taxi service that was linked to the Gallo group.[ccliii] According to this informant, whose identity Seedman never revealed, the real reason for the Colombo murder plot was the belief that he was taking money from the League and not splitting the profits with other Gang bosses.[ccliv] For anyone who actually knew Joe Colombo, this supposed theft of League funds was utterly impossible. His integrity and devotion to the League's work would never have allowed him to steal money intended to help the less fortunate.

Daley added that the plot was "detailed," well planned and "approved only days before" the shooting, and further claimed those involved in the plot would be arrested.[cclv] The NYPD asserted that there were other plots to murder Nicholas "Jiggs" Forlano, Carmine Persico, Hugh McIntosh, and Joseph "Joey Notch" Iannuci.[cclvi] These were all men known to be strong Colombo supporters. Since the police were claiming other Italian gangsters had made out the contracts to kill them, publishing this information could likely have led to a bloody gang war.

One member of the press asked whether the resoluteness with which they spoke was based on arrests, eyewitness testimony or physical evidence. Daley answered, "I can't say."[cclvii] Regardless of the obscure nature of the source, the press conveyed this speculative information to the public. In fact, reporters were encouraged to sensationalize their reports, knowing there would never be a lawsuit for slander or a public rebuttal, because these men want no media attention at all. The only man who'd ever publicly denied his involvement in organized crime had just been silenced, and as long as Joe Colombo was in a coma and unable to defend himself, as far as the media was concerned, the gloves were off.

Seedman's head detective on the case, Sergeant John Weber, wanted to ignore the informant and the police department's theory of a gangland rivalry.[cclviii] He preferred to investigate the case starting only with the hard facts and then draw a conclusion. Seedman wanted the Gallo story to be true, he needed to be right, since he was now responsible for propagating the idea that this was an underworld hit and that they had information that would lead to arrests. Seedman hoped and believed that Weber's further investigation would turn up nothing.[cclix]

Even without any corroborating information from the Gallo group, there were apparent contradictions in the timeline that made it unlikely that Johnson was hired by Gallo. According to a number of friends and relatives, Johnson had claimed months prior that he was working as a photographer for the League.[cclx] In fact, reports of this began before Gallo had even been released from prison. It seems virtually impossible that Gallo would have initiated this intricate plan with Johnson from behind prison walls.

Shortly after Joe was shot, a meeting was called by the "Dons" of the five New York Mob outfits. Albert Gallo was sent for to explain the Gallos role in the shooting. They got word to Albert through an emissary, Vincent "the Chin" Gigante from the Genovese crew. Gigante, the brother of Father Louis Gigante, had been in contact with the Gallo crew for many years and was a trusted ally, but this meeting had Albert worried. Any gangster knew that an unsanctioned hit on a Mob boss would result in death to the shooters and their whole crew. It was all over the press and streets that Joey Gallo had been working with blacks. Whether it was Gallo or an associate behind the shooting, it certainly appeared that the Gallo's were responsible. Albert Gallo and Pete the Greek met the Chin at his apartment in the Bronx. Gigante got right to the point, "About the circle. Well, certain people, myself included, don't know whether you did or you didn't whack Joe C. And I'm telling you now, Blast, they're looking hard."[cclxi] Gigante let Gallo know that the Commission was demanding an explanation, but the last thing they wanted to do was jump the gun and have any

345

members of the Gallo crew killed if they were innocent. Gigante told Gallo, "These people need to be assured, and I feel that you and I have enough trust and faith in one another, and I hope to hear something so I can assure them."[cclxii] They talked for hours until Gigante was convinced they weren't behind it. As much as they had wanted to shoot Colombo, it wasn't their hit. When they discussed the possibility of a lone gunman, Gallo pointed out, "Only a psychopath goes in, pulls a piece, and shoots, nothing prearranged. This was too premeditated." They discussed the phony press pass and credentials, and decided they were easy obstacles to overcome, but pondered how Johnson was convinced he would escape. "It's like a Kennedy assassination."[cclxiii]

The Gambino Theory

The Gambino theory was just an extension of the Gallo theory. It involved the same plot and players, but employed Gambino as the mastermind who gave Gallo permission to do the hit. The FBI's own informants reported back to agents that they had little suspicion that Gambino had any prior knowledge of the shooting.[cclxiv] It was also reported to the FBI that "Mafia leaders are analyzing the background of Jerome Johnson"[cclxv] which further proves the hit was a complete shock to the underworld.

Seedman ignored the underworld informants who insisted that "a lot of people knew Gallo was challenging Colombo and was close to black gangsters so the shooting could have been engineered to point to Gallo."[cclxvi]

Barry Slotnick spoke about the rumors of Gambino being behind this. His uncle had been a very close friend of Gambino's for years. Slotnick was also privy to Joe's personal relationship with Gambino and doubted that this was his doing all along. Gambino knew how close Slotnick was to Colombo, not only personally, but physically; he was next to Joe during all his public appearances. To hire an unknown, unpredictable psychopath to shoot Joe would have meant endangering Slotnick, not to mention thousands of innocent people at the rally. This would include mothers, daughters, and children of IACRL, many of whom were relatives of known mobsters and their associates. Barry argued that Gambino would never have approved this type of action and said that it was simply "not possible."

As far as Seedman was concerned the case had been solved even without prosecutions. Deputy Commissioner Daley said Seedman felt the Colombo shooting was a Mob hit from the very beginning.[cclxvii] Seedman believed it was Gambino and Gallo in tandem. But both NYPD and the FBI reported that Joe Colombo and Carl Gambino had a private meeting one week before the rally and during that meeting addressed the issue of Joey Gallo and his attempts to move in on South Brooklyn rackets. It was reported that Carl and Joe would "fight any attempt by Gallo."[cclxviii]

In addition to the relationship Gambino had with Colombo, other evidence contradicted the theory of Gambino as a mastermind. Daniel P. Hollman, Chief of the Joint Strike Force to Combat Organized Crime, and probably the most respected and experienced federal investigator in New York, disbelieved Seedman's theory and held a press conference to explain his reasoning: "You have to recognize that if Johnson were to change his mind and not go through with this attempted murder at the Italian Unity Day, he may then, under certain stresses reveal what occurred [the plot] to law enforcement agencies. Or he might turn in fact to the Colombo family itself and for money, reveal to them what had been planned. This of course then would have placed that organized crime figure who planned this thing in, shall we say a very precarious position."

Seedman felt challenged and responded to the press immediately. "Whatever we had previously revealed in the Colombo case we are not at this time changing anything as to what we have said. Johnson, if Mr. Hollman labels him a psychopath, we also have said that he is a psychopath. But that doesn't mean that he did it on his own." Fighting to keep leverage, Seedman also told reporters again, "We will make an arrest in this case."[cclxix]

Hollman was not impressed by Seedman's rebuttal, and noted, "Having studied organized crime and attempted slayings over a number of years certain patterns become obvious with respect to these attempted slayings." He then cited the murders of Arnold Schuster and Albert Anastasia. He talked about the selection of the assassin and the period of apprenticeship they go through to be inducted into organized crime and how "they are known to be competent and very professional with respect to assassination attempts." Johnson, according to these established patterns, didn't "fit into this mold at all. He has not the prior background in organized crime. He owes organized crime groups no bit of loyalty. He's never been associated with them. So then if you look further into the Johnson situation, if you assume for a moment that some organized crime figure outside of the Colombo family decided to have Colombo assassinated, he then had to confer and discuss this matter with Johnson at some length. He had to plan it. He had to pay him. He had to probably obtain the murder weapon and a series of meetings would had to have taken place with Johnson." Seedman believed that the hit was put together in one week.[cclxx] Hollman could not believe Johnson was considered dependable for a job of this magnitude. "That is something very doubtful that the organized crime group would permit to happen. You've never had that type of situation prevail before."

When asked by a reporter why he felt so strongly that this was not an underworld hit, Hollman almost insinuated they had other knowledge about the job, "Well there are other things besides that I don't want to get in to. I prefer to leave this now as my own observations. I don't want to get into my sources." Hollman also questioned the exit strategy for Johnson; specifically the fact that there was none. "Obviously, Johnson didn't want to be killed. He would have made every attempt to escape. And had he escaped, he would have again been a possible live witness, someday, against a particular organized crime group. It just doesn't lend and fit into the pattern."

Hollman was not the only federal crime fighter who didn't believe the shooting was linked to the Mob. The government attorney in charge of Joe Colombo's territories of Brooklyn, Queens and Long Island, Joseph F. Lynch told reporters he had "no information to indicate either Johnson was employed by a gangland rival of Colombo or that he was acting alone."[cclxxi]

Regardless of facts and professional opinions offered, Seedman stuck to his gangland theory and said, "We will not reverse ourselves, Colombo was shot by a Mob-hired killer."[cclxxii] He was too invested in the theory and if he changed his course he would have been humiliated in front of his colleagues, the media, and the public. Seedman's story began with a "detailed" plot that involved two hit men, Johnson and the man who hit Johnson." Weeks later Seedman changed his stance claiming Johnson's shooting was made by a bodyguard of Colombo and was a "reaction" to Colombo's shooting.[cclxxiii] The likelihood that Johnson was shot by a Colombo bodyguard, however, was slim, as Colombo's people would certainly want Johnson kept alive to get to the source of the shooting. Also, the escape of Johnson's shooter seemed virtually impossible unless it had been a police officer. Seedman's case showed other inconsistencies, but reporters failed to notice.

Seedman claimed that the gun used to kill Johnson was untraceable, but ballistics reported otherwise. The Colombo case had 500 DD-5's submitted, the complaint forms filled out by police to detail their investigations. The reports represented over 2000 days of investigative work.[cclxxiv] After filing multiple requests for the files with the NYPD's Freedom of Information Law Unit, only five pieces of paper were provided. Accompanying the papers was the following response:

> Redactions were made to the document(s) in that release of the information would represent an unwarranted invasion of personal privacy

> Redactions were made to the document(s) in that release of the information would identify a confidential source/confidential information

One of the pages received was a DD-5 complaint report filed by Patrolman Giovanni Schiozzi of the 14th Precinct. It was a positive identification of Jerome Johnson as the man who shot Joe Colombo. There were some interesting facts in the ballistics reports about the weapons recovered. The gun, which was identified as the weapon used to shoot Joe Colombo, was widely reported as a 7.65-millimeter automatic of "foreign make."[cclxxv] Although eyewitnesses claimed to have seen Johnson shoot the gun, and police claimed to have removed the weapon from Johnson's hand, none of his fingerprints were found on the weapon.[cclxxvi]

Seedman was very careful in avoiding questions about fingerprints on the weapon. An eyewitness to the shooting told the press and police officers that he'd witnessed a policeman pick up the gun, clean it, cock it, shift it to his right hand and put it in his pocket.[cclxxvii] The weapon was identified in police reports as a "Menta" with the serial number 3757.[cclxxviii] It was reported to the press that the weapon was completely untraceable. But, curiously, the ballistics report read:

> UNDER THE NAME "MENTA" THERE IS NO RECORD WITH LOST PROPERTY OR NCIC HOWEVER THERE IS A LISTING WITH THIS DEPT. FOR A 7.65 CAL. LUGAR AUTOMATIC PISTOL SERIAL # 3757. THIS LUGAR IS WANTED IN CHIEF OF DETECTIVES INVESTIGATION # 2426 OF OCT. 16, 1958, INS. HENNING.

One might question why they mentioned in the report the existence of a different make with the same serial number, unless they weren't certain whether they had a Lugar or a Menta in their possession.

When Seedman was asked by reporters, "How do you know it wasn't a cop who killed Johnson?" Seedman answered cautiously, "Because we have the gun that killed Johnson; it's been tested by ballistics and it is not a police gun." That fact hardly clears any cops of the shooting. One can only assume Seedman meant that it wasn't an officer reacting with aggression or nervously shooting Johnson with his police-issued sidearm. If it were a cop in question or an FBI agent, he would have been part of a more secretive plan, thus using a weapon with a mysterious past like the revolver that killed Johnson. Seedman was then asked, "Who was the last owner?" He replied, "No comment on that question."[cclxxix] This was a question he did not want to reveal the answer to. It turned out that last owner was a police officer that had reported the gun lost in transit in 1964.[cclxxx]

Seedman ended up closing the case after the shooting of Joey Gallo on Hester Street in April 1972. Although he never had to answer for his bold press announcements with promises to make arrests, he was already modifying his theory about a month after he made the statements to the media. In an interview with Barbara Campbell of the *New York Times,* he said he would stick to his theory of an underworld rivalry because it came from a "reliable" source, but would not rule out other possibilities.[cclxxxi]

Rumors in the NYPD circled that the FBI had pushed Seedman out of the case. Even former Deputy Police Commissioner Robert Daley could not get to the bottom of who shut down the investigation. Orders from above stated they didn't want to bring any Mob figures before a Grand Jury for questioning.[cclxxxii] This was a peculiar decision, given that during the past 70 years the police department had been doing precisely this; shaking down criminals and holding Grand Jury hearings to extract what they information they could use or issue contempt charges. The Assistant District Attorney Dan Fitzgerald criticized the police department for closing the case, calling the decision a "mistake."[cclxxxiii] Seedman had a gut feeling that one day he would be vindicated in his claim by receiving confirmation from an informant.[cclxxxiv] After forty plus years, no such confirmation has occurred and the reliable source has never been revealed.

The FBI-CIA Theory

Joe was vulnerable to assassination in his position as a political leader. Accusations that the FBI was responsible, although not widely publicized, were prevalent. Even the League's chaplain Rev. Louis Gigante accused the FBI, citing their enmity for Joe and the IACRL. "If he [Johnson] was hired, the CIA has done this before. The FBI has done this before. Maybe he was hired by so-called legitimate forces." There were many aspects of the shooting that matched the method of operations of COINTELPRO. The media campaign that followed the shooting was a perfect distraction. Leutrell Osborne Sr., a twenty-five year CIA case officer commented on the actions of the FBI during the Hoover years. "Agents infiltrated organizations, conducted, 'dirty tricks,' psychological warfare, and used the legal system, break-ins, stalking, assaults and beatings for harassment. They inflicted physical, emotional, and economic damage, and did not stop short of using assassinations to "neutralize their adversaries."

In a 1970 FBI Memorandum to Cartha "Deke" DeLoach, Hoover's assistant director, the crime records division stated an editor of the New York Daily News would be:

> RUNNING AN ARTICLE CONCERNING COLOMBO AND HIS ASSOCIATES, WHICH WILL SHOW JUST WHAT A "BUM" HE IS

With Hoover's approval, in another tactic the Daily News would also "utlize" any source information provided by the FBI with the promise it would leave no trail back to the government.

In 1975 Frank Church became the chairman of the Select Committee to Study Government Operations with Respect to Intelligence Activities (commonly referred to as the Church committee). By this time Hoover had passed on and it was safer to investigate the once "untouchable" FBI. The committee's purpose was to investigate the abuses of power and illegal tactics being used by the CIA and FBI on American citizens.

The committee discovered foul play ranging from negative disinformation campaigns through the news media to murder. The practices employed by these intelligence organizations were highly unethical. They found documented proof that misinformation campaigns were put in play with the hopes of creating violence among rival groups. In 1976 the Church committee concluded, "domestic intelligence activity has threatened and undermined the constitutional rights of American free speech, association and privacy. It has done so primarily because the constitutional system for checking abuses of power has not been applied."[cclxxxv]

This subtle victory against harassment and abuse of power by the CIA and FBI would have been greatly celebrated by Joe and the League. A few years later, Congress did more probing and opened investigations into theories that the CIA and FBI were responsible for assassinations. Before Congress began its interrogations, six top FBI officials under J. Edgar Hoover died within a six-month period. One of the men, a top FBI official, William C. Sullivan was very outspoken about Hoover's illicit operations and was fired from the Bureau without warning in the summer of 1971. He told friends explicitly that he would be killed in an event that would look like an accident, but it would be murder.[cclxxxvi] On November 9, 1977, Sullivan was walking through the woods near his home in New Hampshire when he was shot in the neck and killed instantly. In the early morning dawn, the twenty-two year old shooter had apparently mistaken Sullivan for a deer.[cclxxxvii] Without the testimony of these officials, no one will ever know the extent of Hoover's illegal operations.

On June 30, 1971, the night after Joe's shooting, Barry and Donna Slotnick were watching the news in their Manhattan apartment. When the image of Jerome Addison Johnson appeared on the screen, Donna Slotnick was startled and excitedly told her husband, "Barry, that's him! That is the man I saw in the hallway at the law office! That's him!" Barry knew it had been quite some time since the bombing of his offices. He asked Donna if she was positive. Donna assured him the man on the TV was the same one she had seen holding a black bag in the hallway of the Park Row office moments before the bomb went off. There was no doubt in her mind.

Jerome Johnson had participated in this attack on the League almost a year before Colombo's assassination. At this time, the League was still nascent and had the complete approval of men like Gambino. Gallo was still serving time in prison. It was revealed years later that the FBI had been enlisting blacks to pose as photographers for years during the civil rights movement. In 2010, Memphis civil rights photographer Ernest Withers was exposed as an informant who spied on the movement for the FBI.[cclxxxviii]

True crime writers and news editors all agreed that Colombo's actions against the FBI were attracting too much attention and would create "backlash."[cclxxxix] But this backlash was only imagined to come from organized crime groups. At the time of the shooting, for the majority of the public it was inconceivable that the U.S. government could have played a role in his assassination. People were considered crazy for questioning the death of the President Kennedy in 1963, although there were numerous potential motives behind his assassination. The motive for the FBI to kill Joe Colombo and destroy the League wasn't difficult to imagine.

The media campaign after the shooting was designed to establish a link between the shooter and Joe's life in organized crime. Reporters did less investigating and more echoing of law enforcement. The Gallo theory was simple, making it easy to sell. Gallo disliked Colombo and had allied himself with blacks in prison. Johnson shot Colombo and he was black. Gallo's photo was in every newspaper and all over the TV during the weeks after the shooting. The newspapers even juxtaposed photos of Johnson and Gallo.[ccxc] These articles were selling an idea, not reporting the facts. They even publicized stories that purportedly came from underworld sources. Mob informants who would have had been privy to plans to kill Joe Colombo couldn't substantiate the theory promoted by Seedman or the mass media. These informants, who could have gained a lot of money by endorsing Seedman's theory, never disclosed any information about Joey Gallo or Carl Gambino's involvement. Joey Gallo's associate, Nicky Barnes, a black drug dealer from Harlem turned government informant, completed an autobiography and recalled no connection between Gallo and Colombo's assassination. The same went for snitch biographer Sammy "the Bull" Gravano, Michael Franzese, Joseph Cantalupo, and Gallo's closest associate turned informant Pete the Greek Diapoulos. Not only did they all deny that Gallo orchestrated the hit on Colombo, they also all adopted the theory that the US government was responsible for the shooting, because it had the clearest motive.

When the "Prime Minister of the Underworld," Frank Costello, was questioned in 1972 about who tried to kill Joe, he answered, "All I can tell you is that no Mob guy did the job."[ccxci] Then asked if it was Joey Gallo he responded, "Joe Gallo and his henchmen were small time hoods that spent most of their lives in jail. You remember that crap back in 1957 when the cops said Joe Gallo knocked off Albert Anastasia? Those punks shook at the mention of Anastasia's name."[ccxcii] When Costello was asked about the rumors that were spreading that the "white hats" (government agents) hired and then shot Johnson to silence him, he replied, "All I know is no Mob-connected guy tried to assassinate Colombo. And if he wasn't connected, he'd have to be a real nut to believe he could kill Colombo and make a getaway from those hundreds of cops."[ccxciii]

In 1985 and 1986 Joseph Cantalupo testified against the Mafia Commission, he spent six years wearing a wire around wise guys and was one of Rudolph Giuliani's key players. He never once heard from anyone within the Colombo crew that Gambino or Gallo killed the late boss. He admitted himself, "With all the publicity and stories, I just never believed Gallo could be that stupid to have killed Colombo."[ccxciv]

Sonny Franzese's son, Michael Franzese had no direct knowledge of the conspiracy, but the man purported to have led the Colombo family did discuss his theory in depth with many Colombo loyalists, and it didn't point to Gallo. Carmine Persico believed that "the government had set up Johnson to kill Colombo because they were afraid of the power he was gaining through the Italian-American Civil Rights League."[ccxcv]

Sammy the Bull spoke about the Colombo murder after he became a rat. He was with the Colombos around the time of the shooting and was an active member of the IACRL. He knew about Gallo's animosity towards Colombo and that given the chance Gallo would have liked to kill him. Joey Gallo told plenty of guys that he would have loved to be the guy behind killing Colombo, but he couldn't take the credit because he just didn't do it. Sammy said, "Junior Persico, Shorty, all the top guys in the family believed him. Some guys thought the government had set it up to make it look like the Gallos done it."

This theory that the government had orchestrated the assassination is compelling for one principal reason; any other theory had no plan of escape for Johnson. The only group that could guarantee him safe passage once he'd shot Colombo would be law enforcement. Seedman truly believed Johnson was convinced or duped into thinking one of these mobsters could escort him from the rally unscathed. This seems utterly implausible, however, even for a person who might be tempted by financial reward.

Persico believed the FBI could have told Johnson he would be arrested immediately after the shooting and then possibly given a chance to testify that he was hired by an underworld member to do the shooting. They would then grant him immunity and place him in the witness protection program. Given his extensive rap sheet, and the frequency with which he was released, Johnson might have been in the clutches of the FBI for some time.

Persico personally investigated the shooting using all of his resources in hopes of finding the accomplices that were witnessed at the rally with Johnson. Through Persico, Greg Scarpa furnished the FBI with a color photo obtained of the female that accompanied Johnson to the Rally. He told the FBI he and others were supposed to be on the hunt for the woman so that she could be snatched and made to tell "who hired Johnson to hit Colombo."[ccxcvi] After copying the photos and returning the original to Scarpa the FBI buried the photo instead of turning it into Seedman for his investigation. Their reason stated:

> IT IS NOTED THAT THE ABOVE INFORMATION HAS NOT BEEN DISSEMINATED TO THE NYCPD INASMUCH AS IT IS FELT TO DO SO MIGHT SERIOUSLY JEOPARDIZE INFORMANTS POSITION.[ccxcvii]

The FBI claimed they were not going to investigate the shooting of Joseph Colombo, even though they had already spent millions investigating his life.

The FBI still went door to door in New York questioning every suspected mobster that attended or called in sick to be at the rally. They insisted that they were merely trying to establish the future hierarchy of the family while Joe was sidelined. Frank J. Profaci, brother of the late Joseph Profaci and a suspected Colombo solider was questioned at his home in Brooklyn on July 15, 1971. He told the agents he arrived at the rally around 3 p.m., after the incident had already occurred and "could not offer any information relating to the event."[ccxcviii] The agents then furnished him with a photograph of himself at the time of the shooting, forcing Profaci to recant his statement. Profaci still didn't have much to say about the shooting and ended the interview by telling the FBI "Colombo was a great man who did a lot for the League."[ccxcix]

When the FBI arrived at the home of one of Joe's closest friends, Dominic "Mimi" Scialo, like others, had very little information to offer them about the actual shooting. They asked if Joey Gallo had anything to do with it and Mimi replied, "Your guess is as good as mine." Before the agents left Mimi said, "One of the stories going around is that the CIA had Colombo hit at the request of the FBI. He indicated that the FBI was "too hot" to do it themselves."[ccc]

Mobsters all over Brooklyn discussed the shooting and the probability of it being Gallo's orchestration. An anonymous source stated, "Joey was crazy, but not suicidal. The fact that rats told the cops wise guys were thinking it was an underworld hit only meant the cops were talking to the wrong wise guys. Killing Colombo was the last thing wise guys would have done at the time. The FBI already had three quarters of the Mob under indictment. The only people that believed he [Gallo] did it were John Q. Public." A few weeks after the shooting, after the "bosses" did their own investigation, convicted Lucchese mobster Christopher "Christie Tick" Furnari, Colombo captain Duke Santora, Petey Brush Morello, and a few others were at Furnari's famous hangout, the 19th Hole in Bensonhurst, discussing the shooting. They agreed Gallo using a black guy was comparable to the NYPD using an assassin dressed in a cop uniform. Duke Santora in his hoarse voice said disgustedly, "This was the fucking FBI! Joe spit in Hoover's face and they fucking whacked him."

When Anthony Colombo was approached by an FBI agent in the halls of Roosevelt Hospital, the FBI, not Seedman, warned him of a contract out on his, and his family's lives. Could there have been a link between Seedman's informant and the FBI? Or was it possible Seedman was so sure of the information because it was actually the FBI feeding it to him directly or indirectly? Seedman not only concealed evidence relating to the weapons, but there were also two pieces of evidence from the crime scene that never made it into an official report. The first was in the satchel recovered at the scene. This bag, believed to belong to Joe, was only reported by Seedman's squad to have had a few League pins in it and a revolver. The weapon, not fired was in the official reports, but also in that bag seen by officers at the scene of the crime was an undisclosed amount of money. This was League funds collected that morning from all of the captains. The second piece of evidence that never made it into press reports was the contents of another suitcase found near Jerome Johnson. Officers on the scene that day claimed to have counted $40,000 dollars in the case. It was taken to Roosevelt Hospital with Johnson and the guns, but once removed by Seedman's entourage it was never mentioned again. Officers commented about both of the cases forty years later wondering, "What ever happened to that case? I wonder where it is now?" The officers that tackled Johnson were very surprised that they were never questioned about the shooting. It wasn't until forty years later for this book they were asked to tell their accounts of what happened that day in Columbus Circle.

***

After the police concluded their investigation into the murder of Joe Colombo, claiming that all leads had been exhausted, the government would deliver one final blow to Colombo. On March 13, 1977, a spokesperson for the Justice Department affirmed that the ban on the use of the terms "Mafia" and "Cosa Nostra" had ended. Attorney General Griffin Bell began using the term openly and his spokesperson when interviewed stated, "In view of the fact that the Attorney General had used the term, I think it's safe to say the policy is no longer in effect."[ccci]

For the next forty years, true crime authors would reprint the same two stories about the Unity Day shootings. Some believed that Gallo was responsible, while others would suggest Gambino had arranged for his assassination. A number of books and articles, and even a major motion picture combined the two theories, making Gallo and Gambino co-conspirators. No writer could furnish any real evidence to support these theories, but as is the case with most popular legends, the public would eventually accept them as fact.

***

"During the years after my father's shooting my mother stayed beside him faithfully until the day he died. Our entire lives were changed in a matter of sixty seconds, never to be the same again. I sold his home in Brooklyn and moved my wife and kids upstate. Rumors still circulated about a possible gang war. I would walk around the property with shotguns and rifles loaded and ready to fire. I remember as a kid, I would dream up scenarios pretending I was a cowboy protecting my family's property. Never in a million years could I have guessed the fantasy would become a grim reality.

The FBI continued to investigate my father even years after the shooting. While he was in the hospital, they were afraid he would recover. After the surgeries were performed my father was moved to his home in Brooklyn where he had 24-hour care from nurses and doctors. They heard all kinds of rumors and wanted to know if he could talk, write messages, was he watching TV, any movements or talking? They were so interested they wanted a court-appointed neurologist to give them a medical report. They were continuously offering money to people that knew us, hoping they could get into my father's home and get a report. They ended up getting one from Joseph Cantalupo, the son of my father's good friend Anthony Cantalupo. To think how deeply rooted our families were. Our grandfathers would golf together back in the 20's and this man went to our home for a paycheck from the government duping his father and my mother one afternoon to satisfy the government. The government attorneys and agents can all wear suits and hide behind their badges and law degrees, but they were savages all the same to me.

To this day, I believe the words Carl Gambino spoke to me about my father's shooting. I believe the many other men from the underworld who claimed this shooting was no Mob hit. Men that knew what my father was doing, his political aspirations, men like Dick Capozzola and Meir Kahane believed my father was the victim of a government conspiracy. Even though Hoover escaped prosecution many of his cohorts did not. Those men swore oaths to defend this nation and proved to be corruptible. The newspapers still printed bold headlines about the "Mafia" and similar organizations ruining the moral fiber of our community, my father never bought it, and he died trying to defend it. He died trying to defend people's rights and liberties, knowing crime was not made by Italians; it existed everywhere, within every race and every profession. People can say whatever they want about my father, that he was a Mob boss, part of a five-man hit team, loan shark, but what they can't argue against is that for the last two years of his life he was a civil rights leader. Regardless of his age, occupation, wealth or political preference, he accomplished more than any Italian-American activist did before or after him.

The media did a great job keeping positive stories out of the papers and continuously running negative campaigns against my father and the League. Regardless of their efforts my father touched thousands of people with his hard work and dedication. He left a legacy behind that would take more than a bullet to extinguish. As for my father, what he shared with me was his dream of friendship, family, and living in a world of understanding and giving of oneself. He refused complacency; he insisted on righteousness and justice. If something had to get done no matter how difficult or distasteful; his way was, 'let's just get it done.'"

Epilogue

Forty years after his father's murder, Anthony Colombo walks up the driveway to his house in upstate New York. There are many remarkable similarities between Anthony and his father. He is at once decorous, while evincing a stern demeanor. His stare is intense, as he seems to be analyzing everything he looks at. Like his father, he shares an ardent love for his family and its traditions, especially spending time in the countryside. In the 1970's while caring for his father, Anthony built a home for his wife and children on the family property. He often gazes over the hills and thinks about how the landscape has changed over the years. Despite the passage of time, Anthony still can't help reliving that day over and over again. "On the day he got shot I should have been standing right there. I was changing my clothes because I had to make a speech." He shakes his head and frowns. "Who the hell knows? Maybe I could've pushed his [Johnson's] hand after the first shot. I just can't believe that with all those people right there, nobody did anything. I can't believe it." While he still suffers the pain of losing his father just as Joe lost his, Anthony has managed to break the cycle by surviving to see his grandchildren reach school.

Years after the shooting, Anthony reluctantly and temporarily embarked on a path that his father would have surely forbidden. When asked how his father would have reacted to some of his decisions, he responds, "He would have tried to kill me. This I know for sure. He never wanted that life for me. He would tell me things that at that time I just couldn't believe for myself. Once he died, so many things changed. I know my choices might have broken his heart, and if he were alive I wouldn't have made them. I know he lived through it when his own father was killed. It was something I made sure my children would not have to face." Anthony expresses regret about some of his life's decisions. He felt he needed to make certain sacrifices to protect his family. He has paid for his lawlessness and has since abandoned his belief that crime is a necessary evil in life. One still wonders, however, whether he did not actually believe the abundant stories of his father's involvement in organized crime.

"I heard many of the things that were said about my father, but I wouldn't dare ever say anything about it. I always knew my father was a powerful man; his whole demeanor exuded power. I knew he had a lot of tough friends, but that's how Brooklyn was in those days; a lot of really tough men were in the streets. When the League began is when I really started hearing stories and reading it in the paper. At that time he denied being a member of organized crime so vehemently that it was hard not to believe him. Did I ever ask him, 'Dad, are you in the Mafia?' I would never have done that. It would have been too embarrassing for me to ever ask that. He was my father and I trusted what he said. He made it very easy to believe him. He was a very convincing man. And even if he was involved in the "Mafia," the FBI didn't do a good job of proving it. They would arrest him for petty crimes and write things about him in the press that I knew weren't true. When you see lies presented like that again and again you learn to disregard all the rumors. Many of the things they arrested him for were never even directly linked to him. Whom would you believe; the government or your own father? And so I defended him, with all my heart. When you love someone you're going to believe what they say, whether or not it is true. And after all, the truth is always relative. What is meaningful in the end is one's own experience, and I know my father was an honorable, fair, selfless and loving man. This truth supersedes any of the sensationalized, exaggerated, or fabricated stories that surrounded him during and after his life."

As Marc Antony proclaimed of Julius Caesar, "the evil men do lives after them; the good is oft interred with their bones."

Appendix

There are numerous people who have contributed to the telling of this story. I would like to thank Steve Aiello, Dick Capozzola (RIP), Father Gigante, Nick Gravante, Phillip Rosello, Giuliani "Tony" Schiozzi, Al Ruddy, Bob D'Alessandro, the late John Cook Sr., and the rest of the brave veterans who served on the U.S.S. Falgout, and finally, two of my very dear friends in Harlem, may they rest in peace…they know who they are.

I'd like to thank Mike McLeer and the Verrazano Narrows Coffee shop for lending their time and location to help promote this book. I'd like to give special thanks to Aldo Tambelini and Anna Salamone for their contributions, Barry Slotnick for all of his support from day one of the League's inception, Ti-Grace Atkinson for all of the hours and dedication she lent to this project, and to Ray Vanacore who moved mountains more than once to make this book possible. Extra special thanks to copy editor Tasha Rubinow, who worked tirelessly at taking this story and making it an easy read.

I'd like to thank my first agent who has passed on, Mickey Frieberg, who worked until his last days trying to bring this project to the public.

I want to thank my Aunt Ray-Ray and Uncle Do-Do, and the rest of my family who supported me during the life of this project, and especially my children Joseph, Lucille, Cristine for her dedication to the final edit, and especially my son Anthony to whom I am very grateful for helping me tremendously in making this book happen, without all your hard work and support this couldn't have been possible. I would like to thank God and the Blessed Mother. And last but not least I would like to thank my wife Carol for her constant support of this project that I have sought to realize for forty years. Thank you for staying by my side since 1960, when I first met you at St. Mary's Church in Washingtonville, New York. I still thank God every day for bringing us together.

Bibliography

Aronson, Harvey. The Killing of Joe Gallo. G.P. Putnam's Sons, 1973.

Bart, Peter. Infamous Players: A Tale of Movies, the Mob, (and sex). Weinstein Books, 2011

Bari, Frank with Gribben, Mark C. Under the Williamsburg Bridge: The Story of an American Family

Balsamo, William & John. Young Al Capone, The Untold Story of Scarface in New York 1899-1925. Skyhorse,2011.

Bergreen, Laurence. Capone, The Man and the Era. Simon & Schuster, 1994.

Blackstock, Nelson. Cointelpro The Fbi's secret war on political freedom, New York, The Anchor foundation, 1988

Block, Alan. East Side, West Side, Organizing Crime In New York 1930-1950. Transaction Publishing 1983.

Bonanno, Bill. Bound By Honor, A Mafioso's Story. St. Martin's Press, 1999.

Bonanno, Joesph. A Man of Honor. Buccaneer Books, 1983
Borsella, Cristogianna. On Persecution, Identity & Activism. Dante University Press, 2005.

Cook, Fred, J. Mafia!. Fawcett Gold Medal Book, 1973.

Cantalupo, Joseph & Renner, Thomas C. Body Mike An unsparing Expose by the Mafia Insider who turned on the Mob, New York, Villard Books, 1990

Critchley, David. The Orgin of Organized Crime in America. Routledge, 2009.

Daley, Robert. Target Blue, An Insider's View of the NYPD. Delacorte Press, 1971.

Dash, Mike. The First Family. Random House, 2009.

Davis, John H. Mafia Dynasty: The Rise and Fall of the Gambino Crime Family. New York: HarperCollins, 1993.

Deloach, Cartha D. "Deke" Hoover's FBI the inside story by Hoover's trusted Lieutenant. Washington, DC. Regnery Publishing Inc. 1995

DeVico, Peter. The Mafia Made Easy, The Anataomy and Culture of La Cosa Nostra. Tate Publishing 2007.

Diapoulos, Peter. The Sixth Family. Bantam Books, 1976.

DiStasi, Lawerance. Una Storia Segreta. Heyday Books, 2001.

DiStefano, Paul. Behind Criminal Minds Xlibris Corp. 2011
Downey, Patrick. Gangster City, The History of the New York Underworld 1900-1935. Barricade, 2004.

Folsom, Tom. The Mad Ones: Crazy Joe Gallo and The Revolution at the Edge of the Underworld. Weinstein Books, 2008.

Franzese, Michael. Blood Covenant. Whitaker House, 1992.

Gage, Nicholas. The Mafia is not an equal Opportunity Employer. McGraw-Hill Book Company, 1971.

Gardaphe, Fred L. From Wiseguys to Wise Men. Routledge, 2006.

Gentry, Curt. J. Edgar Hoover: The Man and the Secrets. W.W. Norton & Company, 1991.

Glick, Brian. War at Home: Covert Action Against U.S. Activists. Southend Press, 1989

Goddard, Donald. Joey. Harper & Row, 1974.

Gosch & Hammer, Martin A. & Richard. The Last Testament of Lucky Luciano. Lucky, Brown and Company, 1974.

Griffin, Joe. Mob Nemesis. Prometheus Books, 2002.

Horn, Stacy, The Restless Sleep: Inside New York City's Cold Case Squad. Penguin Books, 2005

Hammond Jr., Charles Montgomery. The Image Decade Television Documentary 1965-1975. Hastings House, 1981.

Homer & Caputo, Frederic D. & David A. Guns and garlic: myths and realities of organized crime. Perdue Research Foundation, 1974.

Johnson, Donald. American Sailors and United Sates Marines at War and Peace: Navy Stories and Marine Corps Legacies. iUniverse, 2011

Kenny & Finckenhauer, Dennis J & James O. Organized Crime in America. Wadsworth, 1995.

LaGumina, Salvatore J. WOP, A Documentarty History of Anti-Italian Discrimination. Guernica, 1973.

LaSorte, Michael. La Merica, Images of Italian Greenhorn Experience. Temple University Press, 1985.

Maas, Peter. The Valachi Papers. Bantam Books, 1968.

Magione & Morreale, Jerre & Ben. La Storia, Five Centuries of the Italian American Experience. Harper Perennial, 1992.

May, Allan R. Gangland Gotham. Greenwood Press, 2009.

Mellen, Joan "A Farewell to Justice: Jim Garrison, JFK' s assassination and the case that should have
changed history" Washington D.C. Potomac Books, 2005.

Mollenhoff, Clark R. Strike Force: Organized Crime and the Government. Prentice Hall, New Jersey. 1972

Novak, Robert D. The Prince of Darkness: 50 Years of Reporting in Washington. Three Rivers Press. 2007

Novak, Michael. Unmeltable ethnics: politics & culture in American life

Newton, Michael. The Encyclopedia of American Law Enforcement. Checkmark Books, 2007.

Pedahzur & Perliger, Ami & Arie. Jewish Terrorism In Israel. Columbia University Press New York, 2009

Puzo, Mario. The God-Father Papers and other Confessions. Pan Books, 1972.

Puzo, Mario. The Godfather. Putnam, 1969

Raab, Selwyn. Five Families. Robson Books, 2006.

Reynolds, John Lawrence. Secret Societies: Inside the Worlds Most Notorious Organizations. Arcade Publishing, New York, 2006.

Reppetto, Thomas. Bringing Down the Mob: The War Against the American Mafia Henry Holt and Company, 2006.

Rieder, Jonathan. Canarsie, The Jews and Italians of Brooklyn Against Liberalism. Harvard University Press, 1985.

Rosenthal, Richard. Rookie cop: deep undercover in the Jewish Defense League. Leapfrog Press, 2000.

Ruth, David E. Inventing The Public Enemy. The University of Chicago Press, 1996.

Salerno & Tompkins, Ralph & John S. The Crime Confederation. Double Day Press 1969.

Schoenberg, Robert J. Mr. Capone, The Real and Complete Story of Al Capone. Quill William Morrow, 1992.

Scarne, John The Mafia Conspiracy. Scarne Enterprises Inc., 1976.

Seedman & Hellman, Albert A. & Peter. CHIEF!. Avon, 1974.

Talese, Gay. Honor thy Father. Harper Perennial, 1971.

Liz Trotta. Fighting for air: in the trenches with television news. Simon & Schuster, 1991.

Villano, Anthony. Brick Agent. Quadrangle, 1977.

    Hugh, Wilford. The Mighty Wurlitzer: How the CIA Played America. Cambridge: Harvard University Press. 2008

Selected articles

Nicholas Pileggi "Risorgimento of Italian Power" *New York Magazine* June 7th 1971.

Nicholas Pileggi "The Mafia: Serving your community since 1890" *New York Magazine* July 24th 1972.

Dick Schaap "The ten most overrated people in New York" *New York Magazine* January 3, 1972.

Peter Hellman "Seven Days of Killing" *New York Magazine* August 28, 1972.

Selected Government Archives

U.S. Department of Justice, Federal Bureau of Investigation, Washington D.C. File No. 92-5509: Joseph Anthony Colombo.

U.S. Department of Justice, Federal Bureau of Investigation, Washington D.C. File No. 92-3405: Carlo Gambino.

U.S. Department of Justice, Federal Bureau of Investigation, Washington D.C. File No. 92-2834: Joseph Profaci.

U.S. Department of Justice, Federal Bureau of Investigation, Washington D.C. File No. 92-1610: Joseph Gregory Gallo.

U.S. Department of Justice, Federal Bureau of Investigation, Washington D.C. File No. 92-6612: Gregory Scarpa.

Supplementary Detailed Staff Reports on Intelligence Activities and The Rights Of Americans. Book 3. Final Report of the Select Committee to Study Governmental Operations With Respect To Intelligence Activities. United States Senate. (April 23, 1976)

National Personnel Records Center: Official Military Personnel File, St. Louis, MO. Colombo, Joseph Anthony

Index

Ocean's Eleven, **131**
A.I.D. (Americans of Italian Descent)
  Organization, 113, 161, 256, 257
Aaron, Robert, **245**
Abbatemarco, Anthony "Tony Shots", **55, 327**
Abbatemarco, Anthony "Tony Shots", **284**
Abbatemarco, Frankie "Shots", **55, 327**
Aiello, Steve, **189, 190, 294, 315, 369**
Aloi, Sebastian "Buster", **85**
Aloi, Vincent, **129**
American Jewish Congress, **292**
Americano Hotel, **133**
Anastasia, Umberto "Albert", **28, 29, 30, 31, 49, 349, 358**
Andolino, Simone, **85**
Angleman, Frances, **136**
Anselmi, Albert, **xv**
Fitzgerald, Dan, **353**
Atkinson, Ti-Grace, **316, 341, 369**
Bell, Griffin, **363**
Mitchell, John, **187, 219, 232, 274, 298**
Aurelio, Richard R., **198, 276, 277**
Barbara, Joe "The Barber", **49**
Barnes, Nicky, **357**

Battista, Vito, **197, 198, 277**
Beam, Abe, **315**
Beetle, Blue, **128**
Bernardo, Tony, **284**
Biaggi, Mario, **315**
Bianco, Nick, **84, 285**
Birth, B'nai, **292**
Bishop, Joey, **131**
Black Revolutionary Attack Team, **322, 341**
Blei, Malvin, **255**
Blood Brothers
  Harlem militant group, 191
Bludhorn, Charlie, **263, 264**
Blue Beetle, **128**
Boland, **110, 120, 130, 153, 154, 158, 224, 225, 243, 244**
Bonanno, Bill, **100, 101, 136**
Bonanno, Joseph, **xiii**
Boriello, Bobby, **284**
Bove, Steve, **127**
Brando, Marlon, **252, 266**
BRAT. *See* Black Revolutionary Attack Team
Bruno, Angelo, **109, 129, 138**
Burke, Fred "Killer", **xv**
C.I.A.O.
  Italian American organization, 187, 292
Cambridge, Godfrey, **223, 224**
Camp Unity, **224, 294, 301,**

302, 312
Camp Webatuck, **14**
Campagna, Frank "Pee Wee", **46**
Campbell, Barbara, **353**
Candarini, Peter, **279**
Candello, Gaspare, **xvii**
Cantalupo Realty, **88, 91, 110, 137, 198, 234, 302, 304**
Cantalupo, Joseph, **88, 89, 177, 312, 357, 358, 364**
Capone, Alphonse "Al", **xiv, xv, 371, 374**
Cappazola, Dick, **224, 259**
Carlino, Leo "Big Leo", **85**
Carpentier, Eugene, **320**
Carter, Jimmy, **190**
Casablanca **City, 23**
Castellamarese War, **xiii, 56**
CBS, **180**
Celler, Emanuel, **274**
CIA, **84, 180, 182, 328, 354, 355, 361, 374**
Central Intelligence Bureau (CIB), **63, 64, 74, 75, 114**
Chaudury, M.N.I. **Pakistani Minister Consul General, 229**
Chief Inspector Codd, **343**
Chubby. *See* Rosello, Phillip "Chubby"
Church committee **to study government operations, 354, 355**
Church, Frank, **354**

Clinton Correctional, **283**
COINTELPRO. *See* Counter Intelligence Program (COINTELPRO)
Collosimo, Jim "Big", **xiv**
Colombo crime organization, **xiii, 144**
Colombo, Anthony
  Durante, Tony, 2, 3, 7, 8, 61, 62
  Tony Durante, 78
Colombo, Anthony Edward, **26, 37, 41, 42, 45, 47, 49, 56, 59, 60, 63, 65, 68, 70, 73, 85, 90, 93, 94, 95, 102, 114, 115, 116, 117, 119, 120, 132, 139, 146, 147, 149, 152, 153, 154, 155, 156, 157, 159, 160, 165, 169, 171, 173, 174, 175, 176, 177, 184, 189, 190, 191, 192, 193, 197, 198, 222, 229, 230, 234, 240, 242, 244, 246, 248, 249, 252, 256, 257, 262, 265, 266, 272, 274, 275, 293, 302, 306, 310, 311, 313, 314, 318, 325, 326, 329, 331, 360, 361, 366, 367, 374, 375, 386**
Colombo, Carol, **69, 90, 102, 103, 114, 115, 119, 120, 121, 132, 133, 150, 157, 158, 318, 320, 370**
Colombo, Cristoforo, **169**
Colombo, Joe, Jr., **30, 45, 159**

Colombo, Joseph Anthony, ix, x, xiv, xvii, xviii, 1, 2, 4, 14, 19, 23, 26, 28, 30, 32, 50, 56, 86, 88, 89, 90, 93, 96, 97, 100, 101, 102, 104, 106, 108, 109, 110, 114, 119, 120, 121, 122, 123, 126, 127, 136, 138, 139, 142, 143, 144, 147, 148, 153, 157, 159, 169, 170, 171, 173, 176, 189, 199, 225, 226, 228, 231, 240, 244, 247, 249, 253, 256, 259, 260, 266, 268, 269, 270, 271, 272, 277, 279, 280, 281, 282, 284, 285, 286, 287, 289, 290, 291, 296, 297, 303, 304, 308, 309, 312, 317, 323, 324, 335, 336, 337, 339, 341, 343, 344, 348, 350, 351, 357, 363

Colombo, Lawrence, 3

Colombo, Lucille "Jo-Jo", 16, 17, 19, 20, 21, 23, 24, 25, 30, 37, 43, 44, 45, 46, 52, 56, 66, 67, 74, 95, 151, 153, 160, 249, 265, 302, 312, 313, 323

Colombo, Vincent Michael, 37

Columbus Circle, New York, NY, x, 264, 274, 316, 317, 321, 362

Commissioner Daley. *See* Daley Robert

Copacabana, 74, 133, 224

Coppola, Francis Ford, **258**
Corona Fighting 69, **196**
Costa, Don, **223**
Costello, Frank, **28, 49, 56, 252, 358**
Counter Intelligence Program (COINTELPRO), **63, 180, 182**
Crazy Joe Gallo. *See* Gallo, Joe
Cristoforo Colombo, **317**
Cudak, Robert F., **298**
Cuomo, Mario, **197**
Cutrone, John, **137**
D'Ambrosio, Salvatore "Sally D.", **85, 142, 144, 145, 146, 147, 149, 153, 254, 255**
D'Aquila, Salvatore "Toto", **xvi**
D'Ambrosio, Salvatore "Sally D.", **144**
D'Ambrosio, Salvatore "Sally D", **85**
Daily News, **147, 176, 181, 245, 326, 386**
Daley, Robert, **343, 347, 353**
Damone, Vic, **223**
Dangerfield, Rodney, **133**
Dannemora. *See* Clinton Correctional
Darren, Bobby, **134**
Davis, Sammy, Jr., **131, 223, 224, 315, 371**
De Lucio, Fred "No Nose", **144, 145, 146, 149**
DeLoach, Cartha "Deke",

181
Reed, Thomas, **319**
Diapoulos, Pete "the Greek", **283, 284, 285, 286, 305, 345, 357**
DiCicco, Joseph, **276**
Dickinson, Angie, **131**
DiGregorio, Gaspar, **92, 101**
Dillon, Dennis, **198, 227, 233, 236, 240, 243, 278, 279, 308**
Dioguardi, Phillip "Fat Philly", **147, 148, 150, 173, 217, 218, 234**
Dioguardi, Phillip "Fat Philly", **147**
Cahn, William, **172, 246**
Dr. Sinatra, **192**
Druker, James O., **233**
Dunbar, William J., Jr., **136**
Durante, Tony. *See* Colombo, Anthony
Evans, Bob, **256, 258, 259, 262, 264, 266**
Faiello, Lucille. *See* Colombo, Lucille "Jo-Jo"
Fat Philly. *See* Dioguardi, Phillip "Fat Philly"
Federal Bureau of Investigation (FBI), **ix, xi, xiii, 3, 18, 49, 50, 51, 52, 63, 77, 78, 84, 85, 86, 87, 88, 89, 90, 91, 92, 93, 99, 101, 102, 104, 105, 106, 107, 108, 109, 111, 112, 113, 114, 115, 119, 120, 121, 122, 123, 127, 129, 130, 135, 136, 137, 138, 142, 143, 144, 145, 146, 147, 148, 149, 153, 154, 157, 158, 159, 160, 161, 162, 168, 169, 170, 171, 172, 177, 178, 179, 180, 181, 182, 183, 186, 189, 218, 219, 225, 226, 227, 230, 231, 232, 235, 236, 237, 242, 243, 244, 246, 248, 252, 257, 268, 271, 272, 273, 274, 278, 279, 280, 291, 297, 298, 300, 301, 302, 303, 304, 305, 307, 308, 313, 315, 316, 319, 324, 328, 329, 332, 337, 338, 341, 342, 347, 348, 352, 353, 354, 355, 356, 357, 359, 360, 361, 362, 364, 367, 372**
Federici, Bill, **176**
Felt Forum, **221, 222, 224, 241, 273**
Fermi, Enrico, **189**
Ferretti, Fred, **295**
Ferrigno, Bartolo "Barioco Bartulucia", **85**
McMullin, David, **316**
Five Points, **xiv**
Fontana, Harry, **85**
Forlano, Nicholas "Jiggs", **74, 85, 344**
Four Seasons, **221**
Francis, Connie, **221, 223, 224**
Frankie 'The Beast", **118**
Frankie "Shots"

Abbatemarco, Frankie "Shots", **54**
Franzese, John "Sonny", **46, 153, 358**
Franzese, Michael, **304, 357, 358**
Freyberg, Michael, **172**
Furnari, Christopher "Christie Tick", **361**
Gagliano, Gaetano "Tommy", **xiii**
Gale, J.H., **181**
Gallinaro, William B., **297**
Gallo Profaci War, **285**
Gallo, Albert, **96, 102, 286, 288, 303, 324, 345**
Gallo, Joe, **ix, 49, 73, 75, 76, 78, 127, 254, 284, 299, 300, 309, 310, 311, 316, 324, 331, 337, 345, 348, 353, 357, 358, 359, 361, 371, 372**
Gallo, Larry, **73, 78, 84, 92, 96, 100, 102, 113, 114, 117, 127, 144, 145, 153, 254, 255, 284**
Gallo, Steve, **284**
Gallo/Profaci Conflict. *See* Gallo/Profaci War
Gallo/Profaci War, **73, 75, 144, 254, 284**
Gallo-Profaci War, **228**
Gambale, Joseph "Joe Smash", **11, 14, 15**
Gambino, Carl, **ix, 76, 78, 81, 104, 105, 106, 111, 126, 129, 177, 179, 193, 273, 308, 309, 332, 335, 337, 348, 357, 364, 375**
Gambino, Carlo. *See* Gambino, Carl
Geraci, Charlie, **323**
Gigante, Louis, Father, **169, 281, 323, 324, 335, 345, 369**
Gigante, Vincent "the Chin", **345**
Gioielli, Joe "Jelly", **55, 73, 74, 78, 127, 145, 254, 255, 284**
Gioielli, Joe "Jelly", **74**
Giuliani, Rudolph, **358**
Goodfella Tapes, **137, 139**
Goodfellas
   1990 movie, **133, 316**
Gottlieb, Mary, **13**
Gravano, Salvatore "Sammy the Bull", **47, 48, 357, 359**
Greater Red Bank of New York, **293**
Greenhaven Prison, **283**
Guida, Thomas, **163**
Gulf and Western Offices, **263, 264, 266**
Gulotta Jr., Frank A., **246**
Hale, David, **136, 219, 237**
Hamil, Pete, **265**
Harvard Inn, **xv**
Harvey, Everett, **240**
Henry, Pat, **118, 223**
Hill, Henry, **133**
Hollman, Daniel P.
   federal investigator, 348
Hoover, J. Edgar, **50, 63,**

105, 106, 112, 136, 180, 182, 227, 246, 274, 325, 328, 354, 355, 361, 364, 372
House of Chan's, **129, 130, 135**
Hubela, Louie "the Syrian", **284**
Humperdinck, Engelbert, **133**
Huntley Brinkley show, **179**
IACRL. See Italian-American Civil Rights League
Iannaccia, Joe " Joe Notch", **11, 137**
Iannaccia, Joe "Joe Notch", **118**
Iannaccia, Joseph "Joe Notch", **11**
Illiano, Frank "Punchy", **327, 328**
Internal Revenue Service (IRS), **227, 236, 243, 300**
Ioele, Francesco. See Uale, Frankie
Italian-American Civil Rights League, **ix, 60, 161, 162, 163, 164, 165, 168, 169, 170, 171, 172, 173, 175, 177, 178, 179, 182, 186, 187, 188, 189, 190, 191, 192, 193, 196, 197, 199, 220, 221, 222, 224, 225, 227, 228, 229, 230, 233, 240, 241, 242, 243, 247, 248, 256, 257, 259, 260, 261, 263, 264, 265, 266, 267, 268, 269, 270, 271,** 272, 273, 274, 275, 276, 277, 280, 291, 294, 295, 298, 302, 303, 305, 306, 307, 309, 312, 315, 316, 331, 333, 335, 337, 343, 345, 354, 355, 356, 357, 358, 361, 365, 367, 369
James, John, **293**
Jeffe, Stanley, **266**
Jewish Defense League, **291, 292, 293, 374**
Joe Notch. See Iannaccia, Joseph "Joe Notch"
Joe Smash. See Gambale, Joseph "Joe Smash"
John Malone, **189, 240**
Johnson, Jerome Addison, **ix, 319, 320, 323, 326, 327, 328, 332, 336, 338, 339, 340, 341, 345, 346, 347, 348, 349, 350, 351, 352, 354, 356, 357, 358, 359, 360, 362, 366, 373**
Jones, Tom, **134, 315**
Baer, Harold, **226, 249, 273, 280**
Frey, William, **219**
Kelly, Paul, **172**
Judge Baer. See Baer, Harold; Judge
Judge Frey. See Frey, William; Judge
Judge Kelly. See Kelly, Paul; Judge
Widlitz, Paul, **246**
Justice Paul Widlitz. See Widlitz, Paul; Justice

Kahane, Meir, **289, 290, 292, 364**
Kennedy, Bobby, **92, 129**
Kennedy, John F., **84, 104, 221, 298, 373**
King, BB, **315**
King, Martin Luther, Jr, **129**
KKK
Ku Klux Klan, 285
Kravitz, Sy, **223**
Kronkite, Walter, **296**
Kunstler, William, **280**
La Cosa Nostra, **86, 87, 91, 106, 107, 108, 111, 137, 177, 186, 190, 192, 261, 265, 271, 372**
Labella, Joe, **266**
Lansky, Meyer, **xiii, 56**
LaRosa, Joe, **51, 58**
Lawford, Peter, **131**
Lee, London, **118**
Lefkowitz, Jacob, **278**
Lennard, David, **236**
Leoni, Sam, Dr., **293**
Leukemia Society, **293, 294**
Licavoli, Peter, **135**
Lindsay, John, **231**
LoCicero, Charles "The Sidge", **87, 125, 126**
Lollobrigida, Gina, **224**
Lonergan, Richard "Peg Leg", **xiv**
Lopez, Trinny, **223**
Luciano, Charlie, **111**
Luciano, Charlie "Lucky", **372**
Luciano, Charlie "Lucky", **xiii**
Ludlow Massacre, **194**
Lynch, Joseph F., **350**
Mafia, **60, 64, 96, 109, 147, 153, 170, 171, 186, 189, 190, 192, 248, 251, 260, 261, 263, 264, 271, 296, 316, 337, 347, 358, 363, 365, 367, 371, 372, 374, 375, 386**
Magaddino, Stefano, **76, 83, 93**
Magliocco, Ambrose, **85**
Magliocco, Joe, **72, 76, 77, 78, 83, 84, 85, 88, 176**
Mainello, Nicholas, **279**
Man of Honor
 Joe Bonanno, 76,
Mano, Tom, **117**
Marchi, John, **188, 265, 277**
Marcone, Nat, **161, 163, 167, 192, 242, 260, 269, 272**
Marino, Gaetano "Toddo", **85**
Martin, Dean, **131**
Martin, Ross, **223**
Marx, Guy, **223**
Massotta, Thomas, **129**
McClellan Subcommittee, **298**
McGurn, Jack "Machine Gun", **xv**
McIntosh, Hugh, **118, 344**
McMahon, Ed, **222, 223**
Michaelson, Judith, **275**
Miraglia, Rocky, **91, 118, 137, 139, 225, 226, 286,**

382

287, 301
Montana, Lenny, **254**
Montemarano, Donny "Shacks", **74**
Morello, Petey Brush, **361**
Morgan, Arthur, **318**
Morgentha, Robert, **92**
Mother of Joe Colombo Sr. Catherine, 3, 6, 9, 75
Mussachio, Salvatore "The Sheik", **72, 85**
NBC, **179, 223, 274**
New York City Hall, **197, 198, 274**
New York Times, **113, 180, 190, 191, 192, 193, 267, 280, 295, 296, 353, 386**
Newman, Al, **289**
Newton, Wayne, **133**
Noonan, Dennis, **198**
NYPD
   New York Police Department, 31, 46, 50, 52, 59, 63, 75, 82, 96, 99, 114, 129, 161, 167, 170, 177, 225, 320, 327, 336, 344, 348, 351, 353, 361, 371
O'Brien, Carol. *See* Colombo, Carol
O'Banion, Charles Dean, **xiv**
O'Brien, Timothy, **119, 120, 121, 318**
Oddo, John "Johnny Bath Beach", **46, 85, 96**
Office of Policy Coordination (OPC), **180**

Schiozzi, Tony, **317, 318, 319, 351, 369**
Oliveri, Christine, **8**
OPC. *See* Office of Policy Coordination (OPC)
Organized Crime Strike Force, **232, 242, 274, 278, 296, 308, 309**
Organized Crime Task Force (OCTF), **50**
Osborne, Leutrell, Sr, **354**
Oswald, Lee Harvey, **84**
Paca, William, **221**
Pacino, Al, **266**
Paramount Pictures, **263, 264**
Park Sheraton Hotel, **49, 164, 168, 259, 272, 281, 308**
Pero, Angelo "Shelly", **50**
Persico, Alphonse "Allie Boy", **127**
Persico, Carmine, **52, 74, 78, 83, 84, 118, 127, 299, 344, 358**
Persico-Orena Wars, **143**
Pete the Greek. *See* Diapoulos, Pete "the Greek"
Pileggi, Nicholas, **295, 327, 375**
Piraino, Giuseppe, **xv, xvi, xvii, 81, 82**
Plum Beach, **17, 21**
Podell, Jules, **134**
Pollack, Michael B., **309**
Procaccino, Mario, **277**
Profaci organization, **xviii, 63, 76, 86, 87, 91, 125**

Profaci, Frank J., **360**
Prohibition, **122**
Prohibition Era, **xiii, xvi,** 127
Puzo, Mario, **251**
Quantico, **135**
R.I.C.O.
  Racketeer Influenced and Corrupt Organizations Act, 135
Kahane, Meir, **291, 324**
Rat Pack, **131**
Red Cross, **293, 294**
Rickles, Don, **133**
Roberts, Ken, **220**
Rockefeller, David, **231**
Rockefeller, Nelson, **x, 188, 194, 231, 275, 276**
Romero, Cesar, **131**
Roselli, Jimmy, **118**
Rosello, Phillip "Chubby", **329**
Rosenthal, Abe, **190, 191, 192, 193, 231**
Royal Box, **133**
Rubertone, James, **87**
Ruddy, Al, **252, 256, 259, 261, 262, 263, 264, 266, 316, 369**
Russo, Gianni, **266**
Sable, Jack M., **306**
Salamone, Richard, **236, 242**
Sally D. *See* D'Ambrosio, Salvatore "Sally D."
Santagelo, Alfred, **307**
Santora, Duke, **361**
Santoro, Modesto, **130, 137**
Scalise, John, **xv**

Scarpa, Greg, **87, 88, 141, 143, 235, 279, 359, 360, 375, 386**
Schipani, Joseph "Joe Ship", **85**
Scialo, Dominic "Mimi", **50, 118, 137, 142**
Scialo, Dominic "Mimi", **11, 46, 361**
Scimone, John, **72, 129, 254**
Scotti, Alfred J., **226**
See Mussachio, Salvatore "The Sheik"io.
Seedman, Albert, **126, 315, 322, 336**
Senator Ervin, **242**
Weber, John, **344**
Shaap, Dick, **231**
Sims, Silvia, **119**
Sinatra, Frank, **114, 131, 134, 192, 220, 223, 224, 257**
Sing Sing Prison, **xvii, 29, 63, 282, 304**
Slater, Sidney, **74, 75**
Slotnick, Barry, **96, 97, 98, 100, 129, 153, 158, 162, 167, 173, 175, 176, 182, 190, 192, 217, 218, 226, 233, 234, 243, 246, 247, 249, 266, 289, 290, 292, 317, 319, 347, 356, 369**
Tallia, Ray, **198, 233, 236, 242, 243**
SS Paul Hamilton, **22**
SS Royal Star, **22**
SS Samite, **22**
SS Stephen F. Austin, **22**

384

Staten Island Advance, **238, 240**
Stein, Charles "Ruby", **74**
Stevens, Paul M., **136**
Storm, Morty, **118, 223**
Sullivan, William C., **143, 181, 355**
Sutton, Percy, **315**
Tambelini, Aldo, **369**
Tambellini, Aldo, **272**
the Chin. *See* Gigante, Vincent "the Chin"
the Commission, **xiii, 50, 76, 83, 92, 101, 107, 121, 137, 138, 197, 253, 298, 345**
the Del Vikings, **118**
The Four Seasons, **223**
The Gang That Couldn't Shoot Straight
   Gallo film project 1971, 303
The Godfather
   1969 novel, 251, 373
   1972 film, 145, 254, 256, 259, 262, 266, 267, 268, 316
   Part II
   1974 film, 145
The Godfather Part II
   1974 film, 254
the League. *See* Italian-American Civil Rights League
the New York Board of Rabbis, **292**
The Order Sons Of Italy, **187**
The Pee Jays, **223**

Tipa, Giuseppe "Joseph Tifa", **85**
Tolson, Clyde, 181
Torrio, Johnny, **xv**
Tramunti, Carmine, **309**
Triangle Shirtwaist Factory, **195**
Tumola, Joseph, **147, 148, 150, 153**
U.S.S. Falgout, **369**
Uale, Frankie, **xiv, xv, xvi, xvii, 28, 82**
Unione Siciliana, **xv**
Unity Day, **163, 166, 168, 175, 178, 186, 274, 293, 303, 305, 306, 307, 309, 310, 312, 314, 315, 323, 339, 348, 363**
Valli, Frankie, **223, 315,** *See* The Four Seasons
Van Arsdale, Harry, **231**
Vario, Paul, **316**
Vietnam War, **154**
Vincent, Mangano, **xiii**
Vingo, Vinnie, **234**
Vitale, Caesar, **147, 148, 151, 164, 175, 184, 192, 217, 261**
Warren, Fran, **118**
Welsh, Bernie, **110, 111, 112, 155, 156, 157, 198, 225, 244, 245, 300**
Willis, Gordon, **258, 267**
Wisner, Frank, **180, 182**
Withers, Ernest, **356**
Youngman, Henny, **133**

Notes

[i] Michael T. Kaufman *"Profacis' Roots Deep In Brooklyn"* New York Times (August 18, 1964) pp.16

[ii] *"Track Capone Gangsters"* New York Times (July, 10 1928) pp. 25

[iii] *"City Gets Demands to End Gang Wars; Issue Put to Mayor"* New York Times (July 11, 1928) pp. 1

[iv] *"Track Capone Gangsters"* New York Times (July, 10 1928) pp. 25

[v] Mark Kriegel. *"More Than a Close Shave in His Chair"* Daily News April 23, 1997.

[vi] "Italians Fight Slurs" *New York Times* (Jan 25, 1960) pp.12

[vii] "Mafia Shows Decried" *New York Times* (Aug 25, 1959)pp.35

[viii] Salerno & Tompkins, Ralph & John S. *The Crime Confederation.* (Double Day Press 1969) pp.131

[ix] Salerno & Tompkins, Ralph & John S. *The Crime Confederation.* (Double Day Press 1969) pp.135

[x] "13 in Gallo Gang Arrested in Raid" *New York Times* (October 11, 1961) pp.35

[xi] Bonanno, Joesph. *A Man of Honor.* (Buccaneer Books, 1983) pp.234-235

[xii] Raab, Selwyn. *Five Families.* (Robson Books, 2006) Pp.163

[xiii] "144 Slain in 1930 in Brooklyn Alone" *New York Times* (Jan. 11, 1931) pp.33

[xiv] "Racketeer is Slain in Brooklyn Street" *New York Times* (March 28, 1930) pp.1

[xv] "Gunman Buried in Pomp" *New York Times* (April 1, 1930) pp. 17

[xvi] "L.I. Autopsy Finds No Poison in Body Of a Mafia Leader" *New York Times* (August 28, 1969) pp.23

[xvii] Villano, Anthony. *Brick Agent.* Quadrangle, 1977. pp.105

[xviii] U.S. Department of Justice, Federal Bureau of Investigation, Washington D.C. File No. 92-6612: Gregory Scarpa. Pg. 39

[xix] U.S. Department of Justice, Federal Bureau of Investigation, Washington D.C. File No. 92-6612: Gregory Scarpa. Pp. 42,65

[xx] U.S. Department of Justice, Federal Bureau of Investigation, Washington D.C. File No. 92-6612: Gregory Scarpa. Pp. 7,14

[xxi] U.S. Department of Justice, Federal Bureau of Investigation, Washington D.C. File No. 92-6612: Gregory Scarpa. Pg. 30
[xxii] Bonanno, Joseph. *"A Man of Honor."* (Buccaneer Books, 1983) pp. 261
[xxiii] "Colombo is Given 30-Day Jail Stay" *New York Times* (April 8, 1966) pp.58
[xxiv] Supreme Court of the United States Joseph Colombo v. NEW YORK No. 175 October 19,1970 (400 U.S. 16) 16, 91 S.Ct. 99, 27 L.Ed. 216
[xxv] Court of Appeals of New York, The PEOPLE of the Sate of New York, Respondent v. Joseph COLOMBO, Appellant. Dec. 29, 1972. (31 N.Y. 2d 947, 293, N.E. 2d 247, 341 N.Y.S. 2d 97)
[xxvi] "Reputed Brooklyn Mafia Head Arrested on Perjury Charges" *New York Times* (March 7, 1970) pp. 20
[xxvii] "Colombo is Given 30-Day Jail Stay" *New York Times* (April 8, 1966) pp.58
[xxviii] "13 Seized in Queens In 'Little Apalachin' *New York Times* (September 23, 1966) pp.1
[xxix] U.S. Department of Jusitce, Federal Bureau of Investigation. Washington D.C. – "Hoodwink" Internal secutiry memorandum.
[xxx] *Ibid*
[xxxi] *Ibid*
[xxxii] *Ibid*
[xxxiii] Smith, Sandy "The Crime Cartel" Life Magazine Vol. 63 No.9 (September 1967) pp.15
[xxxiv] Mangione & Morreale, Jerre & Ben , *La Storia Five Centuries of the Italian American Experience*, (New York, New York: Harper Collins, 1992), pp.347
[xxxv] "Judge Defends Sinatra as Antidefamation Head" *New York Times* (5/13/1967) pp. 36
[xxxvi] Cantalupo, Joseph & Renner, Thomas C. *Body Mike An unsparing Expose by the Mafia Insider who turned on the Mob*. (New York, Villard Books, 1990) pp.66
[xxxvii] Seedman & Hellman, Albert A. & Peter. *CHIEF!*. Avon, 1974. Pg. 343
[xxxviii] Will Lissner "P.B.A. Scores Use Of Gallos By City" *New York Times* (August 15, 1966) pp.28
[xxxix] "Larry Gallo Dies in Sleep at 41, fought in Brooklyn Gang War" *New York Times* (May 19, 1968) pp.66
[xl] Emanuel Perlmutter "Gallo, Gang Leader, Is Buried With Pomp of Prohibition Era" *New York Times* (May 22, 1968) pp.51

[xli] Charles Grutzner "Mafia Increasing Investments in Business on L.I." *New York Times* (October 8, 1967) pp 1, 85
[xlii] Villano, Anthony and Gerald Astor. *Brick Agent*, (New York, New York: Quadrangle/ The New York Times Book Company, 1977), pp.29
[xliii] Gentry, Curt. *J. Edgar Hoover: The Man and the Secrets*. (W.W. Norton & Company, 1991) pp. 607
[xliv] Enric Volante *"Former FBI Agent ends Lengthy Silence The Mafia Bombings"* Arizona Daily Star (February 4, 2004)
[xlv] Cook, Fred, J. *Mafia!*. (Fawcett Gold Medal Book, 1973) pp. 227
[xlvi] Raab, Selwyn. *Five Families*. (Robson Books, 2006) pp.186
[xlvii] Murray Kempton. *"Cosa Nostra- That's Italian for "Our Headache"* Playboy (December, 1970) pp. 274
[xlviii] U.S. Department of Justice, Federal Bureau of Investigation, Washington D.C. File No. 92-6612: Gregory Scarpa.
[xlix] U.S. Department of Justice, Federal Bureau of Investigation, Washington D.C. File No. 92-6612: Gregory Scarpa. Pg. 718
[l] Harvey Aronson, *The Killing of Joey Gallo*, (New York, G.P. Putnam's Sons, 1973): pp. 102
[li] U.S. Department of Justice, Federal Bureau of Investigation, Washington D.C. File No. 92-5509: Joseph Anthony Colombo.
[lii] U.S. Department of Justice, Federal Bureau of Investigation, Washington D.C. File No. 92-5509: Joseph Anthony Colombo.
[liii] Frank Faso and Paul Meskil, "'Torture Room' Raid Stirs Mob-Cops Quiz" *Daily News* (1/20/1970), pp.3
[liv] Irving Lieberman, "Probe Murder in Mafia Club" *New York Post* (1/20/1970), pp. 1
[lv] U.S. Department of Justice, Federal Bureau of Investigation, Washington D.C. File No. 92-5509: Joseph Anthony Colombo.
[lvi] U.S. Department of Justice, Federal Bureau of Investigation, Washington D.C. File No. 92-5509: Joseph Anthony Colombo.
[lvii] Lesley Oelsner "Reputed Brooklyn Mafia Head Arrested on Perjury Charges" *New York Times* (3/7/1970) pp.20
[lviii] Craig R. Whitney "Reputed Mafia Figure linked to Picketing of F.B.I." *New York Times* (6/9/1970) pp.51
[lix] Robert D. McFadden "Italian Pickets At F.B.I. Sued" *New York Times* (6/6/1970) pp.19
[lx] Craig R. Whitney "Reputed Mafia Figure linked to Picketing of F.B.I." *New York Times* (6/9/1970) pp.1
[lxi] Craig R. Whitney "Reputed Mafia Figure linked to Picketing of F.B.I." *New York Times* (6/9/1970) pp.51

[lxii] Robert D. McFadden "Italian Pickets At F.B.I. Sued" *New York Times* (6/6/1970) pp.19
[lxiii] Craig R. Whitney "Reputed Mafia Figure linked to Picketing of F.B.I." *New York Times* (6/9/1970) pg.51
[lxiv] Craig R. Whitney "Pickets at F.B.I. Visited by Judge" *New York Times* (6/10/1970) pg.35
[lxv] "Police Error Seen in F.B.I. Picketing" *New York Times* (6/12/1970) pg.16
[lxvi] Robert E. Tomasson "Judge Curbs Pickets' Din At F.B.I. Hq." *New York Times* (6/16/1970) pg.49
[lxvii] "Italo-Americans Press Unity Day" *New York Times* (6/18/1970) pg.58
[lxviii] Paul L. Montgomery "Italians to Hold Rally Tomorrow" *New York Times* (6/28/1970) pg.34
[lxix] Paul L. Montgomery "Italians to Hold Rally Tomorrow" *New York Times* (6/28/1970) pg.34
[lxx] Anthony Burton, "When a Protest is a picnic" *Daily News* (6/30/1970) pg.3
[lxxi] William Federici, "Joe Colombo, 23 Indicted by L.I. Jury" *Daily News* (7/1/1970) pg.3
[lxxii] *Ibid*
[lxxiii] William Federici "Joe Colombo: Ok, I'll Be a Mafioso for Good" *New York Daily News* (July 3, 1970) pg. 3
[lxxiv] William Federici "Joe Colombo: Ok, I'll Be a Mafioso for Good" *New York Daily News* (July 3, 1970) pg. 3
[lxxv] William Federici "Joe Colombo: Ok, I'll Be a Mafioso for Good" *New York Daily News* (July 3, 1970) pg. 3
[lxxvi] William Federici "Joe Colombo: Ok, I'll Be a Mafioso for Good" *New York Daily News* (July 3, 1970) pg. 24
[lxxvii] William Federici "Joe Colombo: Ok, I'll Be a Mafioso for Good" *New York Daily News* (July 3, 1970) pg. 24
[lxxviii] William Federici "Joe Colombo: Ok, I'll Be a Mafioso for Good" *New York Daily News* (July 3, 1970) pg. 3
[lxxix] U.S. Department of Justice, Federal Bureau of Investigation, Washington D.C. File No. 92-5509: Joseph Anthony Colombo.
[lxxx] U.S. Department of Justice, Federal Bureau of Investigation, Washington D.C. File No. 92-5509: Joseph Anthony Colombo.
[lxxxi] Hugh, Wilford. *The Mighty Wurlitzer: How the CIA Played America.* (Cambridge: Harvard University Press. 2008) pg. 7

[lxxxii] Newton, Michael. *The Encyclopedia of American Law Enforcement.* Checkmark Books, 2007. pg. 34
[lxxxiii] Newton, Michael. *The Encyclopedia of American Law Enforcement.* Checkmark Books, 2007. pg. 35
[lxxxiv] U.S. Department of Justice, Federal Bureau of Investigation, Washington D.C. File No. 92-5509: Joseph Anthony Colombo.
[lxxxv] U.S. Department of Justice, Federal Bureau of Investigation, Washington D.C. File No. 92-5509: Joseph Anthony Colombo.
[lxxxvi] "Ethnic Slurs a No..No..- Justice Dept." *Golden Lion* Volume 1 Number 3 (July-August, 1970) pg. 1
[lxxxvii] "Rockefeller Bars Use of Mafia Term By State Agencies" *New York Times* (August 28, 1970) pg. 32
[lxxxviii] Paul L. Montgomery "Italians Protest Against Mafia Image" *New York Times* (July 5, 1970) pg. 90
[lxxxix] Paul L. Montgomery "Italians Protest Against Mafia Image" *New York Times* (July 5, 1970) pg. 90
[xc] Paul L. Montgomery "Italians Protest Against Mafia Image" *New York Times* (July 5, 1970) pg. 90
[xci] "Italians Protest Against Mafia Image" " *New York Times* (July 5, 1970) pg. 90
[xcii] Dick Schaap "The Ten Most Powerful Men in New York" *New York Magazine* (January 4, 1971) pg. 29
[xciii] "Times Picketed by Protest Group" *New York Times* (July 31, 1970) pg. 20
[xciv] "Times Picketed by Protest Group" *New York Times* (July 31, 1970) pg. 20
[xcv] Murray Schumach "Neighborhoods: 69 Homes in Corona at Stake" *New York Times* (August 11, 1970) pg. 35
[xcvi] "Battista Demands Inquiry on Corona" *New York Times*. (August 26, 1970) pg. 30
[xcvii] "60 From Queens Picket City Hall To Save Homes Due for Razing" *New York Times* (September 9, 1970) pg. 28
[xcviii] Maurice Carroll. "Protesting Groups Scuffle at City Hall" *New York Times* (September 30, 1970) pg. 34
[xcix] Maurice Carroll. "Protesting Groups Scuffle at City Hall" *New York Times* (September 30, 1970) pg. 34
[c] Newton, Michael. *The Encyclopedia of American Law Enforcement.* (Checkmark Books, 2007) pg. 147
[ci] (World Press) "Tucson FBI Bomb-Throwers" *The Challenge.* Volume 1 Issue 7 (December 1970) pg.. 6

[cii] "Mafia This Time Just Like Old West in Arizona" *The Tuscaloosa News* (May 3, 1971) pg. 16
[ciii] "Mafia the target: Bombings By 'FBI Agent'" *San Francisco Chronicle* (August 21, 1969) pg. 10
[civ] (World Press) "Tucson FBI Bomb-Thorowers" *The Challenge*. Volume 1 Issue 7 (December 1970) pg. 6
[cv] Robert E. Tomasson "Colombo is Guilty in Perjury Case" *New York Times*. (December 24, 1970) pg. 1
[cvi] Norma Abrams & Arthur Mulligan "Colombo Irate: FBI Lifted His Membership List" *New York Daily News* (December 18, 1970) pg. 5
[cvii] U.S. Department of Justice, Federal Bureau of Investigation, Washington D.C. File No. 92-5509: Joseph Anthony Colombo.
[cviii] "Italian Rights Group To Again Picket FBI" *The Tri-Boro Post* (February 11, 1971) pg. 3
[cix] "Italian Rights Group To Again Picket FBI" *The Tri-Boro Post* (February 11, 1971) pg. 3
[cx] Charles Grutzner "Colombo Named Man of Year by Paper" *New York Times*. (January 22, 1971) pg. 79
[cxi] Dick Schaap "The Ten Most Powerful Men in New York" *New York Magazine* (January 4, 1971) pg. 24
[cxii] Mollenhoff, Clark R. *Strike Force: Organized Crime and the Government*. Prentice Hall, New Jersey. 1972 pg. 208
[cxiii] "Colombo Acquitted In Conspiracy Case" *New York Times*. (February 27, 1971) pg. 55
[cxiv] U.S. Department of Justice, Federal Bureau of Investigation, Washington D.C. File No. 92-6612: Gregory Scarpa. Pg. 726
[cxv] "Colombo Acquitted In Conspiracy Case" *New York Times*. (February 27, 1971) pg. 55
[cxvi] "Italian League Protests Crime Articles" *Staten Island Advance*. (February 25, 1971) pg. 1
[cxvii] Morris Kaplan. "Jury is Studying Italian Picketing" *New York Times*. (March 4, 1971) pg. 39
[cxviii] Robert Kappstatter. "Colombo at Paper Pocket Quiz" *New York Daily News* (March 4, 1971) pg. 49
[cxix] Department of Justice - Report to Congress on the Activities and Operations of the Public Integrity Section for 1990. pg. 16
[cxx] Department of Justice - Report to Congress on the Activities and Operations of the Public Integrity Section for 1991. pg. 20
[cxxi] Nathan Kanter & Henry Lee. "Finally, Papa Colombo Goes to Jail-No Bail" *New York Daily News* (March 6, 1971) pg. 3

[cxxii] Manny Topol "Five Jailed in Theft; A First for Colombo" *Newsday* (March 6, 1971) pg. 4
[cxxiii] Nathan Kanter & Henry Lee. "Finally, Papa Colombo Goes to Jail-No Bail" *New York Daily News* (March 6, 1971) pg. 3
[cxxiv] Mellen, Joan *"A Farewell to Justice: Jim Garrison, JFK's assassination and the case that should have changed history"* (Washington D.C. Potomac Books 2005). pg. 291
[cxxv] United States of America, Appellee, V. Joseph M. Margiotta, Appellant. No. 1238, Docket 82-1025 United States Court of Appeals, Second Circuit July 27, 1982 Sect. 19
[cxxvi] Frank Lynn. Life after Jail: Politicians Get Help From Their Friends" New York Times (October 23, 1987)
[cxxvii] "Bail to Be Sought For Colombo Sr." *Newsday* (March 8, 1971) pg.7
[cxxviii] "Colombo, Released In Bail, Joins Group Picketing the F.B.I." *New York Times* (March 9, 1971) pg. 39
[cxxix] Puzo, Mario. *The God-Father Papers and other Confessions*. Pan Books, 1972. Pg. 10
[cxxx] Harvey Aronson, *The Killing of Joey Gallo*, (New York, G.P. Putnam's Sons, 1973): pg. 102
[cxxxi] Editorial, *"Italian American Civil Rights League Active On All Fronts"*, The Brooklyn Graphic Vol. 18 No. 12 (March, 24, 1971) pg.1
[cxxxii] Grace Lichtenstien, *"Godfather Film Won't Mention Mafia"*, New York Times (Mar,20,1971) pg.1
[cxxxiii] Bart, Peter. Infamous Players: A Tale of Movies, the Mob, (and sex). (Weinstein Books, 2011) pg.98
[cxxxiv] Ben Calderone "Think Dante, Not Mafia" *New York Times* (April 2, 1971) pg. 38
[cxxxv] "The M---a" *New York Times* (March 28, 1971) pg. E4
[cxxxvi] Pete Hamil "The Bad Guys" *New York Post* (April 1, 1971) pg. 45
[cxxxvii] Ed Lowe & Joe Demma "Guest of Honor: 'I Was Framed'" *Newsday* (March 23, 1971) pg. 4
[cxxxviii] Ed Lowe & Joe Demma "Guest of Honor: 'I Was Framed'" *Newsday* (March 23, 1971) pg. 4
[cxxxix] Patterson, Clayton Resistance: A Radical Social and Political History of the Lower East Side (New York, Seven Stories Press 2006) pg. 65
[cxl] Patterson, Clayton. *Resistance: A Radical Social and Political History of the Lower East Side*. (New York, Seven Stories Press 2006) pg. 66
[cxli] "Celler Says Wiretapping Policy May Be Leading to Police State" New York Times (April 26, 1971) pp.63

[cxlii] NBC News Archives
[cxliii] Judith Michaelson "The Colombo League's VIPs" *New York Post* (April 7, 1971) pp. 2
[cxliv] Judith Michaelson "The Colombo League's VIPs" *New York Post* (April 7, 1971) pp. 64
[cxlv] Judith Michaelson "The Colombo League's VIPs" *New York Post* (April 7, 1971) pp. 64
[cxlvi] "Colombo Sr. Is Indicted Again; Illegal Gambling Activities Are Alleged" *Wall Street Journal* (April 23, 1971) pp. 6
[cxlvii] "Colombo Arrest Spurs Court Row" *Staten Island Advance* Volume 86 No. 16,538 (April 3, 1971) pp. 1
[cxlviii] Mollenhoff, Clark R. *Strike Force: Organized Crime and the Government*. Prentice Hall, New Jersey. 1972 pp. 208
[cxlix] Mollenhoff, Clark R. *Strike Force: Organized Crime and the Government*. Prentice Hall, New Jersey. 1972 pp. 210
[cl] Morris Kaplan "Lawyer for Colombo Says a Tap on U.S. Phone Warned of Arrest" *New York Times* (April 3, 1971) pp. 1
[cli] U.S. Department of Justice, Federal Bureau of Investigation, Washington D.C. File No. 92-6612: Gregory Scarpa. Pg. 730
[clii] Victor S. Navasky "Right On! With Lawyer William Kunstler". *New York Times* (April 19.1970) pp. 217
[cliii] Anthony Burton "Bedroom Bugged: Colombo" *New York Daily News* (April 1, 1971) pp. 4
[cliv] Anthony Burton "Bedroom Bugged: Colombo" *New York Daily News* (April 1, 1971) pp. 4
[clv] Victor Riesel "'Crazy Joe' and Mafia" *Rome-Tribune News* (April 14, 1972) pp.3
[clvi] Diapoulos, Peter. *The Sixth Family*. (Bantam Books, 1976) pp. 25
[clvii] Jay Levin "Word Is Out to Get Gallo" *New York Post* (July 13, 1971) pp. 2
[clviii] Goddard, Donald *"Joey"* (New York Harper & Row 1974) pp. 221
[clix] Jay Levin "Word Is Out to Get Gallo" *New York Post* (July 13, 1971) pp. 2
[clx] Jay Levin "Word Is Out to Get Gallo" *New York Post* (July 13, 1971) pp. 52
[clxi] Diapoulos, Peter. *The Sixth Family*. (Bantam Books, 1976) pp. 5
[clxii] Diapoulos, Peter. *The Sixth Family*. (Bantam Books, 1976) pp. 55
[clxiii] Diapoulos, Peter. *The Sixth Family*. (Bantam Books, 1976) pp. 15
[clxiv] Diapoulos, Peter. *The Sixth Family*. (Bantam Books, 1976) pp. 16
[clxv] Diapoulos, Peter. *The Sixth Family*. (Bantam Books, 1976) pp. 16

clxvi Diapoulos, Peter. *The Sixth Family*. (Bantam Books, 1976) pp. 17
clxvii Morris Kaplan "Kahane and Colombo Join Forces to Fight Reported U.S. Harassment" *New York Times* (May 14, 1971) pg. 1
clxviii Morris Kaplan "Kahane and Colombo Join Forces to Fight Reported U.S. Harassment" *New York Times* (May 14, 1971) pg. 66
clxix Rosenthal, Richard. *Rookie cop: deep undercover in the Jewish Defense League*. Leapfrog Press, 2000. pg. 169
clxx Morris Kaplan "Kahane and Colombo Join Forces to Fight Reported U.S. Harassment" *New York Times* (May 14, 1971) pg. 66
clxxi Fred Ferretti "Italian-American League's Power Spreads" *New York Times* (April 4, 1971) pg. 64
clxxii "Italian American League Active on All Fronts" The Brooklyn Graphic Volume 18 no. 12 (March 24, 1971) pg. 1
clxxiii "Public Relations – A Night For Colombo" *Time Magazine* (April 5, 1971) pg. 16
clxxiv Nicholas Gage "Colombo: The New Look in the Mafia" *New York Times* (May 3, 1971) pg. 1
clxxv Nicholas Gage "Colombo: The New Look in the Mafia" *New York Times* (May 3, 1971) pg. 1
clxxvi Mollenhoff, Clark R. *Strike Force: Organized Crime and the Government*. Prentice Hall, New Jersey. 1972. pp. 210
clxxvii Nicholas Gage "Colombo: The New Look in the Mafia" *New York Times* (May 3, 1971) pp. 1
clxxviii Nicholas Gage "Colombo: The New Look in the Mafia" *New York Times* (May 3, 1971) pp. 54
clxxix Mollenhoff, Clark R. *Strike Force: Organized Crime and the Government*. Prentice Hall, New Jersey. 1972. pp. 211
clxxx Mollenhoff, Clark R. *Strike Force: Organized Crime and the Government*. Prentice Hall, New Jersey. 1972. pp. 211
clxxxi Supplementary Detailed Staff Reports on Intelligence Activities and The Rights Of Americans. Book 3. *Final Report of the Select Committee to Study Governmental Operations With Respect To Intelligence Activities. United Sates Senate*. (April 23, 1976) Section 4 – A1
clxxxii Nicholas Gage "Colombo: The New Look in the Mafia" *New York Times* (May 3, 1971) pp. 54
clxxxiii Supplementary Detailed Staff Reports on Intelligence Activities and The Rights Of Americans. Book 3. *Final Report of the Select Committee to Study Governmental Operations With Respect To Intelligence Activities. United Sates Senate*. (April 23, 1976) Section 4 - B

[clxxxiv] Nicholas Gage "Colombo: The New Look in the Mafia" *New York Times* (May 3, 1971) pp. 54
[clxxxv] Nicholas Gage "Colombo: The New Look in the Mafia" *New York Times* (May 3, 1971) pp. 54
[clxxxvi] Nicholas Gage "Colombo: The New Look in the Mafia" *New York Times* (May 3, 1971) pp. 54
[clxxxvii] U.S. Department of Justice, Federal Bureau of Investigation, Washington D.C. File No. 92-5509: Joseph Anthony Colombo. (HH COVER PAGE)
[clxxxviii] Villano, Anthony. *Brick Agent*. Quadrangle, 1977. pp. 172
[clxxxix] "Acquit Former Co-Defendant In Silver Case" *New York Daily News* (May 5, 1971) pp. 9
[cxc] Cantalupo, Joseph & Renner, Thomas C. *Body Mike An unsparing Expose by the Mafia Insider who turned on the Mob*, New York, Villard Books, 1990. pp. 112
[cxci] U.S. Department of Justice, Federal Bureau of Investigation, Washington D.C. File No. 92-1610: Joseph Gregory Gallo. C. Cover page
[cxcii] U.S. Department of Justice, Federal Bureau of Investigation, Washington D.C. File No. 92-1610: Joseph Gregory Gallo. E. Cover page
[cxciii] Diapoulos, Peter. *The Sixth Family*. (Bantam Books, 1976) pp. 54
[cxciv] Diapoulos, Peter. *The Sixth Family*. (Bantam Books, 1976) pp. 54
[cxcv] Diapoulos, Peter. *The Sixth Family*. (Bantam Books, 1976) pp. 55
[cxcvi] U.S. Department of Justice, Federal Bureau of Investigation, Washington D.C. File No. 92-1610: Joseph Gregory Gallo. Pg.5
[cxcvii] U.S. Department of Justice, Federal Bureau of Investigation, Washington D.C. File No. 92-1610: Joseph Gregory Gallo. Pg.6
[cxcviii] Franzese, Michael. *Blood Covenant*. Whitaker House, 1992. pp. 80
[cxcix] Diapoulos, Peter. *The Sixth Family*. (Bantam Books, 1976) pp. 35
[cc] Diapoulos, Peter. *The Sixth Family*. (Bantam Books, 1976) pp. 35
[cci] Diapoulos, Peter. *The Sixth Family*. (Bantam Books, 1976) pp. 38
[ccii] U.S. Department of Justice, Federal Bureau of Investigation, Washington D.C. File No. 92-1610: Joseph Gregory Gallo. Pg.7
[cciii] "Unity Day: Breather for FBI" *New York Post* (June 16, 1971) pp. 34
[cciv] "Unity Day: Breather for FBI" *New York Post* (June 16, 1971) pp. 34
[ccv] James F. Clarity "Italian-American League Said to Pressure Shops" *New York Times* (June 26, 1971) pp. 15
[ccvi] James F. Clarity "Italian-American League Said to Pressure Shops" *New York Times* (June 26, 1971) pp. 15

[ccvii] Francis X. Clines "20 Other Italian Groups Meet With State Rights Chief in Complaints of bias" *New York Times* (June 26, 1971) pp. 15

[ccviii] William Federici "Some Faces Missing as Italians Complain About Bias" *New York Daily News* (June 26, 1971) pp. 5

[ccix] Francis X. Clines "20 Other Italian Groups Meet With State Rights Chief in Complaints of bias" *New York Times* (June 26, 1971) pp. 15

[ccx] William Federici "Some Faces Missing as Italians Complain About Bias" *New York Daily News* (June 26, 1971) pp. 5

[ccxi] Glick, Brian. *War at Home: Covert Action Against U.S. Activists.* Southend Press, 1989 pp. 10

[ccxii] Lawrence Van Gelder "Reputed Mafiosi Seized in Raids" New York Times (June 12, 1970) pg. 16

[ccxiii] Lawrence Van Gelder "Reputed Mafiosi Seized in Raids" New York Times (June 12, 1970) pg. 1

[ccxiv] Cantalupo, Joseph & Renner, Thomas C. *Body Mike An unsparing Expose by the Mafia Insider who turned on the Mob*, New York, Villard Books, 1990. pp. 116

[ccxv] Daley, Robert. *Target Blue, An Insider's View of the NYPD.* Delacorte Press, 1971. pg. 190

[ccxvi] Seedman & Hellman, Albert A. & Peter. *CHIEF!*. Avon, 1974. pg. 352

[ccxvii] Daley, Robert. *Target Blue, An Insider's View of the NYPD.* Delacorte Press, 1971. pg. 196

[ccxviii] William Federici & Richard Oliver "Ex-Con Shoots Colombo, Dies: Black is Slain at Unity Day Rally After Hitting Mob Boss. Daily News (June 29, 1971) pg. 6

[ccxix] Seedman & Hellman, Albert A. & Peter. *CHIEF!*. Avon, 1974. pg. 357

[ccxx] John Sibley "Hospital Emergency Room a Mixture of Chaos and Efficiency After Shooting" *New York Times* (June 29, 1971) pg. 21

[ccxxi] William Federici & Richard Oliver "Ex-Con Shoots Colombo, Dies: Black is Slain at Unity Day Rally After Hitting Mob Boss. Daily News (June 29, 1971) pg. 6

[ccxxii] Cy Egan & Jerry Capeci "Colombo Improves But Still in Coma" *New York Post* (July 1, 1971) pg. 4

[ccxxiii] (UPI) "Gangland Boss shot at rally" *The Times Herald Record* (June 29, 1971) pp. 7

[ccxxiv] Ed Bowe "Rally Trip Ends In Silent Prayer" *Newsday* (June 29, 1971) pg. 12

ccxxv Pedahzur & Perliger, Ami & Arie. *Jewish Terrorism In Israel.* Columbia University Press New York, 2009. Pg. 95
ccxxvi Diapoulos, Peter. *The Sixth Family.* (Bantam Books, 1976) pp. 53,54
ccxxvii U.S. Department of Justice, Federal Bureau of Investigation, Washington D.C. File No. 92-1610: Joseph Gregory Gallo. (4/7/1971) G Cover Page
ccxxviii Diapoulos, Peter. *The Sixth Family.* (Bantam Books, 1976) pp. 53,54
ccxxix William Federici & Richard Oliver "Ex-Con Shoots Colombo, Dies: Black is Slain at Unity Day Rally After Hitting Mob Boss. Daily News (June 29, 1971) pg. 3
ccxxx Frank Faso, Edward Kirkman, Paul Meskil. "Shooting Attack May Trigger New Gang Bang-Bang" *Daily News.* (June 29, 1971) pg. 4
ccxxxi Tom Renner "Colombo Faced Challenge From Mob" *Newsday* (June 29, 1971) pg. 3
ccxxxii Frank Faso, Edward Kirkman, Paul Meskil. "Shooting Attack May Trigger New Gang Bang-Bang" *Daily News.* (June 29, 1971) pg. 4
ccxxxiii Pileggi, Nicholas "They City Politic: Why they had to shoot Joe Colombo" *New Yorker Magazine* (July 12, 1971) pg. 8
ccxxxiv Diapoulos, Peter. *The Sixth Family.* (Bantam Books, 1976) pg. 54
ccxxxv Diapoulos, Peter. *The Sixth Family.* (Bantam Books, 1976) pg. 58
ccxxxvi Diapoulos, Peter. *The Sixth Family.* (Bantam Books, 1976) pg. 61
ccxxxvii Daley, Robert. *Target Blue, An Insider's View of the NYPD.* Delacorte Press, 1971. Pg. 205
ccxxxviii Daley, Robert. *Target Blue, An Insider's View of the NYPD.* Delacorte Press, 1971. Pg. 202
ccxxxix Sandy Smith "The Mafia: Back to the Bad Old Days?" Time Magazine (July 12, 1971) pg. 18
ccxl U.S. Department of Justice, Federal Bureau of Investigation, Washington D.C. File No. 92-5509: Joseph Anthony Colombo. (June, 1971)
ccxli William Sherman "The Mystery Man Who Shot Joe Colombo" *Daily News* (August 26, 1971) pg. 68
ccxlii John Mullane & Ernest Johnston Jr. "The Triggerman's Past" New York Post (June 29, 2971) pg. 2
ccxliii John Mullane & Ernest Johnston Jr. "The Triggerman's Past" New York Post (June 29, 2971) pg. 2
ccxliv John Mullane & Ernest Johnston Jr. "The Triggerman's Past" New York Post (June 29, 2971) pg. 2

[ccxlv] Patrick Clark & Vincent Lee. "Gunman Record: Arrests for Rape, Robbery & Drugs" *Daily News* (June 29, 1971) pg. 5

[ccxlvi] Sandy Smith "The Mafia: Back to the Bad Old Days?" Time Magazine (July 12, 1971) pg. 17

[ccxlvii] William Sherman "Jerome Johnson: A Real Nowhere Man" *Daily News* (August 27, 1971) pg. 40

[ccxlviii] William Sherman "The Mystery Man Who Shot Joe Colombo" *Daily News* (August 26, 1971) pg. 68

[ccxlix] William Federici, Edward Kirkman, & Henry Lee. "Colombo Rallies after Getting Blood- Cops Hunt Attacker's Contacts; He Was 'Expecting Big Score'" *Daily News* (June 30, 1971-final) pg. 3

[ccl] William Federici & Richard Oliver "Ex-Con Shoots Colombo, Dies: Black is Slain at Unity Day Rally After Hitting Mob Boss. *Daily News* (June 29, 1971) pg. 6

[ccli] Daley, Robert. *Target Blue, An Insider's View of the NYPD*. Delacorte Press, 1971. Pg. 208

[cclii] Daley, Robert. *Target Blue, An Insider's View of the NYPD*. Delacorte Press, 1971. Pg. 211

[ccliii] Seedman & Hellman, Albert A. & Peter. *CHIEF!*. Avon, 1974. Pg. 389

[ccliv] Daley, Robert. *Target Blue, An Insider's View of the NYPD*. Delacorte Press, 1971. Pg. 208

[cclv] Fred Ferretti "Colombo Attack Linked By Police To A Gang Plot" *New York Times* (July 3, 1971) pg. 1

[cclvi] Frank Faso, Edward Kirkman & Henry Lee "Cops: Colombo a Gang Target – Others in Mob Marked For Death. *Daily News* (July 3, 1971) pg. 3

[cclvii] Fred Ferretti "Colombo Attack Linked By Police To A Gang Plot" *New York Times* (July 3, 1971) pg. 52

[cclviii] Daley, Robert. *Target Blue, An Insider's View of the NYPD*. Delacorte Press, 1971. Pg. 215

[cclix] Daley, Robert. *Target Blue, An Insider's View of the NYPD*. Delacorte Press, 1971. Pg. 220

[cclx] Barbara Campbell "Cousin Asserts Jerome Johnson Told Of Job With League" *New York Times* (July 1, 1971) pg. 1

[cclxi] Diapoulos, Peter. *The Sixth Family*. (Bantam Books, 1976) pp. 68

[cclxii] Diapoulos, Peter. *The Sixth Family*. (Bantam Books, 1976) pp. 68

[cclxiii] Diapoulos, Peter. *The Sixth Family*. (Bantam Books, 1976) pp. 69

[cclxiv] Nicholas Gage. "Informants Give Mafia Reaction to Colombo Shooting" *New York Times* (June 30, 1971) pp. 26

[cclxv] Nicholas Gage. "Informants Give Mafia Reaction to Colombo Shooting" *New York Times* (June 30, 1971) pp. 26

[cclxvi] Nicholas Gage. "Informants Give Mafia Reaction to Colombo Shooting" New York Times (June 30, 1971) pp. 26

[cclxvii] Daley, Robert. *Target Blue, An Insider's View of the NYPD.* Delacorte Press, 1971. Pg. 209

[cclxviii] Tom Renner "Colombo Faced Challenge From Mob" *Newsday* (June 29, 1971) pp. 10

[cclxix] Marcia Kramer & William Federici "Mob Ordered Colombo Shot, Cops Insist" Daily News (September 1, 1971) pg.12

[cclxx] Seedman & Hellman, Albert A. & Peter. *CHIEF!.* Avon, 1974. Pg. 380

[cclxxi] Eugene Ruffini "The Police, the Press, & the Legend" The Nation (November 22, 1971) pp. 521

[cclxxii] Marcia Kramer & William Federici "Mob Ordered Colombo Shot, Cops Insist" Daily News (September 1, 1971) pg.12

[cclxxiii] Fred Ferretti "Man Slain Here Linked To Mafia" New York Times (July 22, 1971) pg. 34

[cclxxiv] Daley, Robert. *Target Blue, An Insider's View of the NYPD.* Delacorte Press, 1971. Pg. 222

[cclxxv] William Federici, Edward Kirkman, & Henry Lee. "Colombo Rallies after Getting Blood- Cops Hunt Attacker's Contacts; He Was 'Expecting Big Score'" *Daily News* (June 30, 1971-final) pg. 3

[cclxxvi] Daley, Robert. *Target Blue, An Insider's View of the NYPD.* Delacorte Press, 1971. Pg. 205

[cclxxvii] William E. Farrell "Bullets Found At Johnson Home" New York Times (July 2, 1971) pg. 28

[cclxxviii] New York Police Department. Freedom of Information Law Department – DD-5 Supplementary Complaint Report (June 28, 1971) File # 133 88

[cclxxix] Daley, Robert. *Target Blue, An Insider's View of the NYPD.* Delacorte Press, 1971. Pg. 206

[cclxxx] New York Police Department. Freedom of Information Law Department – DD-5 Supplementary Complaint Report (June 28, 1971) File # 133 88

[cclxxxi] Barbara Campbell "Police Firm on Gang Tie In Shooting" New York Times (August 5, 1971) pg. 35

[cclxxxii] Daley, Robert. *Target Blue, An Insider's View of the NYPD.* Delacorte Press, 1971. Pg. 514

cclxxxiii Daley, Robert. *Target Blue, An Insider's View of the NYPD.* Delacorte Press, 1971. Pg. 515

cclxxxiv Seedman & Hellman, Albert A. & Peter. *CHIEF!.* Avon, 1974. Pg. 390

cclxxxv Supplementary Detailed Staff Reports on Intelligence Activities and The Rights Of Americans. Book 2. Final Report of the Select Committee to Study Governmental Operations With Respect To Intelligence Activities. United Sates Senate. (April 23, 1976)

cclxxxvi Novak, Robert D. *The Prince of Darkness: 50 Years of Reporting in Washington.* Three Rivers Press. 2007 pg. 210

cclxxxvii Novak, Robert D. *The Prince of Darkness: 50 Years of Reporting in Washington.* Three Rivers Press. 2007 pg. 210

cclxxxviii Robbie Brown "Civil Rights Photographer Unmasked as Informer" *New York Times* (September 14, 2010) pg. A14

cclxxxix Raab, Selwyn. *Five Families.* Robson Books, 2006. Pg. 190

ccxc Frank Faso & Paul Meskil "Cops & Mob Wait & Wonder: Who's Next?" *Daily News* (June 30, 1971) pg. 3

ccxci Scarne, John *The Mafia Conspiracy.* Scarne Enterprises Inc., 1976

ccxcii Scarne, John *The Mafia Conspiracy.* Scarne Enterprises Inc., 1976

ccxciii Scarne, John *The Mafia Conspiracy.* Scarne Enterprises Inc., 1976

ccxciv Cantalupo, Joseph & Renner, Thomas C. *Body Mike An unsparing Expose by the Mafia Insider who turned on the Mob*, (New York, Villard Books, 1990) pp.118

ccxcv Franzese, Michael. *Blood Covenant.* Whitaker House, 1992. pp. 81

ccxcvi U.S. Department of Justice, Federal Bureau of Investigation, Washington D.C. File No. 92-6612: Gregory Scarpa. Pg. 790

ccxcvii U.S. Department of Justice, Federal Bureau of Investigation, Washington D.C. File No. 92-6612: Gregory Scarpa. Pg. 790

ccxcviii U.S. Department of Justice, Federal Bureau of Investigation, Washington D.C. File No. 92-5509: Joseph Anthony Colombo. (November 8, 1971) pp.5

ccxcix U.S. Department of Justice, Federal Bureau of Investigation, Washington D.C. File No. 92-5509: Joseph Anthony Colombo. (November 8, 1971) pp.5

ccc U.S. Department of Justice, Federal Bureau of Investigation, Washington D.C. File No. 92-5509: Joseph Anthony Colombo. (July 13, 1971) pp.19

ccci "Feds Renew Ethnic Slur" Italo-American Times (March 14, 1977) pg. 1

Photograph Credits

Robert D'Alessandro, *Joseph Colombo & NYPD*, Front Cover

Estevan Oriol, *Anthony Colombo Central Park*, Rear Cover

UNITY PRESS

CPSIA information can be obtained
at www.ICGtesting.com
Printed in the USA
BVHW04s2156120818
524315BV00010B/104/P